Brother Swaggart, Here Is My Question About The Cross

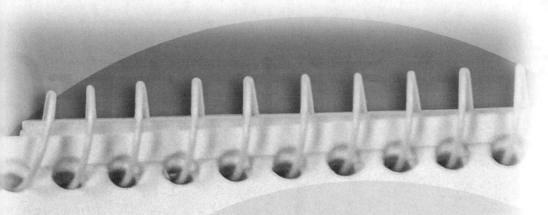

Brother Swaggart, Here Is My Question About The Cross

By Jimmy Swaggart

Jimmy Swaggart Ministries
P.O. Box 262550 • Baton Rouge, Louisiana 70826-2550
Website: www.jsm.org • Email: info@jsm.org
(225) 768-7000

TABLE OF CONTENTS

INTRODUCTION

In 1997, after some six years of two prayer meetings a day (with the exception of Saturday morning), the Lord began to open up to me the Message of the Cross. When I say *"began,"* I'm referring to the fact that I'm still learning about this all-important subject; in fact, the single most important thing the Believer can know.

First of all, the Lord showed me the meaning of the sin nature. I was to find out later that this was the first thing that was shown the Apostle Paul as it regards life and living. It was to Paul that the meaning of the New Covenant was given, which, in essence, is the meaning of the Cross.

Some days later in a morning prayer meeting, the Lord showed me the solution to the sin nature, which is the Cross of Christ. The Lord said three things to me that morning, so simple, but so far-reaching. He said:

"The answer for which you seek is found in the Cross."

And then, *"The solution for which you seek is found in the Cross."*

And then, *"The answer for which you seek is found only in the Cross."*

All of this, the meaning of the sin nature and the solution, which is the Cross of Christ, came out of the Sixth Chapter of Romans.

And then some weeks later, the Lord showed me how the Holy Spirit works in all of this. It is the Cross of Christ which gave and gives the Holy Spirit latitude to work within our lives, and to do all the things which He does. Paul wrote:

"For the Law of the Spirit of Life in Christ Jesus has made me free from the Law of Sin and Death" (Rom. 8:2).

As is obvious, the understanding of the Holy Spirit and the Cross of Christ came from the Eighth Chapter of Romans.

A REVELATION OF UNPRECEDENTED PROPORTIONS

This Revelation, which, as I have stated, continues unto

this hour, has revolutionized my life, my Ministry; in fact, all that I am and do. We set out immediately, and continue unto this hour, doing everything within our power to get this Message to the Church and to the world. The only thing standing between mankind and eternal Hell is the Cross of Christ. When we come to understand that, we then realize how important all of this is.

Unfortunately, the modern Church little preaches the Cross anymore. It has a modicum of understanding as it regards Salvation and the Cross, but, virtually none as it regards Sanctification and the Cross. And yet, virtually the entirety of the Bible is given over to telling individuals how to live for God.

QUESTIONS

We have received, and do receive, I think I can say without fear of exaggeration, thousands of questions into our office regarding the Cross of Christ. Especially considering that this Message is new to the Church, one can readily understand the reason for the inquiries. Plain and simple, the Apostle Paul told us what the Gospel of Jesus Christ really is. He said:

"Christ sent me not to baptize, but to preach the Gospel, not with wisdom of words, lest the Cross of Christ be made of none effect" (I Cor. 1:17).

So, this means, if the Preacher is not preaching the Cross in some way, then whatever it is he is preaching, it's not the Gospel of Jesus Christ, meaning that it will accomplish precious little for the Lord.

I would pray that some of the questions posed in this book, as it regards the Cross, will address some of the questions that possibly you may have. Of necessity, there will be some repetition in the answer because of similarity in some questions.

CHAPTER ONE

Is The Cross Of Christ The Most Important Part Of The Plan Of God?

QUESTION:

IS THE CROSS OF CHRIST THE MOST IMPORTANT PART OF THE PLAN OF GOD?

ANSWER:

Yes!

While anything and everything done by the Lord Jesus Christ is of utmost significance and thereby played its part in this great Redemption Plan, irrespective as to what it might have been, still, the Cross of Christ is by far the pivotal part around which everything else revolves.

How do we know that?

We know that it is the most important part simply because the Cross of Christ is the Foundation on which everything else is built regarding this great Plan of God. It was the first thing formulated in the mind of the Godhead, making it the Foundation.

The Holy Spirit through Simon Peter said this, and I quote directly from THE EXPOSITOR'S STUDY BIBLE:

THE PRECIOUS BLOOD OF CHRIST

"Forasmuch as you know that you were not redeemed with corruptible things, *as* silver and gold *(presents the fact that the most precious commodities [silver and gold] could not redeem fallen man)*, from your vain conversation *(vain lifestyle)* received by tradition from your fathers *(speaks of original sin that is passed on from father to child at conception)*;

"But with the Precious Blood of Christ *(presents the payment, which proclaims the poured out Life of Christ on behalf of sinners)*, as of a Lamb without blemish and without spot *(speaks of the lambs offered as substitutes in the Old Jewish economy; the Death of Christ was not an execution or assassination, but rather a Sacrifice; the Offering of Himself presented a Perfect Sacrifice, for He was perfect in every respect [Ex. 12:5])*:

BEFORE THE FOUNDATION OF THE WORLD

"Who verily was foreordained before the foundation of the world *(refers to the fact that God, in His Omniscience, knew He would create man, man would Fall, and man would be Redeemed by Christ going to the Cross; this was all done before the Universe was created; this means the Cross of Christ is the Foundation Doctrine of all Doctrine, referring to the fact that all Doctrine must be built upon that Foundation, or else it is specious)*, **but was manifest in these last times for you** *(refers to the invisible God Who, in the Person of the Son, was made visible to human eyesight by assuming a human body and human limitations)*,

FAITH

"Who by Him do believe in God *(it is only by Christ and what He did for us at the Cross that we are able to 'Believe in God')*, **Who raised Him** *(Christ)* **up from the dead** *(His Resurrection was guaranteed insomuch as He atoned for all sin [Rom. 6:23])*, **and gave Him Glory** *(refers to the exaltation of Christ)*; **that your Faith and Hope might be in God.** *(This speaks of a heart Faith in God, Who saves sinners in answer to our Faith in the Resurrected Lord Jesus Who died for us)*" **(I Pet. 1:18-21).**

In this statement given by the Holy Spirit through Peter, we have the following:
• **The Cross of Christ as the Foundation Of the Plan of Redemption.**
• **The Cross of Christ addressed in** *"the Precious Blood of Christ."*

• The Resurrection of Christ proclaimed by the fact that God *"raised Him up from the dead."*

• The Exaltation of Christ proclaimed by the short phrase, *"and gave Him Glory."*

Understanding that the Cross of Christ is the Foundation of the great Plan of Redemption, this means that every doctrine must be built upon this Foundation. If it is built on something else, in some way it will be spurious. In fact, all false doctrine stems from a misunderstanding or the ignoring or outright denial of the Cross of Christ. Once we begin to understand this, then we begin to see how important this Message is, insomuch as it was formulated in the mind of the Godhead from before the foundation of the world.

As we stated, God, Who is Omniscient, knew before the foundation of the world that He would make man and that man would Fall, and it would be deemed desirable by the Godhead that God would become Man, the Man Christ Jesus, Who would lay aside the expression of His Deity, while never losing possession of His Deity, all for the express purpose of going to the Cross of Calvary.

THE PRIMARY MISSION OF CHRIST

The Apostle John tells us in the First Chapter of his Gospel exactly Who Jesus is and What Jesus has done. I continue to quote from **THE EXPOSITOR'S STUDY BIBLE:**

> **"In the beginning** (does not infer that Christ as God had a beginning, because as God He had no beginning, but rather refers to the time of Creation [Gen. 1:1]) **was the Word** (the Holy Spirit through John describes Jesus as 'the Eternal Logos'), **and the Word was with God** ('was in relationship with God,' and expresses the idea of the Trinity), **and the Word was God** (meaning that He did not cease to be God during the Incarnation; He 'was' and 'is' God from eternity past to eternity future).

IN THE BEGINNING WITH GOD

"**The same was in the beginning with God** *(this very Person was in eternity with God; there's only one God, but manifested in three Persons — God the Father, God the Son, and God the Holy Spirit)*.

"**All things were made by Him** *(all things came into being through Him; it refers to every item of Creation one by one, rather than all things regarded in totality)*; **and without Him was not any thing made that was made** *(nothing, not even one single thing, was made independently of His cooperation and volition)*.

LIFE

"**In Him was Life** *(presents Jesus, the Eternal Logos, as the first cause)*; **and the Life was the Light of men** *(He Alone is the Life Source of Light; if one doesn't know Christ, one is in darkness)*.

"**And the Light shines in darkness** *(speaks of the Incarnation of Christ, and His coming into this world; His 'Light,' because it is derived from His Life, drives out 'darkness')*; **and the darkness comprehended it not** *(should have been translated, 'apprehended it not'; it means that Satan, even though he tried with all his might, could not stop 'the Light'; today it shines all over the world, and one day soon, there will be nothing left but that 'Light')*" **(Jn. 1:1-5).**

THE REASON FOR GOD BECOMING MAN

"*That* **was the True Light** *(there are many false lights; Jesus is the only True Light)*, **which lights every man who comes into the world** *(if man is to find Light, it will be only in Christ, and it is for 'every man')*.

"**He was in the world** *(the Eternal Logos, the 'Creator')*, **and the world was made by Him** *(as it was originally* *created before the Fall of Lucifer and the Fall of man)*, **and the world knew Him not** *(the world cannot know Christ by wisdom, but only by Revelation)*.

THE WORD MADE FLESH

"And the Word was made flesh *(refers to the Incarnation, 'God becoming man')*, **and dwelt among us** *(refers to Jesus, although Perfect, not holding Himself aloft from all others, but rather lived as all men, even a peasant)*, **(and we beheld His Glory, the Glory as of the Only Begotten of the Father,)** *(speaks of His Deity, although hidden from the eyes of the merely curious; while Christ laid aside the expression of His Deity, He never lost the possession of His Deity)* **full of Grace and Truth** *(as 'flesh,' proclaimed His Humanity, 'Grace and Truth' His Deity)*" **(Jn. 1:9-10, 14).**

THE REASON THE WORD WAS MADE FLESH

"And they which were sent were of the Pharisees *(the Holy Spirit is careful to delineate the source of these questions; the opposition now begins)*.

"And they asked him, and said unto him, Why do you baptize then, if you be not that Christ, nor Elijah, neither that Prophet? *(They were indignant that John not only baptized without ecclesiastical authority, but baptized contrary to the practice of the Pharisees. In other words, he had not asked nor sought their permission, nor did it seem that he cared whether they agreed or not!)*

"John answered them, saying, I baptize with water *(meaning that it was but a temporary symbol of the true, abiding, and effectual baptism of the One Who would baptize with the Holy Spirit)*: **but there stands One among you, Whom you know not** *(points to their spiritual ignorance; Christ was in their very midst, and they did not know!)*.

WHO TAKES AWAY THE SIN OF THE WORLD

"**He it is** *(the Messiah is already here, even though you do not know Him, and He, as stated, is not me)*, **Who coming after me is preferred before me** *(Who existed before me, in fact, has existed eternally)*, **Whose shoe's latchet I am not worthy to unloose** *(by comparison to Christ, the greatest Prophet born of woman labels himself, and rightly so!).*

"**These things were done in Bethabara beyond Jordan, where John was baptizing** *(probably not far from Jericho).*

"**The next day** *(refers to the day after John had been questioned by the emissaries from the Sanhedrin)* **John sees Jesus coming unto him** *(is, no doubt, after the baptism of Jesus, and the temptation in the wilderness)*, **and said, Behold the Lamb of God** *(proclaims Jesus as the Sacrifice for sin, in fact, the Sin-Offering, Whom all the multiple millions of offered lambs had represented)*, **which takes away the sin of the world** *(animal blood could only cover sin, it could not take it away; but Jesus offering Himself as the Perfect Sacrifice took away the sin of the world; He not only cleansed acts of sin, but, as well, addressed the root cause [Col. 2:14-15])*" **(Jn. 1:24-29).**

THREE THINGS HERE SAID

When John introduced Jesus, he said three things of Him that had never been said about another human being. They are:

1. *"The Lamb of God:"* Why did the Holy Spirit through John refer to Christ as *"the Lamb of God?"*

He did so simply because of all the multiple millions of lambs that had been offered in sacrifices before now, even from the dawn of time, which was meant to symbolize the coming Redeemer. He would be the *"Lamb of God"* Who would go to the Cross in order to redeem the fallen sons of Adam's lost race.

2. *"Which takes away the sin of the world:"* Of all the

millions of sacrifices that had been offered previously to this, as stated, even from the dawn of time, those sacrifices did not take away even one sin. The best that animal blood could do was to cover the sin, thereby serving as a stopgap measure until Christ would come. What He did on Calvary's Cross literally took away the sin of the world, at least for all who believe (Jn. 3:16). Truly, every person who is Born-Again, their sins have been taken away. David had prophesied nearly a thousand years earlier:

"As far as the east is from the west, so far has He removed our transgressions from us. *(This is equivalent to 'blotting out our sins' [Acts 3:19; Isa. 43:25; 44:22]. It is impossible to bring the east and the west together; so it is impossible to bring the forgiven sinner and his forgiven sins together. This Divine fact gives to those who believe it a peace which nothing can destroy)*" (Ps. 103:12).

3. *"Sin:"* is used in the singular meaning, not only were all sins atoned but, as well, the root cause of sin was addressed.

CHAPTER TWO

Is Redemption Centered Up In The Cross Of Christ Or The Resurrection Of Christ?

QUESTION:

IS REDEMPTION CENTERED UP IN THE CROSS OF CHRIST OR THE RESURRECTION OF CHRIST?

ANSWER:

Redemption is centered up totally in the Cross of Christ. While everything else after the Cross, the Resurrection, Ascension, and Exaltation of Christ, played a tremendous part, and continues to play a tremendous part, the truth is, all of this is made possible, the Resurrection, Ascension and Exaltation of Christ, because of the Cross.

IT IS FINISHED

Jesus was placed on the Cross at approximately 9 a.m., the time of the morning Sacrifice, and died at approximately 3 p.m., the time of the evening Sacrifice. The Scripture is not completely clear as it regards the last words that He uttered before He died, but most Bible Scholars believe that the following were His final words, *"It is finished, Father, into Your hands I commend My spirit"* (Jn. 19:30; Lk. 23:46). When He said that, the Scripture says, *"He gave up the ghost."* In fact, He didn't die until the Holy Spirit told Him He could die (Heb. 9:14). That's how much the Holy Spirit was in control of His Life.

The words *"it is finished"* proclaim the greatest words, albeit at great price, that any sinner could ever hear; in effect, the world's debt was paid; every iota of the Law had been fulfilled. Concerning that, Paul also wrote:

VICTORY!

"Blotting out the handwriting of Ordinances that was against us *(pertains to the Law of Moses, which was God's standard of Righteousness that man could not reach)*, which was contrary to us *(Law is against us, simply because we are unable to keep its precepts, no matter how hard we try)*, and took it out of the way *(refers to the penalty of the Law being removed)*, nailing it to His Cross *(the Law with its decrees was abolished in Christ's Death, as if Crucified with Him)*;

"*And* having spoiled principalities and powers *(Satan and all of his henchmen were defeated at the Cross by Christ atoning for all sin; sin was the legal right Satan had to hold man in captivity; with all sin atoned, he has no more legal right to hold anyone in bondage)*, He *(Christ)* made a show of them openly *(what Jesus did at the Cross was in the face of the whole universe)*, triumphing over them in it. *(The triumph is complete and it was all done for us, meaning we can walk in power and perpetual victory due to the Cross.)*" (Col. 2:14-15).

When Jesus died on the Cross, two things happened:
1. Totally and completely, He satisfied the demands of the broken Law. Paul wrote:

"Christ has redeemed us from the curse of the Law *(He did so on the Cross)*, being made a curse for us *(He took the penalty of the Law, which was death)*: for it is written, cursed is every one who hangs on a tree *(Deut. 21:22-23)*:

"That the blessing of Abraham *(Justification by Faith)* might come on the Gentiles through Jesus Christ *(what He did at the Cross)*; that we might receive the Promise of the Spirit through Faith. *(All sin was atoned at the Cross which lifted the sin debt from believing man, making it possible for the Holy Spirit to come into the life of the Believer and abide there forever [Jn. 14:16-17].)*" (Gal. 3:13-14).

2. He atoned for all sin, past, present, and future, at least for all who will believe (Jn. 3:16). Paul wrote:

"**But this Man** *(this Priest, Christ Jesus)*, **after He had offered up One Sacrifice for sins forever** *(speaks of the Cross)*, **sat down on the Right Hand of God.** *(Refers to the great contrast with the Priests under the Levitical System, who never sat down because their work was never completed; the Work of Christ was a 'Finished Work,' and needs no repetition.)*" **(Heb. 10:12).**

All of this tells us that Atonement was completed, i.e., *"finished,"* at Calvary.

THE RESURRECTION WAS NEVER IN DOUBT

I realize that some preachers proclaim Jesus having to fight demons and powers of darkness, etc., in order to be resurrected; however, there's nothing like that in the Bible. When Jesus died and His Soul and Spirit went down into the heart of the Earth, He went down there as a Victor, i.e., *"a Conqueror,"* and not as one conquered. In fact, if there had been one single sin unatoned, due to the fact that the Bible tells us that *"the wages of sin is death,"* Jesus could not have risen from the dead (Rom. 6:23), but, due to the fact that God raised Him from the dead, tells us that He atoned for all sin at Calvary and in every capacity. In fact, John the Baptist had prophesied over our Lord when He first entered the Ministry by saying:

"**Behold the Lamb of God** *(proclaims Jesus as the Sacrifice for sin, in fact, the Sin-Offering, Whom all the multiple millions of offered lambs had represented)*, **which takes away the sin of the world.** *(Animal blood could only cover sin, it could not take it away; but Jesus offering Himself as the perfect Sacrifice took away the sin of the world; He not only cleansed acts of sin, but, as well, addressed the root cause [Col. 2:14-15])*" **(Jn. 1:29).**

Jesus had told His Disciples more times than one:

"**The Son of Man shall be betrayed into the hands of men** *(draws the Disciples back to the Mission at hand; that Mission was the Redemption of humanity, which would require the offering of the perfect Sacrifice, which was His Body)*:

"**And they shall kill Him** *(but only because He allowed such [Jn. 10:17-18])*, **and the third day He shall be raised again**" (Mat. 17:22-23).

THE LEGAL PROBLEM OF SIN

Sin was and is the legal right that Satan had to hold man captive; however, with all sin atoned, which Jesus did at the Cross, that legal right was taken away from the Evil One. Now, due to what Jesus did at the Cross, Satan has no more legal right to hold anyone in bondage. If he does so, it is only because mankind, including Believers, does not understand the price that was paid at Calvary and how we are meant to take the benefits of that price unto ourselves.

When Jesus went down into Paradise after His Death, as stated, He went there as a Conqueror. He flung the doors of that place open wide with the intention of bringing everyone out, which He did. He could do this because, as stated, Satan's legal right to hold man captive was now gone. With every sin atoned, and again as we have stated, the legal right the enemy had was forever vanquished. In fact, every Believer in Paradise, which included all from Abel to the Crucifixion of Christ, in a sense was held captive by Satan. That's the reason that Paul wrote:

"**Wherefore He said** *(Ps. 68:18)*, **When He ascended up on high** *(the Ascension)*, **He led captivity captive** *(liberated the souls in Paradise; before the Cross, despite being Believers, they were still held captive by Satan because the blood of bulls and goats could not take away the sin debt; but when Jesus died on the Cross, the sin debt was paid, and now He makes all of these His Captives)*, **and gave**

Gifts unto men. *(These 'Gifts' include all the attributes of Christ, all made possible by the Cross.)*

("Now that He ascended *(mission completed)*, **what is it but that He also descended first into the lower parts of the earth?** *(Immediately before His Ascension to Glory, which would be done in total triumph, He first went down into Paradise to deliver all the believing souls in that region, which He did!)*

"He Who descended is the same also Who ascended *(this is a portrayal of Jesus as Deliverer and Mediator)* **up far above all Heavens** *(presents His present location, never again having to descend into the nether world)*, **that He might fill all things.)** *(He has always been the Creator, but now He is also the Saviour)*" **(Eph. 4:8-10).**

In this account of Jesus going down into Paradise, we do not see one iota of evidence of Him fighting demon spirits, fallen angels, etc., but rather the very opposite. As stated, He went down there as a Victor, as a Conqueror, because at the Cross, Satan was defeated, plus all of his fallen angels, demon spirits, and minions of darkness (Col. 2:14-15).

WHAT DID PAUL SAY?

It must be remembered that the meaning of the New Covenant was given to the Apostle Paul. Concerning this the Scripture says, and I quote from THE EXPOSITOR'S STUDY BIBLE:

"Paul, an Apostle, (not of men, neither by man, but by Jesus Christ, and God the Father, Who raised Him from the dead;) *(This means Paul did not submit the authority of his Apostleship to men, neither was it conferred on him by man.)*

"And all the Brethren which are with me, unto the Churches of Galatia *(refers to all in that region)***:**

"Grace *be* **to you and Peace from God the Father**

(made possible by the Cross), **and *from* our Lord Jesus Christ** *(Who made it possible)*,

"**Who gave Himself for our sins** *(the Cross)*, **that He might deliver us from this present evil world** *(the Cross alone can set the captive free)*, **according to the Will of God and our Father** *(the standard of the entire process of Redemption)*:

"**To Whom *be* Glory forever and ever** *(Divine Glory)*. **Amen.**

NO OTHER GOSPEL

"**I marvel that you are so soon removed from Him** *(the Holy Spirit)* ***Who*** **called you into the Grace of Christ** *(made possible by the Cross)* **unto another gospel** *(anything which doesn't have the Cross as its Object of Faith)*:

"**Which is not another** *(presents the fact that Satan's aim is not so much to deny the Gospel, which he can little do, as to corrupt it)*; **but there be some who trouble you, and would pervert the Gospel of Christ** *(once again, to make the object of Faith something other than the Cross)*.

LET HIM BE ACCURSED

"**But though we** *(Paul and his associates)*, **or an Angel from Heaven, preach any other Gospel unto you than that which we have preached unto you** *(Jesus Christ and Him Crucified)*, **let him be accursed** *(eternally condemned; the Holy Spirit speaks this through Paul, making this very serious)*.

"**As we said before, so say I now again** *(at sometime past, he had said the same thing to them, making their defection even more serious)*, **If any *man* preach any other gospel unto you** *(anything other than the Cross)* **than that you have received** *(which Saved your souls)*, **let him be accursed** *('eternally condemned,' which means the loss of the soul).*

"**For do I now persuade men, or God?** *(In essence, Paul is saying, 'do I preach man's doctrine or God's?')* **or do I seek to please men?** *(This is what false apostles do.)* **for if I yet pleased men, I should not be the Servant of Christ** *(one cannot please both men and God at the same time).*

REVELATION

"**But I certify you, Brethren** *(make known),* **that the Gospel which was preached of me** *(the Message of the Cross)* **is not after man.** *(Any Message other than the Cross is definitely devised by man.)*

"**For I neither received it of man** *(Paul had not learned this great Truth from human teachers),* **neither was I taught it** *(he denies instruction from other men),* **but by the Revelation of Jesus Christ.** *(Revelation is the mighty Act of God whereby the Holy Spirit discloses to the human mind that which could not be understood without Divine Intervention.)*" **(Gal. 1:1-12).**

As it regards the Cross of Christ versus the Resurrection, the great Apostle said:

"For Christ sent me not to baptize, but to preach the Gospel: not with wisdom of words, lest the Cross of Christ should be made of none effect" (I Cor. 1:17). If it is to be noticed, he did not say, *"lest the Resurrection of Christ should be made of none effect."*

He also said, "For the preaching *(Word)* of the Cross is to them who perish foolishness; but unto us which are Saved it is the Power of God" (I Cor. 1:18).

He did not say, *"For the preaching of the Resurrection is to them. . . ."*

The great Apostle also said, *"But we preach Christ Crucified"* (I Cor. 1:23). He did not say, as it regards the Atonement, *"We preach Christ Resurrected. . . ."*

Of course, Paul preached the Resurrection of Christ, even as Chapter 15 of I Corinthians bears out, but not as the Atonement.

He also stated to the Church at Corinth and to all others as well, *"For I determined not to know any thing among you save Jesus Christ, and Him Crucified"* (I Cor. 2:2). He did not say, *"For I determined not to know any thing among you save Jesus Christ, and Him Resurrected. . . ."*

He also stated, *"But God forbid that I should glory, save in the Cross of our Lord Jesus Christ . . ."* (Gal. 6:14). He did not say, *"But God forbid that I should glory, save in the Resurrection of our Lord Jesus Christ. . . ."*

As we have stated, while the Resurrection, and the Ascension, and the Exaltation of Christ were of extreme significance, these three tremendous attributes were the result of the Atonement, i.e., *"the Cross,"* instead of the cause.

Let's look for a moment at the three great attributes of Resurrection, Ascension, and Exaltation.

THE RESURRECTION OF CHRIST

The Resurrection of Christ was not merely an incident. Several things are attributed to His Resurrection.

• Death was defeated: While we do not yet have all the effects of this great Victory over death, that awaiting the coming Rapture of the Church, still, due to the Cross, and the Resurrection of Christ, death has been defeated. When the Trump sounds, we will then be given the full reward of the great Victory won at Calvary's Cross. Paul said:

> "So when this corruptible *(sin nature)* shall have put on incorruption *(the Divine Nature in total control by the Holy Spirit)*, and this mortal *(subject to death)* shall have put on immortality *(will never die)*, then shall be brought to pass the saying that is written, Death is swallowed up in victory *([Isa. 25:8], the full benefits of the Cross will then*

be ours, of which we now have only the Firstfruits [Rom. 8:23])" **(I Cor. 15:54).**

• **The Resurrection of Christ guarantees the coming Resurrection of the Sainted Dead with them given a Glorified Body that will never see death, and with all those in Christ who are alive treated in like manner. So, His Resurrection, while guaranteeing our Resurrection, also guarantees a Glorified Body, actually, like unto Him. John wrote:**

> **"Beloved, now are we the sons of God** *(we are just as much a 'son of God' now as we will be after the Resurrection)***, and it does not yet appear what we shall be** *(our present state as a 'son of God' is not at all like that we shall be in the coming Resurrection)***: but we know that, when He shall appear** *(the Rapture)***, we shall be like Him** *(speaks of being glorified)***; for we shall see Him as He is.** *(Physical eyes in a mortal body could not look upon that Glory, only eyes in Glorified Bodies)*" **(I Jn. 3:2).**

• **His Resurrection guaranteed our Justification. Paul said concerning this:**

> **"Who was delivered for our offences** *(had to do with Jesus dying on the Cross for our sins; He had no sins)***, and was raised again for our Justification** *(we were raised with Him in newness of life [Rom. 6:4-5])*" **(Rom. 4:25).**

Commenting on the words, *"was raised for our Justification,"* Denney says, *"He was delivered up on account of our offences — to make atonement for them; and He was raised on account of our Justification — that it might become an accomplished fact. Paul does ascribe expiatory value to the death or blood of Christ: in a sense it is true the Work of Christ was finished on the Cross. But Paul never thought of that by itself: he knew Christ only as the Risen One Who had died, and Who had the virtue of His atoning death ever in Him; this Christ was One, and all that He did and suffered — The Christ Who had evoked in Him the faith by which he was justified, the only Christ through faith in Whom sinful men ever could be justified; and it is natural, therefore, that he should conceive Him as raised with a view to our justification."*

• **"Know you not, that so many of us as were bap-tized into Jesus Christ** *(plainly says that this Baptism is into Christ and not water [I Cor. 1:17; 12:13; Gal. 3:27; Eph. 4:5; Col. 2:11-13])* **were baptized into His Death?** *(When Christ died on the Cross, in the Mind of God, we died with Him; in other words, He became our Substitute, and our identification with Him in His Death gives us all the benefits for which He died; the idea is that He did it all for us!)*

"Therefore we are buried with Him by baptism into death *(not only did we die with Him, but we were buried with Him as well, which means that all the sin and trans-gression of the past were buried; when they put Him in the Tomb, they put all of our sins into that Tomb as well)***:** **that like as Christ was raised up from the dead by the Glory of the Father, even so we also should walk in new-ness of life** *(we died with Him, we were buried with Him, and His Resurrection was our Resurrection to a 'Newness of Life').*

THE LIKENESS OF HIS DEATH

"For if we have been planted together *(with Christ)* **in the likeness of His Death** *(Paul proclaims the Cross as the instrument through which all Blessings come; consequently, the Cross must ever be the Object of our Faith, which gives the Holy Spirit latitude to work within our lives)***, we shall be also in the** *likeness* **of** *His* **Resurrection** *(we can have the 'likeness of His Resurrection,' i.e., 'live this Resurrec-tion Life,' only as long as we understand the 'likeness of His*

Death,' which refers to the Cross as the means by which all of this is done)" **(Rom. 6:3-5).**

THE ASCENSION OF CHRIST

• **"Of Righteousness, because I go to My Father** *(As far as we know, the First thing that Jesus did after His Ascension, was to present a spotless Righteousness to the Father, namely Himself, which pertained to His Sacrifice at Calvary, that was accepted by God; consequently, that Righteousness is imputed to all who will believe in Him and His Work on the Cross)*, **and you see me no more** *(meaning that His Work was Finished)"* **(Jn. 16:10).**

• **The Ascension of Christ also opened the door for the Holy Spirit to be sent in a new dimension. He said:**

"Nevertheless I tell you the truth; It is expedient for you that I go away *(the Mission and Ministry of the Holy Spirit to the Body of Christ depended upon the return of Christ to the Father)*: **for if I go not away, the Comforter** *(Holy Spirit)* **will not come unto you** *(concerns the respective Office Work of Both Jesus and the Holy Spirit — Jesus as the Saviour of men, and the Holy Spirit as the Power of the Church)*; **but if I depart, I will send Him unto you** *(a Finished Work on the Cross was demanded of Christ, before the Holy Spirit could be sent)"* **(Jn. 16:7).**

THE EXALTATION OF CHRIST

• **Concerning the Exaltation Paul wrote:**

"Has in these last days *(the dispensation of Grace, which is the Church Age)* **spoken unto us by** *His* **Son** *(speaks of the Incarnation)*, **Whom He has appointed Heir of all things** *(through the means of the Cross)*, **by**

Whom also He made the worlds *(proclaims His Deity, as the previous phrase of Him being the 'Heir of all things' proclaims His Humanity)*;

AT THE RIGHT HAND OF THE MAJESTY ON HIGH

"Who being the brightness of *His* Glory *(the radiance of God's Glory)*, **and the express Image of His Person** *(the exact reproduction)*, **and upholding all things by the Word of His Power** *(carries the meaning of Jesus not only sustaining the weight of the universe, but also maintaining its coherence and carrying on its development)*, **when He had by Himself purged our sins** *(which He did at the Cross, dealing with sin regarding its cause, its power, and its guilt)*, **sat down on the Right Hand of the Majesty on high** *(speaks of the Finished Work of Christ, and that the Sacrifice was accepted by the Father)*" **(Heb. 1:2-3).**

GOD HAS HIGHLY EXALTED HIM

• **"And being found in fashion as a man** *(denotes Christ in men's eyes)*, **He humbled Himself** *(He was brought low, but willingly)*, **and became obedient unto death** *(does not mean He became obedient to death; He was always the Master of Death; rather, He subjected Himself to death)*, **even the death of the Cross.** *(This presents the character of His Death as one of disgrace and degradation, which was necessary for men to be redeemed. This type of death alone would pay the terrible sin debt, and do so in totality.)*

"Wherefore God also has highly exalted Him *(to a place of supreme Majesty; Jesus has always been Creator, but now He is Saviour as well)*, **and given Him a Name which is above every name** *(actually says, 'The Name,' referring to a specific Name and Title; that Name, as Verse 11 proclaims, is 'Lord')*:

JESUS CHRIST IS LORD

"**That at the Name of Jesus every knee should bow** *(in the sphere of the Name, which refers to all it entails; all of this is a result of the Cross, the price paid there, and the Redemption consequently afforded)*, **of *things* in Heaven, and *things* in Earth, and *things* under the Earth** *(all Creation will render homage, whether animate or inanimate)*;

"**And *that* every tongue should confess that Jesus Christ is Lord** *(proclaims 'Lord' as the 'Name' of Verse 9; it means 'Master' of all, which again has been made possible by the Cross)*, **to the Glory of God the Father.** *(The acknowledgment of the Glory of Christ is the acknowledgment of the Glory of the Father.)*" **(Phil. 2:8-11).**

THE INTERCESSORY WORK OF CHRIST

The Exaltation of Christ also includes His Intercessory Work, all on our behalf. Paul again wrote:

"**Wherefore He** *(the Lord Jesus Christ)* **is able also to save them to the uttermost** *(proclaims the fact that Christ Alone has made the only true Atonement for sin; He did this at the Cross)* **who come unto God by Him** *(proclaims the only manner in which man can come to God)*, **seeing He ever lives to make intercession for them.** *(His very Presence by the Right Hand of the Father guarantees such, with nothing else having to be done.)*" **(Heb. 7:25).**

THE THRONE OF GRACE

In regard to His Intercessory Work, Paul also said:

"**For we have not an High Priest which cannot be touched with the feeling of our infirmities** *(being Very*

Man as well as Very God, He can do such); **but was at all points tempted like as** *we are, yet* **without sin.** *(His temptation, and ours as well, was to leave the prescribed Will of God, which is the Word of God; but He never did, not even one time.)*

"Let us therefore come boldly unto the Throne of Grace *(presents the Seat of Divine Power, and yet the Source of boundless Grace)*, **that we may obtain Mercy** *(presents that which we want first)*, **and find Grace to help in time of need** *(refers to the Goodness of God extended to all who come, and during any 'time of need'; all made possible by the Cross)*" **(Heb. 4:15-16).**

As should be obvious, while the Resurrection, the Ascension, and the Exaltation of Christ were, as previously stated, of utmost significance, still, these tremendous attributes were the result of what Jesus did at the Cross. This means that it was and is the Cross, which made and makes it all possible.

As I close the answer to the question, *"Is the Atonement found solely in the Cross or the Resurrection?",* the following word given by Oswald Chambers would be appropriate. He titled it, the heading that I will once again use:

IT IS FINISHED

"I have finished the Work which You gave Me to do" (Jn. 17:4).

"The Death of Jesus Christ is the performance in history of the very Mind of God. There is no room for looking on Jesus Christ as a martyr; His death was not something that happened to Him which might have been prevented; His death was the very reason why He came.

"Never build your preaching of forgiveness on the fact that God is our Father and He will forgive us merely because He loves us. It is untrue to Jesus Christ's revelation of God; it makes the Cross unnecessary, and the Redemption 'much ado about nothing.' If God does forgive sin, it is because of the Death of

Christ. God could forgive men in no other way than by the Death of His Son, and Jesus is exalted to be Savior because of His Death. 'We see Jesus because of the suffering of death, crowned with glory and honor.' The greatest note of triumph that ever sounded in the ears of a startled universe was that sounded on the Cross of Christ — 'it is finished.' That is the last word in the Redemption of man.

THE CROSS OF CHRIST

"Anything that belittles or obliterates the holiness of God by a false view of the love of God, is untrue to the Revelation of God given by Jesus Christ. Never allow the thought that Jesus Christ stands with us against God out of pity and compassion; that He became a curse for us out of sympathy with us. Jesus Christ became a curse for us by the Divine Decree. Our portion of realizing the terrific meaning of the curse is conviction of sin, the gift of shame and penitence is given us — this is the great Mercy of God. Jesus Christ hates the wrong in man, and Calvary is the estimate of His hatred."[1]

CHAPTER THREE

Is It Who He Is Or What He Did?

QUESTION:

IS IT WHO HE IS OR WHAT HE DID?

ANSWER:

It is both!
No one but Jesus could have redeemed mankind; however, Redemption was carried out by Jesus going to the Cross.

DEMEANING THE CROSS OF CHRIST

I certainly won't say all, but most people who ask the question, *"Is it Who He is, or what He has done?,"* are demeaning the Cross. They have formed another manner of Redemption, another manner of Sanctification, in their minds till they are rejecting the Cross. It must ever be understood that the Cross of Christ, what Jesus did there, affected the whole of Atonement. That's where the contest took place and that's where the victory was won. The Cross of Christ is not a last minute adjustment, in other words, something that just happened, but rather was formulated in the Mind of God from before the foundation of the world.

BEFORE THE FOUNDATION OF THE WORLD

Peter said:

"Forasmuch as you know that you were not redeemed with corruptible things, as silver and gold *(presents the fact that the most precious commodities [silver and gold] could not redeem fallen man)*, from your vain conversation *(vain lifestyle)* received by tradition from your fathers *(speaks of original sin that is passed on from father to child at conception)*;

"But with the Precious Blood of Christ *(presents the*

payment, which proclaims the poured out Life of Christ on behalf of sinners), **as of a Lamb without blemish and without spot** *(speaks of the lambs offered as substitutes in the Old Jewish economy; the Death of Christ was not an execution or assassination, but rather a Sacrifice; the Offering of Himself presented a Perfect Sacrifice, for He was Perfect in every respect [Ex. 12:5])*:

"**Who verily was foreordained before the foundation of the world** *(refers to the fact that God, in His Omniscience, knew He would create man, man would Fall, and man would be redeemed by Christ going to the Cross; this was all done before the universe was created; this means the Cross of Christ is the Foundation Doctrine of all Doctrine, referring to the fact that all Doctrine must be built upon that Foundation, or else it is specious)*, **but was manifest in these last times for you** *(refers to the invisible God Who, in the Person of the Son, was made visible to human eyesight by assuming a human body and human limitations)*" **(I Pet. 1:18-20).**

We should well understand that something, which was planned in the Mind of the Godhead from eternity past and will extend to eternity future, should not be taken lightly. One must understand, the only thing that stands between mankind and eternal Hell is the Cross of Christ. One could also say, that the only thing that stands between the church and apostasy is the Cross of Christ. It is not possible to make too much of the Cross, but, definitely possible to make too little of the Cross. Unfortunately, despite the clarity of the Word of God, there are enemies of the Cross.

ENEMIES OF THE CROSS

Paul addressed this in many ways, but, perhaps one of his most potent statements is found in his Epistle to the Philippians. He said:

"**Brethren, be followers together of me** *(be 'fellow-imitators')*, **and mark them who walk so as you have us for an example** *(observe intently)*.

"**(For many walk** *(speaks of those attempting to live for God outside of the victory and rudiments of the Cross of Christ)*, **of whom I have told you often, and now tell you even weeping** *(this is a most serious matter)*, **that they are the enemies of the Cross of Christ** *(those who do not look exclusively to the Cross of Christ must be labeled 'enemies')*:

DESTRUCTION

"**Whose end is destruction** *(if the Cross is ignored, and continues to be ignored, the loss of the soul is the only ultimate conclusion)*, **whose god is their belly** *(refers to those who attempt to pervert the Gospel for their own personal gain)*, **and whose glory is in their shame** *(the material things they seek, God labels as 'shame')*, **who mind earthly things.)** *(This means they have no interest in heavenly things, which signifies they are using the Lord for their own personal gain)*" **(Phil. 3:17-19).**

The great Apostle also stated:

APOSTASY

"**Now the Spirit** *(Holy Spirit)* **speaks expressly** *(pointedly)*, **that in the latter times** *(the times in which we now live, the last of the last days, which begin the fulfillment of Endtime Prophecies)* **some shall depart from the Faith** *(anytime Paul uses the term 'the Faith,' in short he is referring to the Cross; so, we are told here that some will depart from the Cross as the means of Salvation and Victory)*, **giving heed to seducing spirits** *(evil spirits, i.e., 'religious spirits,' making something seem like what it isn't)*, **and**

doctrines of devils *(should have been translated, 'doctrines of demons'; the 'seducing spirits' entice Believers away from the true Faith, causing them to believe 'doctrines inspired by demon spirits')*" **(I Tim. 4:1)**

JESUS HAS ALWAYS BEEN GOD

As God, our Lord was unformed, unmade, uncreated, has always been, always is. That might be difficult for us to understand, simply because, as it regards human beings, we always look to the beginning of something or the ending of it. But, our Lord had no beginning. He always was as He always is.

When He became man, while He laid aside the expression of His Deity, He never for a moment laid aside the possession of His Deity. Born in the home of peasants and raised in the same manner, still, He was God. But, I must remind the Bible Student of the following:

As God and God Alone, not a single person was redeemed. Now, the reader must understand that. Man was not redeemed until God became Man, and did so for the purpose of going to the Cross, which He did, in order that man might be redeemed. In other words, for man to be redeemed, Jesus Christ would have to die on the Cross.

Now don't misunderstand, God is Omnipotent, meaning that He is all-powerful, meaning that He can do anything. As well, He is Omniscient, meaning that He knows everything, past, present, and future. As well, he is Omnipresent, meaning that He is everywhere, and for all time. So, this means that God could have redeemed man without becoming man and going to the Cross; however, the Godhead, even from before the foundation of the world, through foreknowledge knew that man would be created and that man would fall. As well, it was deemed necessary that God would become man in order to redeem man. This was the best way in order for man to be Saved.

So, man was not redeemed until Jesus died on the Cross, thereby, paying the price that man could not pay and, thereby, making it possible for man to be Saved.

Jesus came to this world to do many things; however, His primary Objective, which was all-important, and for which was His express purpose, was the Cross.

MESSIAH, THE OBEDIENT SERVANT

"I clothe the Heavens with blackness, and I make sackcloth their covering. *(The assertion here is that if He so chooses, He could leave all nature in absolute darkness — a power necessarily belonging only to Him Who said, 'Let there be light; and there was light' [Gen. 1:3].)*

"The Lord GOD has given Me the tongue of the learned, that I should know how to speak a Word in season to him who is weary: He wakens morning by morning, He wakens My ear to hear as the learned. *(The intent of the Holy Spirit in this Chapter is to portray to man the inexhaustible Power of God that could, if He so chose, use that Power in any capacity, but rather chose to send His Only Son to 'redeem' not only Israel, but the entirety of mankind.*

"In Verse 4, He is presented as the Perfect Disciple. He only spoke the Words, which were given Him by God ['that I should know how to speak']. He asserted this seven times when on Earth [Jn. 7:16; 8:28, 46-47; 14:10, 24; 17:8].

"The phrase, 'He wakens morning by morning, He wakens My ear to hear as the learned,' refers to the fact that God held immediate and constant communication with the 'Servant'— not enlightening Him occasionally, as He did the Prophets by dreams and visions, but continually whispering in His Ear.

"In fact, the phrase, 'Morning by morning,' is not to be narrowed to the bare literal meaning, but to be taken in the sense of 'uninterruptedly.' All of this was not necessarily for His Own benefit, but rather that 'He should know how to speak a Word in season to him who is weary.')

THE TRUE SERVANT

"The Lord GOD has opened My ear, and I was not rebellious, neither turned away back. *(This Verse pertains to the entire willingness of Christ to hear the Father, and to do so as the True Servant, as contrasted with the professed servant, or Children of Israel.*

" 'Neither turned away back,' refers to Him being most tried. Even in the Garden of Gethsemane, His final Word was, 'Not My Will, but Thine, be done' [Lk. 22:42].)

HIS SUFFERING

"I gave My back to the smiters, and My cheeks to them who plucked off the hair: I hid not My face from shame and spitting. *(This Verse addresses itself to the hours before the Crucifixion. Mat. 26:67 and 27:26 fulfill this Passage.*

"That our Lord, of such power as is described in Verse 3, could contain Himself, when His Own People would treat Him thusly, is beyond comprehension! Their response to His Love was their hate. They whipped Him, pulled His beard from His Face, and spit on Him.

"Their doing it was no surprise. By His Omniscience, He knew before He came what the results would be. And yet, He came anyway!)

SET MY FACE LIKE FLINT

"For the Lord GOD will help Me; therefore shall I not be confounded: therefore have I set My face like a flint, and I know that I shall not be ashamed. *(Lk. 9:31, 51 fulfill this Verse. The 'help' that His Father gave Him was that He might finish the task of redeeming mankind. The idea of redeeming someone who responds only with hate cannot be comprehended by the mortal mind, especially* *when one considers what that redemption costs!*

"'I set My face like a flint,' refers to the resolve of accomplishing a certain thing despite all the scorn and hatred)"
(Isa. 50:3-7).

As stated, the Cross was the objective of Christ, in other words, the very reason that He came. While everything else He did was of utmost significance, as should be understood, still, the following must be noted:

THE MINISTRY OF CHRIST

• While the conception of Christ by the Holy Spirit in the womb of Mary was absolutely necessary, still, had it stopped there, no one would have been redeemed.
• While the Life of Christ of total perfection was absolutely necessary, still, if it had stopped there, no one would have been Saved.
• While the Miracles and Healings of Christ were, as well, necessary, still, had it stopped there, no one would have been redeemed.
• While the Incarnation of Christ, God becoming Man, was absolutely necessary, still, had it stopped there, no one would have been Saved.
• In fact, the purpose and reason for everything He did was meant to lead to the Cross where, there the price would be paid, the demands of a thrice-Holy God would be satisfied, that *"whosoever will may come and drink of the water of life freely."*
Let us *say it again. Jesus has always been God and never ceased to be God, not even for a single moment.* Still, had it stopped there without Him going to the Cross, no one would have been Saved.

WHY DID GOD HAVE TO BECOME MAN?

In the first place, due to the fact that the supreme Sacrifice had to be the Cross, this excluded God as God. The reason? God is Spirit and a Spirit cannot die. So, in order to redeem mankind, that is, that the price be paid once and for all, God would have to become Man, which He did, and for the express purpose of going to the Cross. In effect, one might say that the Incarnation, God becoming Man, and the Cross of Christ, might be looked at as one and the same.

JOHN THE BELOVED

Concerning the very thing, John the Beloved wrote, saying:

"**In the beginning** *(does not infer that Christ as God had a beginning, because as God He had no beginning, but rather refers to the time of Creation [Gen. 1:1])* **was the Word** *(the Holy Spirit through John describes Jesus as 'the Eternal Logos')*, **and the Word was with God** *('was in relationship with God,' and expresses the idea of the Trinity)*, **and the Word was God** *(meaning that He did not cease to be God during the Incarnation; He 'was' and 'is' God from eternity past to eternity future)*.

The Apostle then went on to say:

"**And the Word was made flesh** *(refers to the Incarnation, 'God becoming man')* **and dwelt among us** *(refers to Jesus, although Perfect, not holding Himself aloft from all others, but rather lived as all men, even a peasant)*, **(and we beheld His Glory, the Glory as of the Only Begotten of the Father,)** *(speaks of His Deity, although hidden from the eyes of the merely curious; while Christ laid aside the expression of His Deity, He never lost the possession of His Deity)* **full of Grace and Truth** *(as 'flesh,' proclaimed His Humanity, 'Grace and Truth' His Deity)*.

And finally:

"**The next day** *(refers to the day after John had been questioned by the emissaries from the Sanhedrin)* **John sees Jesus coming unto him** *(is, no doubt, after the Baptism of Jesus, and the temptation in the wilderness)*, **and said, Behold the Lamb of God** *(proclaims Jesus as the Sacrifice for sin, in fact, the Sin-Offering, Whom all the multiple millions of offered lambs had represented)*, **which takes away the sin of the world** *(animal blood could only cover sin, it could not take it away; but Jesus offering Himself as the Perfect Sacrifice took away the sin of the world; He not only cleansed acts of sin but, as well, addressed the root cause [Col. 2:14-15])*" **(Jn. 1:1, 14, 29).**

AN EVERLASTING COVENANT

Once again, in order to redeem mankind, at least those who will believe, it was not only Who Jesus was and is, the Son of the Living God, but, as well, it was what He did, which refers to the Cross. In fact, Who Jesus was and is and what He did is, one might say, the very core of the Gospel. To impugn either one of these attributes, Who He is and what He did is, in fact, wicked. But, again we remind the reader, while Who He was presented itself as an absolute necessity, as should be obvious, that for which He came to this world to do, and we speak of the Cross, is what redeemed mankind. God as God did not redeem man. God had to become Man in order for this great Work to be carried out. And, let it be quickly said, what He did at the Cross was of such magnitude, so perfect, that the Apostle Paul said the following:

"**Now the God of Peace** *(proclaims that Peace has been made between God and fallen man, and done so through what Jesus did on the Cross on man's behalf)*, **that brought again from the dead our Lord Jesus** *(presents the only mention of the Resurrection of Christ in this Epistle to the Hebrews)*, **that Great Shepherd of the Sheep** *(presents the*

One Who died for us, and Whom God raised from the dead), **through the Blood of the Everlasting Covenant** *(points to the Cross and proclaims the fact that this Covenant, being perfect, is Eternal)*" **(Heb. 13:20).**

CHAPTER FOUR

Can Faith In The Cross Be Turned Into Works?

QUESTION:

CAN FAITH IN THE CROSS BE TURNED INTO WORKS?

ANSWER:

Yes, it can!

And yet, we must be quick to state, proper Faith in Christ and the Cross, which is the only Faith that God will recognize, will always produce good works. In effect, that's what James was talking about when he said:

"But will you know, O vain man, that Faith without works is dead?" (James 2:20).

The idea is, James is saying, *"If a person claims to have Faith and no proper works are being produced, such a person is deceiving himself."* As stated, proper Faith will always produce proper works. And yet, we must be very careful that we do not try to gain Faith by works. Such cannot be done. Works do not produce proper Faith, but, proper Faith will always produce proper works.

THE MANNER IN WHICH FAITH IN THE CROSS CAN BE TURNED INTO WORKS

• Pride: If anyone hears and understands the Message of the Cross, thereby, understanding the significance of that which has been learned, for such a one to exhibit a prideful attitude, a holier-than-thou attitude, automatically turns the whole body of learning into works. Pride always leads to self-righteousness, and such can be easily brought about if a proper attitude isn't maintained.

We must be ever mindful of the fact that it's a whole lot easier reverting from the Holy Spirit to the flesh, than to revert from the flesh to the Holy Spirit. Pride is ever a possible factor. That's at least one of the reasons that Jesus said:

"Watch and pray, that you enter not into temptation

(a warning of the temptation that was about to come upon them — the temptation to forsake Him): **the spirit** *(spirit of man)* **indeed** *is* **willing, but the flesh is weak** *(this battle can be won only by our Faith being placed exclusively in Christ and His Cross, which then gives the Holy Spirit the latitude to work within our lives [Rom. 6:3-14; 8:1-2, 11])*" **(Mat. 26:41).**

This danger of getting into the *"flesh"* is prevalent at all times with no exemption found, even in the Message of the Cross.

• When the Believer learns and understands the great Message of the Cross and then begins to think that because of His Faith properly placed, God owes him something, he has just turned such Faith into works. Our Lord owes no man anything, while we owe Him everything. Jesus had something to say about this.

UNPROFITABLE SERVANTS

"But which of you, having a servant plowing or feeding cattle, will say unto him by and by *(immediately)*, when he is come from the field, Go and sit down to meat?

"And will not rather say unto him, Make ready wherewith I may sup, and gird yourself, and serve me, till I have eaten and drank; and afterward you shall eat and drink? *(A faithful servant will attend to his duties first, and himself second.)*

"Does he thank that servant because he did the things that were commanded him? I trow not *(I think not!)*.

"So likewise, when you shall have done all those things which are commanded you, say, We are unprofitable servants: we have done that which was our duty to do *(the Lord, in essence, says that having fulfilled all these conditions, which were their duty to do, they would be no better than unprofitable servants; this is a fatal blow to the doctrine of salvation by works; the Disciple is to say,*

'I am an unprofitable servant'; the Master will then say, 'Well done, good and faithful servant')" **(Lk. 17:7-10; Mat. 25:21).**

SELF-RIGHTEOUSNESS

Self-righteousness lurks in the shadows at all times. Whenever the individual is lifted up in religious pride, self-righteousness is always the end result. The Believer should always understand that we have nothing God wants or desires, except our heart. So, the idea of learning and understanding great Biblical Truths and, in fact, that the Message of the Cross is the greatest Truth of all, does not make one immune to the acute danger of our Faith in Christ and the Cross being turned into works. Paul had this to say:

"What shall we say then that Abraham our father, as pertaining to the flesh, has found? *(Having stated that the Old Testament teaches that God justifies the sinner on the Faith principle as opposed to the merit principle, the Holy Spirit now brings forward Abraham.)*
"For if Abraham were justified by works *(which he wasn't)*, **he has** *whereof* **to glory; but not before God** *(the boasting of Salvation by works, which God will not accept)*.

ABRAHAM BELIEVED GOD

"For what says the Scripture? Abraham believed God, and it was counted unto him for Righteousness *([Gen. 15:6] if one properly understands this Verse, he properly understands the Bible; Abraham gained Righteousness by simple Faith in God, Who would send a Redeemer into the world (Jn. 8:56]).*
"Now to him who works *(tries to earn Salvation)* **is the reward** *(Righteousness)* **not reckoned of Grace** *(the Grace of God)*, **but of debt** *(claiming that God owes us*

something, which He doesn't!).

"**But to him who works not** *(doesn't trust in works for Salvation)*, **but believes on Him Who Justifies the ungodly** *(through Christ and the Cross)*, **his faith is counted for Righteousness** *(God awards Righteousness only on the basis of Faith in Christ and His Finished Work)*" **(Rom. 4:1-5).**

HUMILITY

The Truth is, there is only one way that humility, and we speak of Biblical humility, can be brought about in the life of the Believer, and that is by one's Faith being anchored solely in the Cross of Christ. In fact, the Cross strips men of all pretension, all supposed merit, all trust in works, etc. Without Faith properly placed in the Cross of Christ, humility will remain elusive. There is nothing in the world worse than a Believer trying to bring himself to a state of humility by his own efforts. The end result is always the opposite! Paul addressed this by saying:

"**Which things have indeed a show of wisdom in will worship** *(refers to worship devised and prescribed by man, which characterizes most of the modern church)*, **and humility** *(false humility)*, **and neglecting of the body** *(speaks of the human body)*; **not in any honor to the satisfying of the flesh.** *(All ascetic observances, while they appeal to men as indications of superior wisdom and piety, have no value as remedies against sensual indulgence. That can be handled only at the Cross)*" **(Col. 2:23).**

CLOTHED WITH HUMILITY

Peter said:

"**. . . and be clothed with humility** *(refers to the virtue that must grace all other virtues, which can only come by*

Faith in the Cross): **for God resists the proud** *(He sets Himself in array against the proud person)*, **and gives grace to the humble.** *(One who places his Faith exclusively in the Cross of Christ.)*

"**Humble yourselves therefore under the Mighty Hand of God** *(the Cross alone and one's Faith in that Finished Work can make one humble)*, **that He may exalt you in due time** *(proclaims the route to the Blessings of God)*:

"**Casting all your care upon Him** *(refers here to a direct and once-for-all committal to God of all that would give us concern)*; **for He cares for you** *(translated literally, 'for you are His concern')*.

THE FAITH

"**Be sober** *(mentally self-controlled)*, **be vigilant** *(awake and watchful)*; **because your adversary the Devil, as a roaring lion, walks about, seeking whom he may devour** *(we are faced with a very powerful adversary)*:

"**Whom** *(the Devil)* **resist steadfast in the Faith** *('the Faith' always refers to what Jesus did at the Cross; our Faith must be ever anchored in that Finished Work)*, **knowing that the same afflictions are accomplished in your Brethren who are in the world.** *(Every true Christian faces the onslaught of the Evil One)*" **(I Pet. 5:5-9)**.

BE THANKFUL

Always be thankful to the Lord that you have had the privilege of knowing and understanding the great Message of the Cross, which is God's Prescription, one might say, for life and living. Instead of allowing the flesh to produce pride, allow Grace to produce humility.

"Ten thousand times ten thousand, In sparkling raiment bright;

"The armies of the ransomed Saints, Throng up the steeps of light:
"'Tis finished, all is finished, Their fight with death and sin;
"Fling open wide the Golden Gates, And let the Victors in."

"What rush of Alleluias, Fills all the Earth and sky!
"What ringing of a thousand harps, Bespeaks the triumph nigh!
"O day, for which creation, And all its tribes were made!
"O joy, for all its former woes, A thousandfold repaid!"

"O, then what raptured greetings, On Canaan's happy shore,
"What knitting severed friendships up, Where partings are no more;
"Then eyes with joy shall sparkle, That brimmed with tears of late;
"Orphans no longer fatherless, Nor widows desolate."

"Bring near Thy great Salvation, Thou Lamb for sinners slain;
"Fill up the roll of Thine elect, Then take Thy Power, and reign;
"Appear, Desire of nations, Thine exiles long for home;
"Show in the heavens Thy promised Sign, Thou Prince and Savior, come."

CHAPTER FIVE

Will Proper Faith In The Cross Of Christ Ultimately Bring The Believer To Sinless Perfection?

QUESTION:

WILL PROPER FAITH IN THE CROSS OF CHRIST ULTIMATELY BRING THE BELIEVER TO SINLESS PERFECTION?

ANSWER:

No!

The Bible does not teach sinless perfection; however, it most definitely does teach that the sin nature is not to have dominion over us. Paul said:

"**For sin shall not have dominion over you** *(the sin nature will not have dominion over us if we as Believers continue to exercise Faith in the Cross of Christ; otherwise, the sin nature most definitely will have dominion over the Believer)*: **for you are not under the Law** *(means that if we try to live this life by any type of law, no matter how good that law might be in its own right, we will conclude by the sin nature having dominion over us)*, **but under Grace** *(the Grace of God flows to the Believer on an unending basis only as long as the Believer exercises Faith in Christ and what He did at the Cross; Grace is merely the Goodness of God exercised by and through the Holy Spirit, and given to undeserving Saints)*" **(Rom. 6:14).**

WHAT IS THE DIFFERENCE IN COMMITTING ACTS OF SIN AND THE DOMINION OF SIN?

That's a good question!

The word *"dominion"* in the Greek is *"kurieuo,"* and means *"to rule, to exercise lordship over."*

Sin dominating a person refers to a particular type of sin over which the Believer cannot seemingly get victory. It could be lust, gambling, drugs, alcohol, nicotine, jealousy, envy, uncontrollable temper, etc.

Before any person comes to Christ, they are ruled by the sin nature 24 hours a day, 7 days a week. In other words, totally and completely. This is the cause of all war, hunger, crime, man's inhumanity to his fellowman, etc. But, when the person comes to Christ, in effect, and immediately, they are set free from all type of sin irrespective as to what it is. In other words, the sin nature, one might say, is unplugged. It is meant to stay that way, but, unfortunately, it never does.

The moment the Believer places his faith in something (anything) other than the Cross of Christ or in conjunction with the Cross of Christ, such activity greatly limits the Holy Spirit. Such a person, even though they don't realize it, is now living in a state of spiritual adultery. This means that the Believer is being unfaithful to Christ. As stated, this greatly hinders the Holy Spirit and so, such a Believer is now left to his own devices. That's when the sin nature begins to have a revival, actually lording it over the person, ruling the person's life in some way and, in fact, getting worse month by month, etc. Such dominion can be broken only by the individual placing his or her faith exclusively in the Cross of Christ, which then gives the Holy Spirit, Who is God, latitude to work within our lives, which He will instantly begin to do. What is impossible for us is very much possible for Him. The sad fact is, most modern Christians, virtually all, are ruled by the sin nature, which makes life almost unbearable.

How do I know that?

I know it because the only remedy for this dilemma is the Cross, and that is not being preached. In fact, if the Message of the Cross is not outright denied, as it is with the Word of Faith people, so-called, then it is ignored in most circles. Even those who believe in the Cross and preach it strongly, regarding Salvation, have no knowledge whatsoever as it regards the Cross pertaining to Sanctification; in other words, how we live this life for the Lord.

Even with the sin nature inactive, so to speak, which can only be brought about by the Believer placing his faith exclusively in Christ and the Cross, still, such a Believer will in some way fail the Lord. We make a grave mistake when we limit sin to what I refer to as the big five — nicotine, alcohol, immorality, gambling, drugs.

COMING SHORT OF THE GLORY OF GOD

The truth is, every single Believer on the face of the Earth, even the godliest, is constantly coming short of the Glory of God. Paul said:

"**For all have sinned** *(presents all men placed in the same category)***, and come short of the Glory of God** *(the Greek Text infers that even the most Righteous among us continue to come short of the Glory of God on a continuing basis)*" **(Rom. 3:23).**

All of this means that we would have no standing at all before God without the Lord Jesus Christ and our Faith in Him and what He did for us at the Cross. The Believer remains Saved on the premise of two particulars. They are:

1. "**But if we walk in the Light, as He is in the Light, we have fellowship one with another** *(if we claim fellowship with Him, we will at the same time walk in the Light, which is the sphere of His Walk)***, and the Blood of Jesus Christ His Son cleanses us from all sin.** *(Our Faith being in the Cross, the shed Blood of Jesus Christ, constantly cleanses us from all sin. In other words, as we are constantly coming short of the Glory of God, the Blood of Jesus Christ is constantly cleansing)*" **(I Jn. 1:7).**
2. "**Wherefore He** *(the Lord Jesus Christ)* **is able also to save them to the uttermost** *(proclaims the fact that Christ Alone has made the only true Atonement for sin; He did this at the Cross)* **who come unto God by Him** *(proclaims the*

only manner in which man can come to God), **seeing He ever lives to make intercession for them.** *(His very Presence by the Right Hand of the Father guarantees such, with nothing else having to be done [Heb. 1:3])*" **(Heb. 7:25).**

THE ANSWER OF PAUL THE APOSTLE
TO SINLESS PERFECTION

Even Paul, who wrote nearly half the New Testament, who was given the meaning of the New Covenant, which is the meaning of the Cross, did not claim sinless perfection.
He said:

"That I may know Him *(referring to what Christ did at the Cross)*, **and the Power of His Resurrection** *(refers to being raised with Him in 'Newness of Life' [Rom. 6:3-5])*, **and the fellowship of His sufferings** *(regarding our trust and Faith placed in what He did for us at the Cross)*, **being made conformable unto His Death** *(to conform to what He did for us at the Cross, understanding that this is the only means of Salvation and Sanctification)*;
"If by any means I might attain unto the Resurrection of the dead. *(This does not refer to the coming Resurrection, but rather the believing sinner being baptized into the Death of Christ [refers to the Crucifixion], and raised in 'Newness of Life,' which gives Victory over all sin [Rom. 6:3-5, 11, 14])*.

PAUL NEVER CLAIMED SINLESS PERFECTION

"Not as though I had already attained, either were already perfect *(the Apostle is saying he doesn't claim sinless perfection)*: **but I follow after** *(to pursue)*, **if that I may apprehend** *(Paul is pursuing absolute Christlikeness)* **that for which also I am apprehended of Christ Jesus.** *(He was Saved by Christ for the purpose of becoming Christlike,* *and so are we!)*

"**Brethren, I count not myself to have apprehended** *(in effect, repeats what he said in the previous Verse)*: **but** *this* **one thing I** *do***, forgetting those things which are behind** *(refers to things the Apostle had depended upon to find favor with God, and the failure that type of effort brought about [Phil. 3:5-6])***, reaching forth unto those things which are before** *(all our attention must be on that which is ahead, and not on what is past; 'those things' consists of all the victories of the Cross)***,**

"**I press toward the mark** *(this represents a moral and Spiritual Target)* **for the prize of the high calling of God (Christlikeness) in Christ Jesus** *(proclaims the manner and means in which all of this is done, which is the Cross [I Cor. 1:17-18; 2:2])*" **(Phil. 3:10-14).**

WHY IS THE SIN NATURE ALLOWED TO REMAIN IN THE NATURE OF THE BELIEVER?

The sin nature has been allowed by the Lord to remain in the nature of believing man in order that we might learn God's Way of Victory and, as well, exercise our Faith and Trust in Him.

Everything the Lord does is for a reason, and is always for our good. He does nothing intended to hurt us but only to help us.

Peter said:

"**You therefore, beloved, seeing you know** *these things* **before** *(the Holy Spirit, through Peter, tells those to whom the Apostle was writing that they were not without understanding regarding what was being taught)***, beware lest you also, being led away with the error of the wicked** *(refers to being led away from the Cross)***, fall from your own steadfastness** *(refers here to the proper application of one's Faith; the Cross of Christ must always be the Object of the Saint's Faith; if we shift our Faith to anything else,* we 'fall' *[Gal. 5:4])*.

The great Apostle then said:

"**But grow in Grace** *(presents the only way the Saint can grow)*, **and** *in* **the knowledge of our Lord and Saviour Jesus Christ.** *(This 'knowledge' refers not only to Who Christ is [the Lord of Glory], but, as well, what He did in order that we might be Redeemed, which points to the Cross.)* **To Him** *be* **Glory both now and forever. Amen.** *(This refers to such belonging to Him, because He is the One Who paid the price for man's Redemption)*" **(II Pet. 3:17-18).**

NOT YET GLORIFIED

Besides that which we have just given, the Lord allows the sin nature to remain because we aren't yet Glorified. Concerning that, the Apostle Paul said:

"**. . . and we shall be changed** *(put on the Glorified Body)*.

"**For this corruptible** *(sin nature)* **must put on incorruption** *(a Glorified Body with no sin nature)*, **and this mortal** *(subject to death)* **must put on immortality** *(will never die)*.

"**So when this corruptible** *(sin nature)* **shall have put on incorruption** *(the Divine Nature in total control by the Holy Spirit)*, **and this mortal** *(subject to death)* **shall have put on immortality** *(will never die)*, **then shall be brought to pass the saying that is written, Death is swallowed up in Victory** *([Isa. 25:8], the full benefits of the Cross will then be ours, of which we now have only the Firstfruits [Rom 8:23])*" **(I Cor. 15:52-54).**

TEMPTATION

There's nothing the Believer can do that will eliminate the

sin nature out of his or her life. Likewise, there is nothing the Believer can do to stop all temptation.

However, concerning temptation, we do have this Promise of the Lord:

"**Wherefore let him who thinks he stands** *(is addressed to all Believers)* **take heed lest he fall.** *(This means to not merely fall from fellowship as some teach, but to fall from Eternal Salvation. This won't happen if the Cross is ever in view.)*

"**There has no temptation taken you but such as is common to man** *(refers to the limitations God has placed upon Satan respecting that which he can or cannot do)*: **but God is faithful, Who will not suffer you to be tempted above that you are able** *(we have His Promise; all temptation is overcome by our Faith remaining constant in Christ and the Cross, which gives the Power of the Holy Spirit to help us [Rom. 8:2])*; **but will with the temptation also make a way to escape, that you may be able to bear** *it. (As stated, the 'way of escape' is always the Cross [Eph. 6:10-18])*.

"**Wherefore, my dearly beloved, flee from idolatry.** *(Anything in which we place our Faith, other than the Cross of Christ, becomes an idol)*" **(I Cor. 10:12-14).**

The short phrase that says, *"That you may be able to bear it,"* and concerning temptation, is interesting indeed!

This means that the Lord has allowed Satan to present the temptation, whatever it might be, and, as well, it is the Lord Who sets the limits as it regards how much Satan is able to do. In other words, the Evil One can only do what the Lord allows him to do.

WHY DOES THE LORD ALLOW TEMPTATION REGARDING HIS PEOPLE?

The Lord allows temptation for the same reason that He

allows the sin nature to remain in the life of the Believer. He wants us to learn trust in Him and to have Faith in Christ and what Christ has done for us at the Cross.

Overcoming such temptation increases our Faith. Even if we don't overcome it, such serves as a teacher as it regards our inadequacy, causing us to take stock as to what is wrong! As it regards the Child of God, everything is a test. How will we act? How will we react?

JESUS WASHES THE DISCIPLES' FEET

This, the foot washing episode, as carried out by Christ, completely abolishes the idea of sinless perfection. The Scripture says:

"**Jesus knowing that the Father had given all things into His Hands** *(portrays two things in His heart as He girded Himself, His conscience Deity and the heartless conduct of Judas)*, **and that He was come from God, and went to God** *(was something that He knew, at least from the time that He was twelve years old)*;

"**He rose from supper** *(He rose from the table when the preparation had been completed)*, **and laid aside His garments** *(physically, His outer Robe; spiritually, He laid aside the expression of His Deity, while never losing the possession of His Deity)*; **and took a towel** *(refers to the action of the lowliest slave or servant in a household; it represents the servant spirit possessed by Christ)*, **and girded Himself** *(wrapped Himself in the towel; spiritually speaking, it refers to His Human Body provided for Him by the Father [Heb. 10:5] in order to serve as a Sacrifice on the Cross for sin)*.

"**After that He poured water into a basin** *(spiritually, it referred to the Holy Spirit, which would pour from Him like a River [Jn. 7:38-39])*, **and began to wash the Disciples' feet** *(presenting the servant principle which we* *are to follow, but even more particularly the cleansing guaranteed by the Holy Spirit concerning our daily walk, which comes about according to our Faith in Christ and what He did for us at the Cross)*, **and to wipe** *them* **with the towel wherewith He was girded** *(refers to the Incarnation, which made possible His Death on Calvary that atoned for all sin and made cleansing possible for the human race)*.

PETER'S RESPONSE

"Then comes He to Simon Peter *(seems to indicate it was Peter to whom He first approached)*: **and Peter said unto Him, Lord, do you wash my feet?** *('The flesh' cannot understand Spiritual realities; it is either too backward or too forward, too courageous or too cowardly; it is incapable of ever being right, and it is impossible to improve, consequently, it must 'die.')*

"Jesus answered and said unto him, What I do you know not now; but you shall know hereafter *(when Peter was filled with the Spirit, which he was on the Day of Pentecost)*.

CONSTANT CLEANSING NEEDED

"Peter said unto Him, You shall never wash my feet *(the Greek Text actually says, 'Not while eternity lasts'; Calvin said, 'With God, obedience is better than worship')*. **Jesus answered him, If I wash you not, you have no part with Me** *(the statement as rendered by Christ speaks to the constant cleansing needed regarding our everyday walk before the Lord, which the washing of the feet [our walk], at least in part, represented)*.

"Simon Peter said unto Him, Lord, not my feet only, but also *my* **hands and** *my* **head** *(Chrysostom said, 'In his deprecation he was vehement, and his yielding more vehement, but both came from his love')*.

"Jesus said to him, he who is washed needs not save to wash his feet *(as stated, pertains to our daily walk before God, which means that the Believer doesn't have to get Saved over and over again; the 'head' refers to our Salvation, meaning that we do not have to be repeatedly Saved, while the 'hands' refer to our 'doing,' signifying that this doesn't need to be washed because Christ has already done what needs to be done; all of this is in the Spiritual sense)*, **but is clean every whit** *(refers to Salvation, and pertains to the Precious Blood of Jesus that cleanses from all sin; the infinite Sacrifice needs no repetition)*: **and you are clean, but not all** *(refers to all the Disciples being Saved with one exception, which was Judas)*" **(Jn. 13:3-10).**

THE POLLUTION OF THIS WORLD

Jesus, washing only their feet, was telling His Disciples that this world is polluted. Our walk through it, which refers to how we order our behavior, how we live for God, in other words, how we live this Christian life, proclaims the fact of spiritual contamination. It does not so much speak of failure on the part of the Believer as it does the evil around us that, which at times, attaches itself to us in some way. That being the case, our Lord is teaching us that constant cleansing is needed.

HOW IS THIS CONSTANT CLEANSING EFFECTED?

Paul said:

"This I say then, **Walk** *(order your behavior)* **in the Spirit** *(we do so by placing our Faith exclusively in Christ and the Cross, through which the Spirit works exclusively [Rom. 8:1-2])*, **and you shall not fulfill the lust of the flesh.** *(This proves the existence of the sin nature in the Believer. It declares the consciousness of corrupt desires. As stated, the only way to not fulfill the lust of the flesh is for our Faith* to be placed exclusively in the Cross.)

"For the flesh *(in this case, evil desires)* **lusts against the spirit** *(is the opposite of the Holy Spirit)***, and the Spirit against the flesh** *(it is the Holy Spirit Alone, Who can subdue the flesh; He does so, as we have repeatedly stated, by our Faith being placed exclusively in the Cross)***: and these are contrary the one to the other** *(these two can never harmonize; as Paul has stated, the old nature must be cast out, which the Holy Spirit Alone can do)***: so that you cannot do the things that you would.** *(Without the Holy Spirit, Who works by the Cross, the Believer cannot live a Holy Life.)*

"But if you be led of the Spirit, you are not under the Law. *(One cannot follow the Spirit and the Law at the same time, but regrettably that's what most modern Christians are attempting to do. Unless one properly understands the Cross as it regards Sanctification, one cannot be properly 'led of the Spirit,' Who works exclusively within the framework of the Finished Work of Christ)"* **(Gal. 5:16-18).**

THE CRUCIFIXION OF THE FLESH WITH THE AFFECTIONS AND LUSTS

Paul also said:

"And they who are Christ's have crucified the flesh with the affections and lusts. *(This can be done only by the Believer understanding it was carried out by Christ at the Cross, and our being 'baptized into His Death' [Rom. 6:3-5]. That being the case, and as repeatedly stated, the Cross must ever be the Object of our Faith, which alone will bring about these results.)*

"If we live in the Spirit, let us also walk in the Spirit *('walk' refers to our lifestyle; this Passage declares both life and Holiness to be the work of the Holy Spirit; He operates Salvation and He operates Sanctification; both are realized* *on the Principle of Faith, and that refers to the Cross ever being the Object of our Faith; many know they have received Spiritual Life, as it regards Salvation through Faith, but they think they can only secure Sanctification by works; this is a great error; it never brings victory; believing in Christ and the Cross for Sanctification, as well as for Justification, introduces one into a life of power and victory, which is the only way it can be accomplished)"* **(Gal. 5:24-25).**

CHAPTER SIX

Is Faith In The Cross Of Christ The Only Way Sin Can Be Defeated?

QUESTION:

IS FAITH IN THE CROSS OF CHRIST THE ONLY WAY SIN CAN BE DEFEATED?

ANSWER:

Yes!

Other than the Cross of Christ, there is no Atonement for sin, no forgiveness of sin, no eradication of guilt, no Eternal Life, no new birth, no Baptism with the Holy Spirit, no Mercy, and no Grace, etc. In other words, every single thing we receive from God comes to us by and through Jesus Christ and what He did at the Cross. Perhaps the following little formula will help us to understand it better:

• Jesus Christ is the Source of all things that we receive from God (Jn. 14:6; Col. 2:10).

• The Cross of Christ is the Means and, in fact, the only Means by which these things are given to us (Rom. 6:3-5; I Cor. 2:2).

• The Cross of Christ and the Cross of Christ alone must be the Object of our Faith in order for us to receive what has been given (I Cor. 1:17, 23; Gal. 6:14).

• The Holy Spirit, Who works exclusively within the parameters of the Finished Work of Christ, oversees all of this (Rom. 8:1-2, 11; Eph. 2:13-18).

Let us establish the fact that it is the Cross of Christ alone which addresses sin. And please understand, when we are speaking of the Cross of Christ, we aren't actually speaking of the wooden beam on which He died. We are rather speaking of the great victories He purchased there with His Own Blood, in other words, the benefits accrued to us. Benefits, I might quickly add, which will never cease, hence, Paul referring to the Cross as *"The Everlasting Covenant"* (Heb. 13:20).

ANIMAL BLOOD WAS INSUFFICIENT

Paul said:

"For *it is* not possible that the blood of bulls and goats should take away sins. *(The word 'impossible' is a strong one. It means there is no way forward through the blood of animals. As well, it applies to all other efforts made by man to address the problem of sin, other than the Cross.)*

"Wherefore when He *(the Lord Jesus)* comes into the world *(presents Christ coming as the Savior, Who undertakes in Grace to meet every claim the Throne of God has against penitent sinners)*, He said, *(Ps. 40:6)* Sacrifice and Offering You would not *(refers to the fact that He would pay for sin, but not with animal sacrifices)*, but a Body have You prepared Me *(God became man with the full intention that His Perfect Physical Body was to be offered up in Sacrifice on the Cross, which it was; the Cross was ever His Destination)*:

"In Burnt Offerings and *sacrifices* for sin *(proclaims the root of the problem which besets mankind — it is 'sin'; the idea is, that the sacrifices were not sufficient as it regards 'sin'; therefore, God took no pleasure in them in that capacity)* You have had no pleasure.

THE WILL OF GOD

"Then said I, Lo, I come, (in the Volume of the Book it is written of Me,) *(the entirety of the Old Testament points exclusively to Christ, and in every capacity)* to do Your Will, O God. *(The Cross was the Will of God because it had to be if man was to be Redeemed.)*

"Above when He said, Sacrifice and Offering and Burnt Offerings and *Offering* for sin You would not *(refers to the fact that animal sacrifices could not cleanse from sin)*, neither had pleasure therein *(concerns the insufficiency of the sacrifices)*; which are offered by the Law *(refers to the fact that all these Offerings were included in the Mosaic Law; even though instigated by God, they were meant to point to Christ)*;

"Then said He, Lo, I come to do Your Will, Oh God. *(The doing of the Will of God, as it regards Christ, pertained totally and completely to His Sacrifice of Himself on the Cross.)* He takes away the First *(the Old Covenant, which He did by the Sacrifice of Himself)*, that He may establish the Second *(the New Covenant, which He did by going to the Cross, the only way it could be established)*.

THE NEW COVENANT

"By the which will *(the Sacrifice of Christ took away the First Covenant, satisfying its demands, and established the New Covenant)* we are Sanctified through the Offering of the Body of Jesus Christ once *for all*. *(This proclaims unequivocally that the only way the Believer can live a victorious life is by the Cross ever being the Object of his Faith.)*

"And every Priest stands daily ministering and offering oftentimes the same sacrifices, which can never take away sins *(proclaiming the insufficiency of this method)*:

"But this Man *(this Priest, Christ Jesus)*, after He had offered One Sacrifice for sins forever *(speaks of the Cross)*, sat down on the Right Hand of God *(refers to the great contrast with the Priests under the Levitical System, who never sat down because their work was never completed; the Work of Christ was a 'Finished Work,' and needed no repetition)*;

"From henceforth expecting till His enemies be made His footstool. *(These enemies are Satan and all the fallen Angels and demon spirits, plus all who follow Satan.)*

FOR OUR SANCTIFICATION

"For by one Offering He has perfected forever them who are Sanctified. *(Everything one needs is found in the Cross of Christ [Gal. 6:14].)*

"*Whereof* the Holy Spirit also is a witness to us *(a witness to the Cross)*: for after that He had said before *(refers to the fact that the Holy Spirit has always witnessed to the veracity of the Finished Work of Christ)*,

"This *is* the Covenant that I will make with them after those days *(proclaims its distinctive feature as being the Sanctifying Work of the Holy Spirit Who would be caused to take up His permanent Abode in the Believer, all made possible by the Cross)*, says the Lord, I will put My Laws into their hearts, and in their minds will I write them *(the work of the New Covenant, which accompanies the born-again experience)*;

"And their sins and iniquities will I remember no more. *(He has taken them all away, and did so by the Cross.)*

"Now where remission of these is *(with all sins atoned, the argument is settled)*, there is no more offering for sin. *(No more offering is necessary, for Christ paid it all)*" (Heb. 10:4-18).

THE CHRISTIAN AND VICTORY OVER SIN

There is only One Way the Child of God can have Victory over sin, and I mean only One Way, and that is that the Cross of Christ, and the Cross of Christ alone, ever be the Object of our Faith.

SIN IS THE PROBLEM!

Unfortunately, sin is little looked at presently as the problem, but other things entirely. For instance, the Word of Faith people claim that sin is no longer the problem with the Believer, inasmuch as he is a new creation man. They claim that sin should not even be mentioned behind the pulpit. If so, they say, such will create a sin consciousness in people's minds, which will cause them to sin. So, according to their reckoning, the way to have victory over sin is to never mention it.

That seems strange when one realizes that the Apostle Paul mentioned sin seventeen times in the Sixth Chapter of Romans alone. We will deal with that Chapter momentarily.

The seeker sensitive churches, so-called, do not mention sin, or the Cross, or the Blood of Christ, etc., because, as they say, *"it might offend people."* In effect, they refuse to admit that man is a fallen creature and if unredeemed, completely ruled by the sin nature, which is the cause of all war and man's inhumanity to man, which, in fact, ever has been. So, these churches are little more than social centers; and the preachers, social workers. While the carnal ear desires to hear such a message, the truth is, under such proclamation, no lives are changed, no sins are dealt with and forgiven, no one is Born-Again. Before man can be Saved, he has to realize that he is lost and, in fact, realize just exactly how lost he actually is. Admittedly, it's not a pretty picture, but, that's the way it is.

THE SYNOPSIS OF THE FIRST
SIX CHAPTERS OF ROMANS

Paul wrote the Epistle to the Romans while at Corinth. It is believed that he sent this Epistle to Rome by *". . . Phoebe our sister, who is a servant of the Church which is at Cenchrea"* (Rom. 16:1).

The word *"servant"* in the Greek is *"diakonos,"* with our words *"deacon"* and *"deaconess"* derived from it. This shows that it is Scriptural for a woman to serve in this capacity as well as a man. Cenchrea was the Port of Corinth, about 9 miles from that city.

Evidently, Phoebe was going to Rome from Cenchrea, a distance of approximately 500 miles. She was entrusted by Paul with the Epistle to the Romans and that it be delivered to the Saints in that city.

Renan says of her, and at this time, *"Phoebe carried under the folds of her robe the whole future of Christian Theology."*[1]

A brief outline of the First Six Chapters of Romans is

necessary here in order to properly address our subject.

• Chapter 1: Paul deals with the Gentile world. It's not a very pretty picture.

• Chapters 2 and 3: Paul deals with the Jew and, thus, Israel; likewise, the picture is not very positive. In fact, he puts both Gentiles and Jews in the same category, their desperate need for a Redeemer. In fact, what Paul said in these two Chapters about the Jews incurred the hate of those people against himself. In their thinking, the idea that the Jews, who had given the world the Word of God (Genesis through Malachi) as well as the Prophets, needed a Redeemer the same as the Gentiles, was to them preposterous! In other words, the Holy Spirit through Paul found the whole world guilty before God and with no way to save themselves. In fact, he would say of Israel in the Tenth Chapter of Romans the following:

"Brethren, my heart's desire and prayer to God for Israel is, that they might be Saved *(Israel, as a Nation, wasn't Saved, despite their history; what an indictment!).*

"For I bear them record that they have a zeal of God *(should read, 'for God'; they had a zeal which had to do with God as its Object)*, but not according to knowledge *(pertains to the right kind of knowledge)*.

IGNORANT OF GOD'S RIGHTEOUSNESS

"For they being ignorant of God's Righteousness *(spells the story not only of ancient Israel, but almost the entirety of the world, and for all time; 'God's Righteousness' is that which is afforded by Christ, and received by exercising Faith in Him and what He did at the Cross, all on our behalf; Israel's ignorance was willful!)*, and going about to establish their own Righteousness *(the case of anyone who attempts to establish Righteousness by any method other than Faith in Christ and the Cross)*, have not submitted themselves unto the Righteousness of God

(God's Righteousness is ensconced in Christ and what He did at the Cross).

"For Christ is the end of the Law for Righteousness *(Christ fulfilled the totality of the Law)* **to everyone who believes.** *(Faith in Christ guarantees the Righteousness which the Law had, but could not give)*" **(Rom. 10:1-4).**

JUSTIFICATION BY FAITH

• **Man's terrible dilemma of not being able to save himself was solved in Chapters 4 and 5. Paul proclaims the answer, as given by God, as** *"Justification by Faith."* **He said:**

"Therefore being Justified by Faith *(this is the only way one can be justified; refers to Faith in Christ and what He did at the Cross)*, **we have peace with God** *(justifying peace)* **through our Lord Jesus Christ** *(what He did at the Cross)*:

"By Whom also we have access by Faith into this Grace *(we have access to the Goodness of God by Faith in Christ)* **wherein we stand** *(wherein alone we can stand)*, **and rejoice in hope** *(a hope that is guaranteed)* **of the Glory of God** *(our Faith in Christ always brings Glory to God; anything else brings glory to self, which God can never accept)*" **(Rom. 5:1-2).**

A thrice-Holy God can justify an obviously guilty sinner by the means of that sinner evidencing Faith exclusively in Christ, Who paid every debt at Calvary's Cross.

• **Chapter 6: After Paul has addressed man's dilemma and then the Solution, which is** *"Justification by Faith,"* **he now addresses the Christian and how that we are to live for God. He begins by telling us that the problem is** *"sin."* **He said:**

THE PROBLEM IS SIN!

"What shall we say then? *(This is meant to direct*

attention to Rom. 5:20.) **Shall we continue in sin, that Grace may abound?** *(Just because Grace is greater than sin doesn't mean that the Believer has a license to sin.)*

"God forbid *(presents Paul's answer to the question, 'Away with the thought, let not such a thing occur').* **How shall we, who are dead to sin** *(dead to the sin nature),* **live any longer therein?** *(This portrays what the Believer is now in Christ)***" (Rom. 6:1-2).**

We must understand now, while Paul was addressing the unredeemed in Chapters 4 and 5, in the balance of this Epistle, beginning with Chapter 6, he is addressing Believers. The Holy Spirit through him tells us clearly and plainly that sin is the problem, even as it regards the Child of God.

And now he will tell us how to have Victory over sin. While he doesn't teach sinless perfection, he most definitely does teach that, *". . . sin shall not have dominion over us: for we are not under the Law, but under Grace"* (Rom. 6:14). He teaches us that this victory can be achieved, can be attained, can be brought about, in only One Way. That One Way is the Cross of Christ. He then says:

THE CROSS

"Know you not, that so many of us as were baptized into Jesus Christ *(plainly says that this Baptism is into Christ and not water [I Cor. 1:17; 12:13; Gal. 3:27; Eph. 4:5; Col. 2:11-13])* **were baptized into His Death?** *(When Christ died on the Cross, in the Mind of God, we died with Him; in other words, He became our Substitute, and our identification with Him in His Death gives us all the benefits for which He died; the idea is that He did it all for us!)*

"Therefore we are buried with Him by baptism into death *(not only did we die with Him, but we were buried with Him as well, which means that all the sin and transgression of the past were buried; when they put Him in the*

Tomb, they put all of our sins into that Tomb as well): **that like as Christ was raised up from the dead by the Glory of the Father, even so we also should walk in Newness of Life** *(we died with Him, we were buried with Him, and His Resurrection was our Resurrection to a 'Newness of Life')*.

RESURRECTION LIFE

"For if we have been planted together *(with Christ)* **in the likeness of His Death** *(Paul proclaims the Cross as the instrument through which all Blessings come; consequently, the Cross must ever be the Object of our Faith, which gives the Holy Spirit latitude to work within our lives)*, **we shall be also** *in the likeness* **of** *His* **Resurrection** *(we can have the 'likeness of His Resurrection,' i.e., 'live this Resurrection Life,' only as long as we understand the 'likeness of His Death,' which refers to the Cross as the Means by which all of this is done)*:

WHAT WE USED TO BE WAS
CRUCIFIED WITH CHRIST

"Knowing this, that our old man is Crucified with *Him* *(all that we were before conversion)*, **that the body of sin might be destroyed** *(the power of the sin nature made ineffective)*, **that henceforth we should not serve sin** *(the guilt of sin is removed at conversion, because the sin nature no longer rules within our hearts and lives)***"** **(Rom. 6:3-6).**

WE ARE COMPLETE IN HIM

"Beware lest any man spoil you through philosophy and vain deceit *(anything that pulls the Believer away from the Cross is not of God)*, **after the tradition of men** *(anything that is not of the Cross is of men)*, **after the**

rudiments of the world, and not after Christ. *(If it's truly after Christ, then it's after the Cross.)*

"For in Him *(Christ)* dwells all the fullness of the Godhead bodily. *(This is Godhead as to essence. Christ is the completion and the fullness of Deity and in Him the Believer is complete.)*

"And you are complete in Him *(the satisfaction of every spiritual want is found in Christ, made possible by the Cross)*, which is the Head of all principality and power *(His Headship extends not only over the Church, which voluntarily serves Him, but over all forces that are opposed to Him as well [Phil. 2:10-11])*:

WITHOUT HANDS

"In Whom also you are circumcised with the Circumcision made without hands *(that which is brought about by the Cross [Rom. 6:3-5])*, in putting off the body of the sins of the flesh by the Circumcision of Christ *(refers to the old carnal nature that is defeated by the Believer placing his Faith totally in the Cross, which gives the Holy Spirit latitude to work)*" **(Col. 2:8-11).**

The great Apostle then said:

WORKS!

"Let no man therefore judge you in meat, or in drink, or in respect of an holyday, or of the new moon, or of the Sabbath *Days (the moment we add any rule or regulation to the Finished Work of Christ, we have just abrogated the Grace of God)*:

"Which are a shadow of things to come *(the Law, with all of its observances, was only meant to point to the One Who was to come, Namely Christ)*; but the Body *(Church) is* of Christ *(refers to 'substance and reality,' as opposed to shadow).*

THE BEGUILING OF BELIEVERS

"**Let no man beguile you of your reward** *(concerns false doctrine)* **in a voluntary humility** *(refers to self-abasement)* **and worshipping of Angels** *(pertained to the Gnostic teaching; this false teaching claimed a man could not go directly to God through Jesus Christ, but rather must reach after God through successive grades of intermediate beings, i.e., 'Angels!')*, **intruding into those things which he has not seen** *(refers to going outside the revealed Word of God)*, **vainly puffed up by his fleshly mind** *('mind of the flesh,' which means it's not the Mind of God)*" **(Col. 2:16-18).**

SOME FALSE WAYS

Anything that becomes the object of our Faith, even good things, other than the Cross of Christ, will bring forth no positive results. Not understanding the Cross of Christ as it refers to Sanctification, the sad fact is, the modern church simply does not know how to live for God. It jumps from one fad to the other.

• For instance, sometime back a young man told me that the key to victory over sin was fasting. Now, while fasting is definitely Scriptural and will definitely be of help, it will not give one victory over sin. As we have shown, and I think amply so, there's no victory over sin outside of the Cross.

• Another said that the Believer should take the Lord's Supper and do so very often. The doing of this, he went on to say, *"Would give one victory in every capacity."* Again, while the Lord's Supper *is a viable Christian Ordinance and* should be taken by every Believer, still, there is no victory over sin in that capacity.

• Others have claimed that if a person is stuck down by the Power of God, in other words, *"falling out under the power,"* that this is the key to all victory. While, again, at times the Lord will definitely knock someone off their feet, still, if they do not know the truth of the Cross, regrettably, they will get up in the same condition in which they fell down.

• *Another says the Family Curse* is the problem. While most definitely there are all types of curses on people who are unredeemed, the fact is, as it regards Believers, all of that was handled at the Cross. Paul said:

"Christ has redeemed us from the curse of the Law *(He did so on the Cross)*, being made a curse for us *(He took the penalty of the Law, which was death)*: for it is written, Cursed is everyone who hangs on a tree *(Deut. 21:22-23)*:

"That the blessing of Abraham *(Justification by Faith)* might come on the Gentiles through Jesus Christ *(what He did at the Cross)*; that we might receive the Promise of the Spirit through Faith. *(All sin was atoned at the Cross which lifted the sin debt from believing man, making it possible for the Holy Spirit to come into the life of the Believer and abide there forever [Jn. 14:16-17])*" (Gal. 3:13-14).

While it is admitted that something is definitely wrong as it regards the Christians who involve themselves in such, still, the reason for the difficulty is because they have made something other than the Cross of Christ the object of their Faith. As a result, Satan has given them a hard time, and will continue to do so, despite being prayed for, as it regards the rebuking, so-called, of the family curse. Regarding Believers, there is no such thing as a family curse.

• Many have claimed that if a Christian is having problems, that means that he has a demon spirit which is causing the problem. In other words, if there is a lust problem, then he has a demon of lust; a gossip problem, then a demon of gossip, etc.

While demon spirits most definitely can and do oppress Believers, demon spirits cannot possess Believers. We must understand that.

Paul said:

"**Know you not that you are the Temple of God** *(where the Holy Spirit abides)*, **and** *that* **the Spirit of God dwells in you?** *(That makes the Born-Again Believer His permanent Home)*" **(I Cor. 3:16).**

The Apostle also said:

"**You cannot drink the Cup of the Lord, and the cup of devils** *(if we are going to associate with demons, the Lord will not remain)*: **you cannot be partakers of the Lord's Table** *(the Lord's Supper)*, **and of the table of devils** *(that which the world offers)*" **(I Cor. 10:21).**

WHAT DOES IT MEAN FOR ONE TO PLACE ONE'S FAITH EXCLUSIVELY IN CHRIST AND THE CROSS?

It means that we understand that every single thing we receive from God comes through Jesus Christ by the means of the Cross. In fact, the Cross of Christ is the only thing that stands between mankind and eternal Hell. As well, the Cross of Christ is the only thing that stands between the Church and Apostasy.

While a Believer can be Saved without understanding the Cross as it refers to Sanctification, to be sure, such a Believer cannot live a victorious life.

The Truth is, whatever we need done within our hearts and lives, the Holy Spirit Alone can do it. Considering that He works exclusively within the parameters of the Finished Work of Christ and will not work outside of those parameters (Rom. 8:2), we should from that understand the absolute necessity of us placing our Faith exclusively in Christ and the Cross.

While I love my Church, the truth is, the Church didn't die on the Cross of Calvary for me. While good works are important, the truth is, one cannot reach God by the means of good works. One can reach the Lord only by the means of Faith, but it must be Faith in Christ and the Cross, or else, it will not be recognized by the Lord.

The following is a little formula that might help you to understand this great Message a little better:

- FOCUS: THE LORD JESUS CHRIST (Jn. 14:6).
- OBJECT OF FAITH: THE CROSS OF CHRIST (Rom. 6:3-5).
- POWER SOURCE: THE HOLY SPIRIT (Rom. 8:1-2, 11).
- RESULTS: VICTORY! (Rom. 6:14).

Now I want to give you the same little formula but, rather, turn it around in the manner in which the modern church is now functioning.

- FOCUS: Works.
- OBJECT OF FAITH: Our Performance.
- POWER SOURCE: Self.
- RESULTS: Defeat!

Yes, Faith in the Cross of Christ on the part of the Believer is the only way sin can be defeated.

CHAPTER SEVEN

What Happened To Jesus From The Cross To The Throne?

QUESTION:

WHAT HAPPENED TO JESUS FROM THE CROSS TO THE THRONE?

ANSWER:

FANCIFUL STORIES!

The subject concerning the happenings which took place with Christ from the Cross to the Throne has produced all types of fanciful stories. In these stories, Jesus is pictured as becoming a sinner on the Cross, actually one with Satan, and then going to the burning side of Hell as all unredeemed do, where He was beaten by demons for 3 days and nights, until God said it was enough, with Jesus then being born again, as all sinners are Born-Again, when they come to Christ. He is pictured as throwing off the demon spirits and then being raised from the dead.

The truth is, there is not a shred of evidence of any of this found in the Bible. One dear lady preacher made the statement concerning these claims, *"You won't find this in the Bible; it has to be revealed to you by the Holy Spirit."*

Now, think about that statement for just a moment.

The greatest event in the annals of human history, the Redemption of man, the time when the price was paid, as predicted by the Sages, the Patriarchs, and the Prophets of old, yet, according to this preacher, it's not found in the Bible! How foolish can we be?!

It's not found in the Bible simply because none of it ever happened.

• Jesus did not become a sinner on the Cross; however, he did take the penalty of sin on the Cross, which was death, thereby, atoning for all sin, past, present, and future, at least for all who will believe (Col. 2:14-15).

• He did not take upon Himself the nature of Satan on the Cross.

• God did not forsake Him while He was on the Cross, at least as they teach.

• Jesus did not go to the burning side of Hell when He died.

• He was not tormented there by demon spirits for 3 days and 3 nights.

• He was not *"born again"* in Hell or, in fact, any other place.

All of this is, as we have stated, something made out of whole cloth, so to speak. In other words, everything listed above is, pure and simple, a fabrication.

WHAT EXACTLY DID JESUS DO WHILE ON THE CROSS?

One might say that He did two things, which had eternal consequences:

1. He satisfied the demands of the broken law, at least for all who will believe. Concerning this, Paul wrote:

"**Blotting out the handwriting of Ordinances that was against us** *(pertains to the Law of Moses, which was God's Standard of Righteousness that man could not reach)*, **which was contrary to us** *(Law is against us, simply because we are unable to keep its precepts, no matter how hard we try)*, **and took it out of the way** *(refers to the penalty of the Law being removed)*, **nailing it to His Cross** *(the Law with its decrees was abolished in Christ's Death, as if Crucified with Him)*" **(Col. 2:14).**

All of this was done to satisfy the demands of a thrice-Holy God. Man owed a debt that he could not pay, so, in effect, Jesus paid it for us by going to the Cross and giving Himself as a Sacrifice, actually, a Perfect Sacrifice. God could accept no less.

Paul also said:

"**Christ has redeemed us from the curse of the Law** *(He did so on the Cross)*, **being made a curse for us** *(He* *took the penalty of the Law, which was death)*: **for it is written, Cursed** *is* **everyone who hangs on a tree** *(Deut. 21:22-23)*:

"**That the Blessing of Abraham** *(Justification by Faith)* **might come on the Gentiles through Jesus Christ** *(what He did at the Cross)*; **that we might receive the Promise of the Spirit through Faith.** *(All sin was atoned at the Cross, which lifted the sin debt from believing man, making it possible for the Holy Spirit to come into the life of the Believer and abide there forever [Jn. 14:16-17])*" **(Gal. 3:13-14).**

AT THE CROSS, OUR LORD DEFEATED SATAN!

2. It was at the Cross that Satan, all demon spirits, all fallen Angels, etc., were totally and completely defeated.

How were they defeated?

Sin provided the legal right that Satan had to hold man captive, but, with Jesus atoning for all sin on the Cross, past, present, and future, this left Satan and his henchmen with no legal means to do anything. So, if anyone presently is held captive by the powers of darkness, it is because, in some way, they have consented to the captivity.

For instance, every unredeemed person in the world is held captive by Satan, but, they are held captive simply because they will not avail themselves of the Salvation afforded by Christ. And, tragically, most modern Christians fall into the same category. They do not understand God's Prescribed Order of Life and Living, i.e., *"victory,"* **so they are captives as well. But, the Truth is, Satan has already been defeated. The Scripture says, and concerning this very thing:**

"***And*** **having spoiled principalities and powers** *(Satan and all of his henchmen were defeated at the Cross by Christ atoning for all sin; sin was the legal right Satan had to hold man in captivity; with all sin atoned, he has no more legal right to hold anyone in bondage)*, **He** *(Christ)* **made**

a show of them openly *(what Jesus did at the Cross was in the face of the whole universe)*, **triumphing over them in it.** *(The triumph is complete and it was all done for us, meaning we can walk in power and perpetual Victory due to the Cross)*" **(Col. 2:15).**

So, all Victory, and in every capacity, was won at the Cross. That Victory did not await the Resurrection. In fact, if there had been one sin left unatoned, Jesus could not have risen from the dead, for the Scripture says, *"The wages of sin is death"* (Rom. 6:23). But, due to the fact that all sin was atoned (past, present, and future), the Resurrection of Christ was a foregone conclusion.

THE ANNOUNCEMENT TO THE SPIRITS IN PRISON

When Jesus died His Soul and Spirit went down into the heart of the Earth, which is where all souls went at that time. The first thing recorded that Jesus did was to *"preach unto the spirits in prison."* Concerning this, we quote from THE EXPOSITOR'S STUDY BIBLE. Peter said:

"**For Christ also has once suffered for sins** *(the suffering of Christ on the Cross was but for one purpose, and that was 'for sins'; while we as Believers might suffer for sins as well, such is never in the realm of Atonement; the price has been fully paid, which means there is nothing left owing)*, **the just for the unjust** *(Christ was the Perfect Sacrifice, the One Who was born without original sin, and Who lived a Perfect Life, never failing in even one point; He Alone was the 'Just')*, **that He might bring us to God** *(refers to the way being opened for sinful man to come into the very Presence of God)*, **being put to death in the flesh** *(refers to the fact that Jesus died physically in order to serve as a Sacrifice, which means He didn't die spiritually, as some claim!)*, **but quickened by the Spirit** *(raised from the dead by the Holy Spirit [Rom. 8:11])*" **(I Pet. 3:18).**

DISOBEDIENT ANGELS

Peter went on to say:

"**By which also He went** *(between the time of His Death and Resurrection)* **and preached** *(announced something)* **unto the spirits in prison** *(does not refer to humans, but rather to fallen Angels; humans in the Bible are never referred to in this particular manner; these were probably the fallen Angels who tried to corrupt the human race by cohabiting with women [II Pet. 2:4; Jude, Vss. 6 and 7]; these fallen Angels are still locked up in this underworld prison)*;

"**Which sometime** *(in times past)* **were disobedient** *(this was shortly before the Flood)*, **when once the long-suffering of God waited in the days of Noah** *(refers to this eruption of fallen Angels with women taking place at the time of Noah; this was probably a hundred or so years before the Flood)*, **while the Ark was a preparing** *(these fallen Angels were committing this particular sin while the Ark was being made ready, ever how long it took; the Scripture doesn't say!)*, **wherein few, that is, eight souls were saved by water.** *(This doesn't refer to being saved from sin. They were saved from drowning in the Flood by being in the Ark)*" **(I Pet. 3:19-20).**

As to exactly what Jesus said to these fallen Angels, we aren't told. But, due to the fact that their efforts had been to stop the coming of Christ into the world by corrupting the human race, He, no doubt, told them, as was obvious, that they had failed. Their throwing in with Satan in his revolution against God had produced nothing but failure. In fact, these particular Angels will be locked up in this underworld prison, where they are at this moment, until they are ultimately transferred to the Lake of Fire, where they will be with Satan, all demon spirits, and all people who followed him, forever and forever (Rev. 20:10).

PARADISE

Before the Cross, and due to the fact that the blood of bulls and goats could not take away sins, the sin debt remained with all Believers, which included all of the Old Testament Greats. Consequently, when they died, they were not then taken to Heaven, but, rather, went to Paradise, referred to by Jesus as *"Abraham's bosom"* (Lk. 16:22). While it is true that all Believers were *"comforted in this place"* (Lk. 16:25), still, they were held captive by Satan. In fact, Paradise was also referred to as *"Hell,"* because it was a part of the underworld. The only thing that separated Believers during that time from hellfire itself was *"a great gulf"* (Lk. 16:26). Actually, the deliverance for all of these Old Testament Saints was dependent totally and completely on the Cross of Christ and what it would accomplish. The Cross would atone for all sin, which meant that Satan would have no more hold over them.

When Jesus went into Paradise, He didn't go there as one conquered, but, rather, as the Conqueror. One might even say that He kicked those gates of Paradise open in order that it may proclaim the fact that the Victory was won.

This is what He partially meant when He said:

"**When Jesus came into the coasts** *(borders)* **of Caesarea Philippi** *(about 30 miles north of the Sea of Galilee),* **He asked His Disciples, saying, Whom do men say that I the Son of Man am?** *(The third form of unbelief manifested itself in popular indifference, indolence, or mere curiosity respecting the Messiah Himself. Upon the answer to this all-important question, hinges the Salvation of man.)*

"**And they said, Some** *say that You are* **John the Baptist: some, Elijah; and others, Jeremiah, or one of the Prophets** *(this form of unbelief manifests itself in the frivolity of the natural heart).*

"**He said unto them, But whom say you that I am?** *(Addressed personally to the Twelve.)*

THE SON OF THE LIVING GOD

"And Simon Peter answered and said, You are the Christ, the Son of the Living God *(the Great Confession).*
"And Jesus answered and said unto him, Blessed are you, Simon Bar-jonah *(Peter is the son of Jonah, as Jesus is the Son of God)*: **for flesh and blood have not revealed it unto you** *(mere human ingenuity)*, **but My Father Who is in Heaven** *(all Spiritual knowledge must be by revelation).*

THE GATES OF HELL SHALL NOT PREVAIL AGAINST IT

"And I say also unto you, That you are Peter *(the Lord changed his name from Simon to Peter, which means 'a fragment of a rock')*, **and upon this rock** *(immovable mass; Jesus is the Living Rock on which the Redeemed as living stones are built; for other foundation can no man lay [I Cor. 3:11])* **I will build My Church** *(the Church belongs to Christ, and He is the Head [Col. 1:18])*; **and the gates of Hell shall not prevail against it** *(the power of death caused by sin, shall not prevail against it, which victory was won at the Cross)*" **(Mat. 16:13-18).**

The word *"prevail"* indicates that Satan and his fallen Angels would have kept that gate closed, if they could have; however, there was nothing they could do. Jesus Christ is Lord!

JESUS LED CAPTIVITY CAPTIVE

Concerning this event, the Scripture says:

"Wherefore He said *(Ps. 68:18)*, **when He ascended up on high** *(the Ascension)*, **He led captivity captive** *(liberated the souls in Paradise; before the Cross, despite being Believers, they were still held captive by Satan because the* *blood of bulls and goats could not take away the sin debt; but when Jesus died on the Cross, the sin debt was paid, and now He makes all of these His Captives)*, **and gave Gifts unto men.** *(These 'Gifts' include all the Attributes of Christ, all made possible by the Cross.)*

"Now that He ascended *(mission completed)*, **what is it but that He also descended first into the lower parts of the Earth?** *(Immediately before His Ascension to Glory, which would be done in total triumph, He first went down into Paradise to deliver all the believing souls in that region, which He did)*" **(Eph. 4:8-9).**

"Leading captivity captive," is a strange statement; however, it means the following:

As stated, all the Old Testament Saints were in Paradise, in essence, held captive by Satan, hence, Jesus using the word *"captivity"* as it regards these people. He, in effect, made them His Captives and there was nothing that Satan could do about it because the Cross had spelled his defeat.

Now, since Jesus has gone to the Cross and has paid the terrible sin debt, when Believers die, they instantly go to be with the Lord Jesus Christ in Heaven (Phil. 1:23).

Jesus preaching to the spirits (fallen Angels) in prison locked away in the heart of the Earth, then going into Paradise and delivering all of the souls who were there, presents, according to the Word of God, everything that Jesus did during the 3 days and nights that our Lord was in the heart of the Earth. And yet, this certainly was not a journey that He desired to take, which should be overly obvious; however, everything He did was done for us. We must never forget that.

HIS SUFFERINGS ON THE CROSS

Likewise, we must never forget, at least as far as we can understand, what He went through on the Cross. The entirety of His 6 hours spent there was horrible to say the least; however, the last 3 hours, from 12 noon until 3 p.m., were the hardest of all. In fact, it was so bad that God blackened the Earth at that time, because He could not look upon His Only Son, Who was suffering as the Sin-Offering for mankind. The Twenty-second Psalm gives us some insight into this most horrible time. Even though it is quite lengthy, I think it would be profitable for me to give the entirety of this Psalm, which I will do, from THE EXPOSITOR'S STUDY BIBLE.

PSALM 22

David said:

"My God, My God, why have You forsaken Me? Why are You so far from helping Me, and from the words of My roaring? *(The stark reality of this Psalm portrays the Crucifixion of the Lord Jesus Christ. The Gospels narrate the fact of the Crucifixion, this Psalm the feelings of the Crucified.*

"Jesus cried this Word while hanging on the Cross [Mat. 27:46]. This portrayal glorifies Him as the Sin-Offering.

"It presents a sinless Man, the Lord Jesus Christ, forsaken by God, but only in the sense that God allowed Him to die. Such a fact is unique in history and will never need to be repeated. This sinless Man — Himself God manifest in the flesh — was made to be a Sin-Offering, in effect, the penalty of sin, which, in this case, was physical death [II Cor. 5:21], and thereby pierced with a sword of Divine Wrath [Zech. 13:7]. In that judgment, God dealt infinitely with sin and, in so dealing with it in the Person of His Beloved Son, showed His Wrath against sin and His Love for the sinner. Thus, He vindicated Himself and, as well, redeemed man. God revealed Himself at Calvary as in no other place or way.

"What the depth of horror was to which the sinless soul of Jesus sank under the Wrath of God as the Sin-Offering is

unfathomable for men or Angels; therefore, our efforts to explain these sufferings will, of necessity, fall short of that which He really experienced.)

THE SIN OFFERING

"O My God, I cry in the daytime, but You hear not; and in the night season, and am not silent *(as a Sin-Offering and Perfect, still, God could not hear or answer prayer from such, at least at this particular time, but could only pour His Judgment as He had done so through the centuries on the slain lamb).*

YOU ARE HOLY

"But You are Holy, O You Who inhabits the praises of Israel. *(This is the closest that the Scripture comes to the statement, 'God inhabits the praises of His People.' During Christ's Earthly Ministry, He spoke of God as His 'Father,' and resumed the title after He had triumphantly shouted, 'Finished.' But while suffering Divine Wrath as the Sin-Offering, He addressed Him as 'God.' Because God is so Holy, He could not even look upon this particular 'Sin-Offering,' much less hear and answer prayer, but only for the time when He was bearing the sin penalty on the Cross [Mk. 15:33-34].)*

DELIVERANCE

"Our fathers trusted in You: they trusted, and You did deliver them. *(However, Christ could not be delivered from this terrible act. Had He been delivered, humanity could not be delivered.*

"Had the Messiah been only Man, He would have put His physical Sufferings first, and His Spiritual Sufferings last. But to Him, as the Only Begotten Son of God, there was

no anguish so infinite as the hiding of the Father's Face.)

"They cried unto You, and were delivered: they trusted in You, and were not confounded *(this teaches God's People to cling in confidence to the Lord when circumstances seem to say that God has abandoned them; the infinite care of God for us is made possible by what Christ did for us at the Cross, and by no other means)*.

A REPROACH

"But I am a worm, and no man; a reproach of men, and despised of the people *(the word 'worm,' as used here by Christ, means that He took the lowest place among men, to be rejected, scorned, spit upon, and even humiliated in infamy and shame [I Pet. 2:24; Isa. 49:7; 52:14; 53: 1-12])*.

"All they who see Me laugh Me to scorn: they shoot out the lip, they shake the head, saying *(this was done by His Own People while He hung on the Cross in bitter suffering; they had no kind word for Him; they only laughed and mocked Him [Mat. 27:39-43])*,

HE TRUSTED THE LORD

"He trusted on the LORD that He would deliver Him: let Him deliver Him, seeing He delighted in Him *(at the Cross, the enemies of Christ, His Own People, actually used the very words as recorded in this Eighth Verse [Mat. 27:43])*.

"But You are He Who took Me out of the womb: You did make Me hope when I was upon My mother's breasts *(these two Verses [9-10] show the relationship between the Father and the Son, even from the womb of the Virgin Mary; and yet, this relationship that had never before been broken would now be broken, at least for a short period of time, because He was bearing the sin penalty of the world)*.

"I was cast upon You from the womb: You are My

God from My mother's belly. *(In a certain sense, this is true of all; but, of the Holy Child, it was most true [Lk. 2:40, 49, 52].)*

"Be not far from Me; for trouble is near; for there is none to help *('all the Disciples forsook Him and fled' [Mat. 26:56] — He was truly One Who 'had no helper').*

THE RELIGIOUS LEADERS OF ISRAEL

"Many bulls have compassed Me: strong bulls of Bashan have beset Me round *('bulls' here symbolize the demon-possessed religious leaders of Israel, who were determined to kill the Messiah [Mat. 27:1-66; Acts 2:36]).*

"They gaped upon Me with their mouths, as a ravening and a roaring lion.

"I am poured out like water, and all My bones are out of joint: My heart is like wax; it is melted in the midst of My bowels *(Crucifixion was one of the most, if not the most, horrible forms of death ever devised by evil men; coupling that with the spiritual torture, which was even far worse, we have suffering that is unimaginable).*

STRENGTH IS GONE

"My strength is dried up like a potsherd; and My tongue cleaves to My jaws; and You have brought Me into the dust of death *(but yet, His death would be totally unlike any other death that had ever been experienced; it would be the death of a Perfect One, Who purposely laid down His Life as a Sacrifice).*

"For dogs have compassed Me *(refers to the Gentiles, who carried out the Crucifixion):* **the assembly of the wicked have inclosed Me** *(refers to the Scribes, Priests, and the Pharisees, actually, the religious leaders of Israel):* **they pierced My hands and My feet** *(nailing Him to the Cross).*

"**I may tell all My bones: they look and stare upon Me** *(Christ hung on the Cross in complete humiliation, in other words, totally naked)*.

"**They part My garments among them, and cast lots upon My vesture** *(uttered a thousand years before the fact [Mat. 27:35, Mk. 15:24, Lk. 23:34; Jn. 19:24] all record its fulfillment)*.

"**But be not You far from Me, O LORD: O My strength, haste You to help Me.** *(Jesus was placed on the Cross at 9 a.m. [Mk. 15:25]. From 12 noon until 3 p.m., the latter being the time when Jesus died and also the time of the evening sacrifice, darkness covered the land for that three-hour period — the period when Jesus was bearing the sin penalty of the world [Mat. 27:45]. During that three-hour period, the Lord would not answer the Prayers of Christ, nor help Him in any way; however, at the moment He died, the sin penalty was paid [Mat. 27:51], and the Lord could, and in fact most definitely did, answer His Prayers from that moment on [Jn. 19:30; Lk. 23:46].)*

DELIVER MY SOUL

"**Deliver My soul from the sword; My darling** *(My soul)* **from the power of the dog** *(the Gentiles, and more particularly Pilate)*.

"**Save Me from the lion's mouth** *(religious leaders of Israel)*: **for You have heard Me from the horns of the unicorns** *(wild bulls, again typifying the religious leaders of Israel)*.

"**I will declare Your Name unto My brethren: in the midst of the congregation will I praise You.** *(Verses 1 through 21 present to us the sufferings of the Messiah, while Verses 22 through 31 present to us the Exaltation and Glory of the Messiah. We are to declare His Name all over the world, and praise Him for what He has done in redeeming man)*" **(Ps. 22:1-22).**

THE ASCENSION OF CHRIST

Some twenty days after the Crucifixion of our Lord, He ascended to the Father. He did two things at that time. They are:

1. He presented to the Father a perfect, spotless Righteousness, which He had gained by perfectly keeping the Law, which no other human being had ever done. While there definitely was righteousness in the Law, fallen man could not attain to that righteousness, simply because he was fallen, thereby, made ineffective. But Jesus wasn't fallen and all on our behalf, He kept the Law perfectly, thereby, gaining its Righteousness. He said:

". . . He *(the Holy Spirit)* will reprove the world of . . . Righteousness, because I go to My Father *(Jesus presented a spotless Righteousness to the Father, namely Himself, which pertained to His Sacrifice at Calvary, that was accepted by God; consequently, that Righteousness is imputed to all who will believe in Him and His Work on the Cross)* . . ." (Jn. 16:8, 10).

THE HOLY SPIRIT

2. When Jesus arrived at the Throne, with His Righteousness totally and completely accepted by God, then He could send the Holy Spirit back to this Earth in a new dimension. He said:

"Nevertheless I tell you the truth; It is expedient for you that I go away *(the Mission and Ministry of the Holy Spirit to the Body of Christ depended upon the return of Christ to the Father)*: for if I go not away, the Comforter *(Holy Spirit)* will not come unto you *(concerns the respective Office Work of Both Jesus and the Holy Spirit — Jesus as the Saviour of men, and the Holy Spirit as the Power of the Church)*; but if I depart, I will send Him unto you *(a Finished Work on the Cross was demanded of Christ, before the Holy Spirit could be sent)*" (Jn. 16:7).

THE EXALTATION OF CHRIST

Accepted by the Father, meaning the great Plan of Redemption was complete, Jesus, the Scripture says, was highly exalted. Paul said:

"**Wherefore God also has highly exalted Him** *(to a place of supreme Majesty; Jesus has always been Creator, but now He is Saviour as well)*, **and given Him a Name which is above every name** *(actually says, 'The Name,' referring to a specific Name and Title; that Name, as Verse 11 proclaims, is 'Lord')*" **(Phil. 2:9).**

Beautifully enough, the great Twenty-second Psalm, given to us by David, proclaims the Sufferings of Christ on the Cross. The last 10 Verses of that great Psalm proclaim His Exaltation. The idea is, the Crucified was raised from the dead and highly exalted. David wrote:

PRAISE THE LORD

"**I will declare Your Name unto My brethren: in the midst of the congregation will I praise You.** *(Verses 1 through 21 present to us the sufferings of the Messiah, while Verses 22 through 31 present to us the Exaltation and Glory of the Messiah. We are to declare His Name all over the world, and praise Him for what He has done in redeeming man).*

FEAR THE LORD

"**You who fear the LORD, praise Him; all you the seed of Jacob, glorify Him; and fear Him, all you the seed of Israel** *(all Believers are to praise the Lord for what He has done; Jesus is the Source, and the Cross is the Means).*
"**For He** *(God the Father)* **has not despised nor**

abhorred the affliction *(suffering)* of the afflicted *(His Only Begotten Son)*; neither has He hid His Face from Him *(not permanently, actually for only about three hours)*; but when He *(our Savior)* cried unto Him *(God the Father)*, He heard *(cried out of the death world, and the Lord heard Him, and raised Him from the dead)*.

"My praise shall be of You in the great congregation *(every Saint is to praise God for what Jesus has done for us at the Cross)*: I will pay My vows *(devotions)* before them who fear Him.

"The meek shall eat and be satisfied: they shall praise the LORD who seek Him: your heart shall live forever *(the Cross afforded us eternal life)*.

ALL THE WORLD WILL TURN TO THE LORD

"All the ends of the world shall remember and turn unto the LORD: and all the kindreds of the nations shall worship before You *(when Jesus died on the Cross, He died not only for Israel, but for the entirety of mankind)*.

"For the kingdom is the LORD's: and He is the governor among the nations *(this privilege is afforded Him because of Calvary)*.

"All they that be fat upon Earth shall eat and worship: all they who go down to the dust shall bow before Him: and none can keep alive his own soul *(life is Christ's gift; the soul cannot be kept spiritually alive except through Him, by His quickening Spirit [Jn. 6:53, 63])*.

"A seed shall serve Him; it shall be accounted to the LORD for a generation *(what Jesus did at the Cross shall be told of the Lord to generation after generation)*.

HIS RIGHTEOUSNESS

"They shall come, and shall declare His Righteousness unto a people who shall be born, that He has done

this *(the words, 'that He has done this,' speak of the great price He paid for man's Redemption; it is done; 'It is Finished' [Jn. 19:30]; this shall be told from generation to generation, and so has it been)*" **(Ps. 22:22-31).**

That is the Bible account of what Jesus did from the Cross to the Throne.

CHAPTER EIGHT

What Does The Word "Flesh" Mean Relative To The Cross, Even As Paul Used The Word?

QUESTION:

WHAT DOES THE WORD "FLESH" MEAN RELATIVE TO THE CROSS, EVEN AS PAUL USED THE WORD?

ANSWER:

The word *"flesh,"* as the Holy Spirit used this word through the Apostle Paul, refers to that which is indicative to human beings. In other words, it speaks of the Believer's personal talent, efforts, ability, power, education, motivation, intellectualism, etc. It's what we can do as human beings. Over and over again, the Holy Spirit through the Apostle tells us that we cannot successfully live for the Lord by the means of the *"flesh,"* i.e., our own ability, etc. That doesn't mean the things mentioned are wrong, for they aren't. It merely means that these things are inadequate. As it regards what you as a Child of God are facing, and I speak of the spirit world of darkness and its power, you are going to have to have more than your own ability. And, thank God, more has been provided, and I speak of the Holy Spirit. Paul said:

"For he who sows to his flesh shall of the flesh reap **corruption** *(those who make something else the object of their Faith, rather than the Cross, which means they are now depending on self-will)*; **but he who sows to the Spirit** *(does so by trusting exclusively in Christ and what Christ did at the Cross)* **shall of the Spirit reap life everlasting.** *(God's Prescribed Order of Victory)*" **(Gal. 6:8).**

IF THE OBJECT OF FAITH FOR THE BELIEVER IS NOT THE CROSS, THEN THE OBJECT OF FAITH IS THE FLESH

If the Believer's Faith is in the Cross of Christ exclusively, then such a Believer is looking to the Holy Spirit to help him as it regards living this life. If the Believer is making anything the object of his faith other than the Cross, and it doesn't matter what it is, then such a Believer is functioning in the flesh. Understanding that the Cross of Christ is so little preached presently and, as it regards Sanctification, almost none at all, then we have to conclude that the majority of the modern church is walking after the flesh instead of after the Spirit. Let us say it again:

There is no other place for the Believer to be other than the flesh or the Holy Spirit. And, we must realize that it's impossible for us to *"walk after the Spirit,"* with our Faith in something other than the Cross of Christ.

Getting back to what Paul said, if the Believer *"sows to his flesh,"* without fail, he *"shall of the flesh reap corruption."* This means that such a Believer will live a life of spiritual failure no matter how hard he tries otherwise. Listen again to Paul as he relates his own experience as he tried to live for God by the means of the flesh.

I'm going to quote from THE EXPOSITOR'S STUDY BIBLE. It will be quite lengthy, but I know that it will be very profitable for the Bible student to carefully study the Text and the notes.

PAUL'S LIFE BEFORE HE WAS GIVEN THE REVELATION OF THE NEW COVENANT

Let us say this first of all about Paul. When he wrote the Seventh Chapter of Romans, he full well knew and understood the meaning of the New Covenant, in other words, how to live this life. He is giving us a page out of his own history, which pertained to the length of time he served the Lord before this great Revelation was given to him. And please understand, if Paul could not live a victorious life, without doing it God's Way, how in the world do we think that we can!

To be sure, every single Believer will in some measure go through the Seventh Chapter of Romans. It is inevitable! It is a period that the Believer has to pass through in order that he be shown that he cannot live a victorious life unless he does it God's Way, which is the Way of the Cross (I Cor. 1:17-18, 23; 2:2). But, it is certainly not God's Will that the Believer remain in the Seventh Chapter of Romans all his life. However, that's exactly what most of the modern church is doing, and we are speaking of those who are truly Saved. Let's see what Paul said.

"**For that which I do** *(the failure)* **I allow not** *(should have been translated, 'I understand not'; these are not the words of an unsaved man, as some claim, but rather a Believer who is trying and failing)*: **for what I would, that do I not** *(refers to the obedience he wants to render to Christ, but rather fails; why? as Paul explained, the Believer is married to Christ, but is being unfaithful to Christ by spiritually cohabiting with the Law, which frustrates the Grace of God [Rom. 7:1-4]; that means the Holy Spirit will not help such a person, which guarantees failure [Gal. 2:21])*; **but what I hate, that do I** *(refers to sin in his life which he doesn't want to do and, in fact, hates, but finds himself unable to stop; unfortunately, due to the fact of not understanding the Cross as it refers to Sanctification, this is the plight of most modern Christians)*.

THE LAW EXPOSES WHAT IS IN A PERSON

"**If then I do that which I would not** *(presents Paul doing something against his will; he doesn't want to do it, and is trying not to do it, whatever it might be, but finds himself doing it anyway)*, **I consent unto the Law that** *it is* **good** *(simply means that the Law of God is working as it is supposed to work; it defines sin, portraying the fact that the sin nature will rule in man's heart if not addressed properly)*.

"**Now then it is no more I that do it** *(this has been misconstrued by many! it means, 'I may be failing, but it's not* *what I want to do'; no true Christian wants to sin because now the Divine Nature is in his life and it is supposed to rule, not the sin nature [II Pet. 1:4])*, **but sin** *(the sin nature)* **that dwells in me** *(despite the fact that some preachers claim the sin nature is gone from the Christian, Paul here plainly says that the sin nature is still in the Christian; however, if our Faith remains constant in the Cross, the sin nature will be dormant, causing us no problem; otherwise, it will cause great problems; while the sin nature 'dwells' in us, it is not to 'rule' in us).*

WILLPOWER

"For I know that in me (that is, in my flesh,) dwells no good thing *(speaks of man's own ability, or rather the lack thereof in comparison to the Holy Spirit, at least when it comes to spiritual things)***: for to will is present with me** *(Paul is speaking here of his willpower; regrettably, most modern Christians are trying to live for God by means of willpower, thinking falsely that since they have come to Christ, they are now free to say 'no' to sin; that is the wrong way to look at the situation; the Believer cannot live for God by the strength of willpower; while the will is definitely important, it alone is not enough; the Believer must exercise Faith in Christ and the Cross, and do so constantly; then he will have the ability and strength to say 'yes' to Christ, which automatically says, 'no' to the things of the world)***; but *how* to perform that which is good I find not** *(outside of the Cross, it is impossible to find a way to do good)***"** (Rom. 7:15-18).

WHY IS THE FLESH INADEQUATE?

As we have quoted, Paul said, *"For I know that in me, that is, in my flesh, dwells no good thing."* Why did he say that?

It all has to do with the Fall. The great Apostle also said:

"And if Christ *be* in you *(He is in you through the Power and Person of the Spirit [Gal. 2:20])*, the body *is* dead because of sin *(means that the physical body has been rendered helpless because of the Fall; consequently, the Believer trying to overcome by willpower presents a fruitless task)*" (Rom. 8:10).

This problem with our physical body, i.e., *"the flesh,"* will not be corrected until the coming Resurrection of Life. At that time, the Apostle also said:

"Behold, I show you a mystery . . . we shall all be changed . . . For this corruptible *(sin nature)* must put on incorruption *(a Glorified Body with no sin nature)*, and this mortal *(subject to death)* *must* put on immortality *(will never die)*" (I Cor. 15:51, 53).

But, until then, this is a problem that we have to live with.

LIVING AFTER THE FLESH

Paul also said:

"Therefore, Brethren *(means that Paul is addressing Believers)*, we are debtors *(refers to what we owe Jesus Christ for what He has done for us on the Cross)*, not to the flesh *(we do not owe anything to our own ability, meaning that such cannot save us or give us victory)*, to live after the flesh *('living after the flesh' pertains to our works, which God can never accept, and which can never bring us victory, but rather defeat)*.
"For if you live after the flesh *(after your own strength and ability, which is outside of God's Prescribed Order)*, you shall die *(you will not be able to live a victorious, Christian life)*: but if you through the Spirit *(by the Power of the Holy Spirit)* do mortify the deeds of the body *(which*

the Holy Spirit Alone can do), **you shall live** *(shall walk in victory; but once again, even at the risk of being overly repetitive, we must never forget that the Spirit works totally and completely within the confines of the Cross of Christ; this means that we must ever make the Cross the Object of our Faith, giving Him latitude to work)*" **(Rom. 8:12-13).**

WALKING AFTER THE FLESH AND
WALKING AFTER THE SPIRIT

The moment the believing sinner comes to Christ, the Holy Spirit begins His Work of trying to bring the Believer from dependence on the flesh to dependence on the Holy Spirit. To be sure, it's not an easy or a quick journey, so to speak.

Invariably, after the new convert comes to Christ, at a point in time, the convert will fail the Lord. There has never been an exception to this. When it happens, the new Believer is shocked and sets about designing fence laws, so to speak, so the failure does not happen again.

Such a Believer will never gravitate toward the Holy Spirit, but always toward the flesh. Again, there are no exceptions.

Why?

The *"flesh"* is that which is indicative of human beings. It's what we are and what we do. In other words, one does not have to learn how to walk after the flesh; it comes naturally. Conversely, one has to learn how to walk after the Spirit, which, as stated, is not something quickly or easily done, but it must be done.

THE REVIVAL OF THE SIN NATURE

The failure on the part of the new Believer does not cause the sin nature, which was unplugged, so to speak, at conversion, to be revived. The cause of that is the Believer placing his or her Faith in something (anything) other than the Cross of Christ. Due to the fact that the flesh can be very, very religious, the

Believer is fooled into believing that he's doing the right thing. But, he isn't! Concerning this, Paul said:

DECEPTION

"For sin *(the sin nature)*, taking occasion by the Commandment *(in no way blames the Commandment, but that the Commandment actually did agitate the sin nature, and brought it to the fore, which it was designed to do)*, deceived me *(Paul thought, now that he had accepted Christ, by that mere fact alone he could certainly obey the Lord in every respect; but he found he couldn't, and neither can you, at least in that fashion)*, and by it slew *me (despite all of his efforts to live for the Lord by means of Law-keeping, he failed; and again, I say, so will you!)*" (Rom. 7:11).

After Paul's conversion on the road to Damascus, and considering that he was baptized with the Holy Spirit some three days later, he felt surely that he could now keep the Commandments of the Lord. So, that's the direction in which he went; in other words, that became the object of his faith. When that happened, the sin nature revived, began to control him, and he found himself sinning even more. What he did the Bible does not say, and it really doesn't matter. In fact, he fought this thing until the Lord finally revealed to him the meaning of the New Covenant, which, in effect, is the meaning of the Cross (Heb. 13:20).

WHAT DID THE LORD SHOW PAUL?

The Revelation, which the Lord gave to the Apostle, was the greatest Revelation that the world has ever known, even greater, far greater, than the Law of Moses. The Lord gave to Paul the meaning of the New Covenant, which, in effect, and as stated, was the meaning of the Cross (Gal. 1:12).

This Revelation, in fact, elucidates what Jesus did at the

Cross. In other words, the Victory He purchased there for you and me. Let the reader understand, when we speak of the Cross of Christ, we aren't speaking of a wooden beam, but rather the benefits of what Jesus did there.

As we have also stated, what He did there was to satisfy the demands of the broken law which, in effect, defeated Satan and all of his demon spirits and fallen Angels, due to the fact that all sin was atoned (Col. 2:14-15).

Almost immediately after conversion, the Holy Spirit begins the task of pulling the Believer from dependence on the flesh to, as stated, dependence on the Holy Spirit.

If the Believer doesn't have proper teaching on the subject, in other words, how to walk after the Spirit, there is no way that such will come about accidentally. And, that's the tragedy of these modern times. The Cross is understood somewhat respecting Salvation, but not at all respecting Sanctification. As a result, Believers are condemned, so to speak, to live all of their lives in the Seventh Chapter of Romans. But to be sure, that's not God's Will!

WHAT DOES IT MEAN TO
WALK AFTER THE FLESH?

As we have explained, the word *"flesh,"* as used by Paul, refers to the personal ability, talent, self-help, education, intellectualism, motivation, etc., of the individual. Even though the Believer loads such up with Scriptures, still, it is *"flesh,"* meaning that such cannot please the Lord (Rom. 8:8). *"Walking after the flesh"* pertains to the Believer making anything other than the Cross of Christ the object of his or her faith. *"Walking after the Spirit"* is the very opposite.

It means for one to place their Faith exclusively in Christ and what Christ has done for us at the Cross and not allow it to be moved elsewhere. That is *"walking after the Spirit,"* in other words, how the Holy Spirit works. Over and over again, Paul tells us this. He said:

THE LAW OF THE SPIRIT OF LIFE
IN CHRIST JESUS

"**For the Law** *(that which we are about to give is a Law of God, devised by the Godhead in eternity past [I Pet. 1:18-20]; this Law, in fact, is 'God's Prescribed Order of Victory')* **of the Spirit** *(Holy Spirit, i.e., 'the way the Spirit works')* **of Life** *(all life comes from Christ, but through the Holy Spirit [Jn. 16:13-14])* **in Christ Jesus** *(any time Paul uses this term or one of its derivatives, he is, without fail, referring to what Christ did at the Cross, which makes this 'life' possible)* **has made me free** *(given me total Victory)* **from the Law of Sin and Death** *(these are the two most powerful Laws in the universe; the 'Law of the Spirit of Life in Christ Jesus' alone is stronger than the 'Law of Sin and Death'; this means that if the Believer attempts to live for God by any manner other than Faith in Christ and the Cross, he is doomed to failure)*" **(Rom. 8:2).**

AFTER THE SPIRIT

The Apostle then said:

"**That the Righteousness of the Law might be fulfilled in us** *(the Law finding its full accomplishment in us can only be done by Faith in Christ, and what Christ has done for us at the Cross)*, **who walk not after the flesh** *(not after our own strength and ability)*, **but after the Spirit** *(the word 'walk' refers to the manner in which we order our life; when we place our Faith in Christ and the Cross, understanding that all things come from God to us by means of the Cross, ever making it the Object of our Faith, the Holy Spirit can then work mightily within us, bringing about the Fruit of the Spirit; that is what 'walking after the Spirit' actually means!)*" **(Rom. 8:4).**

MINDING THE THINGS OF THE SPIRIT

And then:

"For they who are after the flesh do mind the things of the flesh *(refers to Believers trying to live for the Lord by means other than Faith in the Cross of Christ)*; but they who are after the Spirit the things of the Spirit *(those who place their Faith in Christ and the Cross, do so exclusively; they are doing what the Spirit desires, which alone can bring Victory)*" **(Rom. 8:5).**

SPIRITUALLY MINDED

He then said:

"For to be carnally minded *is* death *(this doesn't refer to watching too much television, as some think, but rather trying to live for God outside of His Prescribed Order; the results will be sin and separation from God)*; but to be Spiritually Minded *is* life and peace *(God's Prescribed Order is the Cross; this demands our constant Faith in that Finished Work, which is the Way of the Holy Spirit)*" **(Rom. 8:6).**

THE SPIRIT OF GOD

He then said:

"But you are not in the flesh *(in one sense of the word is asking the question, 'Since you are now a Believer and no longer depending on the flesh, why are you resorting to the flesh?')*, but in the Spirit *(as a Believer, you now have the privilege of being led and empowered by the Holy Spirit; however, He will do such for us only on the premise of our Faith in the Finished Work of Christ)*, **if so be that the**

Spirit of God dwell in you *(if you are truly Saved)*. **Now
if any man have not the Spirit of Christ, he is none of
His** *(Paul is saying that the work of the Spirit in our lives
is made possible by what Christ did at Calvary, and the
Resurrection)*" **(Rom. 8:9).**

THE SPIRIT IS LIFE

Paul continues:

"**And if Christ** *be* **in you** *(He is in you through the
Power and Person of the Spirit [Gal. 2:20])*, **the body** *is*
dead because of sin *(means that the physical body has been
rendered helpless because of the Fall; consequently, the
Believer trying to overcome by willpower presents a fruitless task)*; **but the Spirit** *is* **life because of Righteousness**
*(only the Holy Spirit can make us what we ought to be, which
means we cannot do it ourselves; once again, He performs
all that He does within the confines of the Finished Work
of Christ)*" **(Rom. 8:10).**

THE WORK OF THE HOLY SPIRIT

And finally:

"**But if the Spirit** *(Holy Spirit)* **of Him** *(from God)*
Who raised up Jesus from the dead dwell in you *(and He
definitely does)*, **He Who raised up Christ from the dead
shall also quicken your mortal bodies** *(give us power in
our mortal bodies that we might live a victorious life)* **by
His Spirit Who dwells in you** *(we have the same Power
in us, through the Spirit, that raised Christ from the dead,
and is available to us only on the premise of the Cross and
our Faith in that Sacrifice)*" **(Rom. 8:11).**

We have by no means covered all of the teaching that Paul

gave on this all-important subject, but I think what we have given spells it out graphically so, that whatever must be done in our lives, can only be done by the Holy Spirit. Every true Believer should ardently desire the Working of the Holy Spirit in his or her life. The way this can be done, and the only way it can be done, is for the Believer to place his or her faith exclusively in Christ and what Christ has done for us at the Cross. Then and then only can the Holy Spirit function in our lives as He should, bringing us from the position of the *"flesh"* to the position of the *"Holy Spirit"* and the great victory that He Alone can give.

For the Believer to cease *"walking after the flesh"* and to *"walk after the Spirit,"* he must understand the following:

1. He must understand what *"walking after the flesh"* actually is and, at the same time, what *"walking after the Spirit"* actually is.

2. He must come to the end of himself, which means that he has repeatedly tried and failed and now realizes that what the Lord demands we within ourselves simply cannot accomplish.

3. He must have proper teaching on the subject because faith comes by hearing, and hearing by the Word of God (Rom. 10:17).

THE RESULTS OF WALKING AFTER THE SPIRIT

Let the reader understand that even though he presently understands what *"walking after the Spirit"* actually means and, even though his Faith is placed securely in the Cross of Christ, let not such a Believer think that Satan is going to cease all activity against him. In fact, the efforts of the Evil One very well could be increased and more than likely will be increased. The Believer will even experience failure again, possibly many times, but if he will stay on this path, the path of the Cross of Christ, ultimately he will find that *"sin no longer has dominion over him"* (Rom. 6:14).

That doesn't mean *"sinless perfection,"* but it does mean

that there is no dominating factor of sin within his or her life.
"Walking after the flesh" is the way of man, which always fails.
"Walking after the Spirit" is the way of God, and always succeeds.

CHAPTER NINE

What Is The Difference In The Cross For Salvation And The Cross For Sanctification?

QUESTION:

WHAT IS THE DIFFERENCE IN THE CROSS FOR SALVATION AND THE CROSS FOR SANCTIFICATION?

ANSWER:

As it regards the Cross — none! But, as it regards the believing sinner coming to Christ and the Saint of God who already belongs to Christ, there is a great deal of difference.

The believing sinner coming to Christ knows absolutely nothing about the Lord or the Cross. He just knows he's under conviction and, as someone has said, he feels like he's hanging over Hell on a rotten stick. All he has to do is believe in Christ and call on the Lord, and he will be Saved. Paul said:

"That if you shall confess with your mouth the Lord Jesus *(confess that Jesus is the Lord of Glory, and the Saviour of men, and that He died on the Cross that we might be Saved)*, and shall believe in your heart that God has raised Him from the dead *(pertains to the Bodily Resurrection of Christ, as is obvious)*, you shall be Saved *(it is that simple!)*.

BELIEVING UNTO RIGHTEOUSNESS

"For with the heart man believes unto Righteousness *(presents the word 'believing' in a mode of 'thinking,' not of feeling; the 'believing' has to do with believing Christ, and that His Sacrifice of Himself Atoned for all sin)*; and with the mouth confession is made unto Salvation *(when Faith comes forth from its silence to announce itself and proclaim the Glory and the Grace of the Lord, its voice 'is confession')*.

"For the Scripture says *(combining parts of Isa. 28:16 with 49:23)*, Whosoever believes on Him *(proclaims the fact that Salvation is reachable by all)* shall not be ashamed *(in essence, says, 'shall not be put to shame,' but rather will receive what is promised).*

NO DIFFERENCE BETWEEN THE JEW
AND THE GENTILE

"For there is no difference between the Jew and the Greek *(should read, 'between the Jew and the Gentile'; all must come the same way, which is by and through Christ and what He did at the Cross on our behalf)*: for the same Lord over all is rich unto all who call upon Him *(the riches of Grace will be given to all who truly call upon the Lord).*

"For whosoever *(anyone, anywhere)* shall call upon the Name of the Lord shall be Saved *(speaks of the sinner coming to Christ, but can refer to any Believer and with whatever need; the Cross is the means by which all of this is done)*" (Rom. 10:9-13).

THE SAINT OF GOD

As it regards the person who is already Saved who, in fact, has trusted the Lord for Salvation, which came by the Means of the Cross, he must come to understand that Sanctification comes from the same Source. Regrettably, it's much more difficult for the Saint of God to place his faith exclusively in the Cross than the believing sinner who is initially coming for Salvation.

Why? That's a good question!

While most every Believer, including preachers, who is truly Saved and has at least a modicum of understanding as it regards the Cross of Christ respecting Salvation, the truth is, modern Christians, and again we are speaking of those who are truly Saved, have virtually no knowledge whatsoever as it regards the Cross of Christ respecting Sanctification. For anyone to know the great Truths of the Word of God, those Truths must be taught by capable and anointed Preachers of the Gospel. Regrettably, while the Cross of Christ is somewhat preached as it regards Salvation, it is preached not at all as it regards

Sanctification; consequently, this modern generation of Believers simply do not know how to live for God. The Scripture says, and concerning this very thing:

"So then Faith *comes* by hearing *(it is the publication of the Gospel which produces Faith in it)*, and hearing by the Word of God *(Faith does not come simply by hearing just anything, but rather by hearing God's Word, and believing that Word)*" (Rom. 10:17).

THE CHRISTIAN IS TO EXCLUSIVELY MAKE THE CROSS THE OBJECT OF HIS FAITH

That may seem simple and, in fact, is; however, to do so means that the Believer must lay aside every other object of faith, whatever it might be. Please note the following:

The world in its rejection of God has from the dawn of time tried to manufacture another god, a god of its own making.

Believers, regrettably, have ever tried to manufacture another sacrifice, other than the Cross of Christ. But, let all hear and understand, the Sacrifice of Christ on the Cross dealt and deals with every single problem that faces the human race. Please note the following very carefully:

• Jesus Christ is the Source of all things that we receive from God (Jn. 14:6).

• The Cross of Christ is the Means by which those things are given to us (Rom. 6:3-5).

• Placing our Faith exclusively in the Cross of Christ provides the means by which we receive what is given (I Cor. 1:17-18, 23; 2:2).

• The Holy Spirit superintends all of this (Eph. 2:13-18).

WHAT THE SAINT OF GOD NEEDS, THE HOLY SPIRIT ALONE CAN DEVELOP

Knowing they have been changed by the new birth and,

with many, even baptized with the Holy Spirit, one of the most favorite Scriptures voiced by such Believers is, *"I can do all things through Christ Who strengthens me"* (Phil. 4:13). The Truth is, most Believers do not even really know what Paul was talking about as it regards that particular Verse.

He is saying that he can be abased or he can abound, whichever he is called upon to do, but only *"through Christ Who strengthens me."* In other words, if he has to go hungry, that he can do with the help of the Lord, etc. As well, he can relish the bountiful Blessings that come his way, should the Lord desire such.

SIN IS THE PROBLEM

The church doesn't want to admit that the real problem in our lives as Believers is sin. One group claims that the best way to overcome sin is to never mention it because, if it is mentioned, they say, this will create a sin consciousness in the hearts and lives of Believers and cause them to sin. So, in their thinking, the way not to sin is just simply never mention the subject.

That's somewhat strange when we realize that the Apostle Paul mentions sin some seventeen times in the Sixth Chapter of Romans alone. But, perhaps Paul didn't have the great knowledge that some of these modern Believers have.

Others claim that once we are now Believers, sin is no longer a problem or even claim that it should not be mentioned because it may offend people.

Irrespective of the foolishness of some preachers, sin is the problem. To cope with this problem, the church comes up with one fad after the other.

One day it's the Purpose Driven Life; the next day it's the Government of Twelve; and, then the next day it's the confession message, with the family curse following that.

THE CROSS IS THE ONLY ANSWER FOR SIN

There is only one answer for sin and that is the Cross of

Christ. Paul said:

"**But this Man** *(this Priest, Christ Jesus)*, **after He had offered One Sacrifice for sins forever** *(speaks of the Cross)*, **sat down on the Right Hand of God** *(refers to the great contrast with the Priests under the Levitical system, who never sat down because their work was never completed; the Work of Christ was a 'Finished Work,' and needed no repetition)*;

"**From henceforth expecting till His enemies be made His footstool.** *(These enemies are Satan and all the fallen Angels and demon spirits, plus all who follow Satan.)*

"**For by one Offering He has perfected forever them who are Sanctified.** *(Everything one needs is found in the Cross [Gal. 6:14]).*

THE WITNESS OF THE SPIRIT

"*Whereof* **the Holy Spirit also is a witness to us** *(a witness to the Cross)*: **for after that He had said before** *(refers to the fact that the Holy Spirit has always witnessed to the veracity of the Finished Work of Christ)*,

"**This** *is* **the Covenant that I will make with them after those days** *(proclaims its distinctive feature as being the Sanctifying Work of the Holy Spirit Who would be caused to take up His permanent abode in the Believer, all made possible by the Cross)*, **says the Lord, I will put My Laws into their hearts, and in their minds will I write them** *(the work of the New Covenant, which accompanies the Born-Again experience)*;

"**And their sins and iniquities will I remember no more.** *(He has taken them all away, and did so by the Cross.)*

"**Now where remission of these** *is* *(with all sins atoned, the argument is settled)*, *there is* **no more offering for sin.** *(No more offering is necessary, for Christ paid it all)*" **(Heb. 10:12-18).**

As it regards this terrible problem of sin, the Believer, as stated, cannot bring about by his or her actions the victory that we need. It is impossible! Simply put, self cannot improve self!

To prove the point, let's look at the Apostle Paul.

THE APOSTLE PAUL

The Ninth Chapter of Acts records the conversion of Paul. It is probably one of the most remarkable conversions ever recorded.

Jesus Christ appeared to him in such Glory that Paul was blinded. Nevertheless, he was gloriously Saved in that phenomenal experience.

Some three days later, Ananias, having been spoken to by the Lord, and according to directions from the Lord, went to where Paul was staying and prayed for him, *"that he might receive his sight, and be filled with the Holy Spirit"* (Acts 9:17). Immediately he began to *"preach Christ in the Synagogues"* (Acts 9:20). The point is this:

Despite the phenomenal experience that Paul had regarding his conversion, and despite now being baptized with the Holy Spirit and preaching the Gospel, even then an Apostle, still, the record shows that he could not successfully live for the Lord. The Seventh Chapter of Romans bears this out, and graphically so!

This was before the Lord had revealed the meaning of the New Covenant which, in fact, was revealed to the Apostle Paul (Gal. 1:12). But, the facts are, if the Apostle Paul couldn't successfully live for the Lord as one should live before this great Revelation was given to him, how in the world do we think that we can do what he could not do? Let us say it again:

It was to Paul that the Lord gave the meaning of the New Covenant, which, in effect, is the meaning of the Cross. As the Lord gave the Revelation of the New Covenant to Paul, the great Apostle then gave it to us in his Epistles.

Before we touch on the meaning of the New Covenant, let's see exactly why the Believer within himself cannot be what we ought to be, no matter how hard we try.

THE FALL

Any number of times, Paul alludes to this, but the Passage that I will now give will give us the reason for our inability, meaning that we must have the help of the Holy Spirit. The great Apostle said:

"And if Christ *be* in you *(He is in you through the Power and Person of the Spirit [Gal. 2:20]),* the body *is* dead because of sin *(means that the physical body has been rendered helpless because of the Fall; consequently, the Believer trying to overcome by willpower presents a fruitless task)*; but the Spirit is life because of Righteousness *(only the Holy Spirit can make us what we ought to be, which means we cannot do it ourselves; once again, He performs all that He does within the confines of the Finished Work of Christ).*

"But if the Spirit *(Holy Spirit)* of Him *(from God)* Who raised up Jesus from the dead dwell in you *(and He definitely does),* He Who raised up Christ from the dead shall also quicken your mortal bodies *(give us power in our mortal bodies that we might live a victorious life)* by His Spirit Who dwells in you *(we have the same Power in us, through the Spirit, that raised Christ from the dead, and is available to us only on the premise of the Cross and our Faith in that Sacrifice)*" (Rom. 8:10-11).

Let us say it again:

THE HOLY SPIRIT ALONE CAN MAKE US WHAT WE OUGHT TO BE

Self cannot improve self, and no matter how hard we try. This means that all of the efforts, and I mean all, which ignore the Cross of Christ and Faith in that Finished Work, which then gives the Holy Spirit latitude to work within our hearts and lives, present a wasted effort. It is the Cross of Christ, which gives the Holy Spirit the legal right to do all that He does. Before the Cross, the Holy Spirit was greatly limited due to the fact that the blood of bulls and goats could not take away sins (Heb. 10:4).

What the Believer is facing, and I speak of that which is in the spirit world of darkness, is far beyond our capacity to cope. So, for the Believer to face these things with no more than willpower simply won't work. The Holy Spirit is God and, as such, and as should be obvious, He can do anything. But, most Christians don't know how He works. As a result, most Christians are trying to live this life without the aid and help of the Holy Spirit. Don't misunderstand; the Holy Spirit does not leave the Believer, irrespective as to what erroneous course he might take. But, at the same time, erroneous courses stop Him from doing what He Alone can do.

SPIRITUAL ADULTERY!

In the first four Verses of the Seventh Chapter of Romans, Paul addresses himself to spiritual adultery. What do we mean by the term *"spiritual adultery"*?

Paul tells us that we as Believers are married to Christ. At least that's the way that God looks at the situation. Paul wrote:

> "Wherefore, my Brethren, you also are become dead to the Law *(the Law is not dead per se, but we are dead to the Law because we are dead to its effects; this means that we are not to try to live for God by means of 'Law,' whether the Law of Moses, or religious laws made up by other men or of ourselves; we are to be dead to all religious law)* by the Body of Christ *(this refers to the Crucifixion of Christ, which satisfied the demands of the broken Law we could not satisfy; but Christ did it for us; having fulfilled the Mosaic*

Law in every respect, the Christian is not obligated to religious law in any fashion, only to Christ and what He did at the Cross); **that you should be married to another** *(speaking of Christ)*, **even to Him Who is raised from the dead** *(we are raised with Him in Newness of Life, and we should ever understand that Christ has met, does meet, and shall meet our every need; we look to Him exclusively, referring to what He did for us at the Cross)*, **that we should bring forth fruit unto God** *(proper fruit can only be brought forth by the Believer constantly looking to the Cross; in fact, Christ must never be separated from the Work of the Cross; to do so is to produce 'another Jesus')*" **(Rom. 7:4).**

ONE HUSBAND, THE LORD JESUS CHRIST

The Apostle said:

"Would to God you could bear with me a little in *my* folly: and indeed bear with me. *(In effect, the Apostle is saying, 'indulge me.')*

"For I am jealous over you with godly jealousy *(refers to the 'jealousy of God' [Ex. 20:5; 34:14; Nah. 1:2])*: **for I have espoused you to one husband** *(not jealous of the Corinthians' affection for himself, but of their affection for Christ)*, **that I may present *you* as a chaste virgin to Christ.** *(They must not commit spiritual adultery, which refers to trusting in things other than Christ and the Cross)*" **(II Cor. 11:1-2).**

Let us say it again, if the Believer places his faith and trust in anything except Christ and the Cross, no matter how religious or spiritual the other things may be, such a Believer is being unfaithful to Christ. That's what we mean by *"spiritual adultery."* I should think it would be obvious that the Holy Spirit cannot rightly work in such circumstances. Yet, *"spiritual adultery"* is the position and condition of most modern Believers.

AN ABBREVIATED FORMULA

The following will possibly help us to understand the great Plan of God to a greater degree. It is as follows:

• THE CROSS OF CHRIST: When we speak of the *"Cross of Christ,"* I would certainly hope the reader would understand that we are not speaking of a wooden beam. We are speaking of what Jesus did there, i.e., *"the benefits of the Cross."* In the Atonement, our Lord addressed every single thing that man lost in the Fall and even addressed Satan and all powers of darkness (Col. 2:15; Eph. 1:10). Christ is the Source of all things, even as we have stated, and the Cross is the Means.

• OUR FAITH: To have the benefits of all that Christ accomplished at Cross, it requires only Faith on our part; however, without fail, it must be Faith exclusively in the Cross of Christ. To say it another way, the Cross of Christ must be the Object of our Faith. That's all that God requires of us (Rom. 5:1-2; Eph. 2:8-10; Rom. 4:3, 14; 6:11). As well, our Faith must not be divided between the Cross of Christ and other things. It must be the Cross of Christ exclusively. In fact, the only kind of faith that God will recognize is Faith, which is rested in His Son, our Saviour, the Lord Jesus Christ, Who must always be linked to the Atonement — Who He was and is, and what He did, which refers to the Cross. Everyone has faith, but it's not faith that God will recognize. The Cross is the Means by which we receive all things from the Lord.

• THE HOLY SPIRIT: Once our Faith is properly placed in the Cross, and maintained in the Cross, the Holy Spirit, Who works exclusively within the parameters of the Finished Work of Christ, will then go to work on our behalf. And, to be sure, considering that the Holy Spirit is God, there is nothing that He cannot do; however, for Him to do what He Alone can do, we must, and without fail, have our Faith anchored squarely in the Cross of Christ (Rom. 8:1-2, 10-11).

CHAPTER TEN

Can The Believer Live A Victorious Life Without Understanding The Cross Of Christ Relative To Sanctification?

QUESTION:

CAN THE BELIEVER LIVE A VICTORIOUS LIFE WITH-OUT UNDERSTANDING THE CROSS OF CHRIST RELATIVE TO SANCTIFICATION?

ANSWER:

No! One can be Saved and can make Heaven their Eternal Home without understanding this great Truth, actually, a greater part of the meaning of the New Covenant, but, one cannot live a victorious life.

It should be understood, considering the price paid by our Lord on Calvary's Cross, that He most definitely would want us to have all that we can have at this present time. Admittedly, in this particular Dispensation, the Dispensation of the Church, we can only have the *"firstfruits,"* with the balance given to us at the Resurrection of Life (the Rapture). Paul said:

"The Spirit itself *(Himself)* bears witness with our spirit *(means that He is constantly speaking and witnessing certain things to us)*, that we are the Children of God *(meaning that we are such now, and should enjoy all the privileges of such; we can do so if we will understand that all these privileges come to us from God, by the means of the Cross)*:

JOINT HEIRS WITH JESUS CHRIST

"And if children *(Children of God)*, then heirs *(a privilege)*; heirs of God *(the highest enrichment of all)*, and joint-heirs with Christ *(everything that belongs to Christ belongs to us through the Cross, which was done for us)*; if so be that we suffer with *Him (doesn't pertain to mere suffering, but rather suffering 'with Him,' referring to His Suffering at the Cross, which brought us total*

Victory), **that we may be also glorified together** *(He has been glorified, and we shall be glorified; all made possible by the Cross)*:

THE GLORY

"For I reckon that the sufferings of this present time *(speaks of the world and its condition because of the Fall)* **are not worthy to be compared with the glory** *(the glory of the coming future time will bear no relation to the misery of this present time)* **which shall be revealed in us** *(our Glory will be a reflective Glory, coming from Christ)***.**

"For the earnest expectation of the creature *(should have been translated, 'for the earnest expectation of the Creation')* **waits for the manifestation of the sons of God** *(pertains to the coming Resurrection of Life)***.**

THE CREATION

"For the creature *(Creation)* **was made subject to vanity** *(Adam's Fall signaled the fall of Creation)***, not willingly** *(the Creation did not sin, even as such cannot sin, but became subject to the result of sin, which is death)***, but by reason of Him Who has subjected** *the same* **in Hope** *(speaks of God as the One Who passed sentence because of Adam's Fall, but at the same time gave us a 'Hope'; that 'Hope' is Christ, Who will rectify all things)***,**

DELIVERED FROM THE BONDAGE OF CORRUPTION

"Because the creature *(Creation)* **itself also shall be delivered** *(presents this 'Hope' as effecting that Deliverance, which He did by the Cross)* **from the bondage of corruption** *(speaks of mortality, i.e., 'death')* **into the glorious liberty of the Children of God** *(when man fell, Creation fell! When man shall be delivered, Creation will* *be delivered as well, and is expressed in the word 'also').*

"For we know that the whole Creation *(everything has been affected by Satan's rebellion and Adam's Fall)* **groans and travails in pain together until now** *(refers to the common longing of the elements of the Creation to be brought back to their original perfection).*

THE FIRSTFRUITS OF THE SPIRIT

"And not only *they (the Creation and all it entails),* **but ourselves also** *(refers to Believers),* **who have the Firstfruits of the Spirit** *(even though Jesus addressed every single thing lost in the Fall at the Cross, we only have a part of that possession now, with the balance coming at the Resurrection),* **even we ourselves groan within ourselves** *(proclaims the obvious fact that all Jesus paid for in the Atonement has not yet been fully realized),* **waiting for the Adoption** *(should be translated, 'waiting for the fulfillment of the process, which Adoption into the Family of God guarantees'),* **to wit, the Redemption of our body** *(the glorifying of our physical body that will take place at the Resurrection)"* **(Rom. 8:16-23).**

However, in the *"Firstfruits"* that we now have, there is enough and more to help us live a victorious life and, as our Early Church Fathers coined the phrase, *"Victorious over the world, the flesh, and the Devil."* As stated, the balance will come at the Resurrection, because Paul also said the following:

WE SHALL BE CHANGED

"Behold, I show you a mystery *(a new Revelation given by the Holy Spirit to Paul concerning the Resurrection, i.e., Rapture);* **We shall not all sleep** *(at the time of the Resurrection [Rapture], many Christians will be alive),* **but we shall all be changed** *(both those who are dead and those* *who are alive),*

"In a moment, in the twinkling of an eye *(proclaims how long it will take for this change to take place),* **at the last trump** *(does not denote by the use of the word 'last' that there will be successive trumpet blasts, but rather denotes that this is the close of things, referring to the Church Age):* **for the trumpet shall sound** *(it is the 'Trump of God' [I Thess. 4:16]),* **and the dead shall be raised incorruptible** *(the Sainted dead, with no sin nature),* **and we shall be changed** *(put on the Glorified Body).*

THE GLORIFIED BODY

"For this corruptible *(sin nature)* **must put on incorruption** *(a Glorified Body with no sin nature),* **and this mortal** *(subject to death)* **must put on immortality** *(will never die).*

"So when this corruptible *(sin nature)* **shall have put on incorruption** *(the Divine Nature in total control by the Holy Spirit),* **and this mortal** *(subject to death)* **shall have put on immortality** *(will never die),* **then shall be brought to pass the saying that is written, Death is swallowed up in Victory** *(Isa. 25:8 — the full benefits of the Cross will then be ours, of which we now have only the Firstfruits [Rom. 8:23])"* **(I Cor. 15:51-54).**

IGNORANCE

The truth is, the modern church, and we speak of those who are truly Born-Again, knows precious little about the Cross of Christ as it refers to Sanctification, in other words, how we live for God. Putting it in plain and clear English, the modern church simply doesn't know how to live for God.

As a result, the church is subjected to every type of scheme and every type of gimmick that one can think, purporting to be the key to victory.

The church is told that if there is a problem in the life of a Believer, this means that the person is possessed by a demon spirit. In other words, if one is having problems with lust, it's the demon of lust, or if one is having problems with unforgiveness, it's the demon of unforgiveness, etc.

Is that correct?

No! While demon spirits most definitely oppress the Saints of God, which every one of us has experienced, it is not possible for a demon spirit to possess a Child of God. Paul said:

"**Know you not that you are the Temple of God** *(where the Holy Spirit abides)*, **and** *that* **the Spirit of God dwells in you?** *(That makes the Born-Again Believer His permanent Home)*" **(I Cor. 3:16).**

The Apostle also said:

"**Do you not know that your bodies are the members of Christ?** *(When a person is Saved, they are Saved holistically, meaning spirit, soul, and body. We become a member of Christ as a unity, with the Holy Spirit looking at the triune being of man as 'one.')* **Shall I then take the members of Christ, and make** *them* **the members of an harlot?** *(This constitutes every part of the physical body, including the sex organs, as belonging to Christ.)* **God forbid** *(may it never be!)*

The Apostle went on to say:

"**But he who is joined unto the Lord** *(indicates the closest possible union, symbolized by the sexual union of a Christian husband and wife)* **is one spirit** *(reflects the same union with Christ, albeit in a spiritual sense, as a husband and wife have in a physical sense)*" **(I Cor. 6:15, 17).**

So, I think from these Passages, and more could be given,

it should be obvious that a person cannot be possessed by the Lord and demon spirits at the same time.

DEMONIC OPPRESSION

However, it is definitely possible for a Believer to be oppressed by demon spirits. This affects one's emotions, the nervous system, plus even the physical body, at times causing sickness. Fear and depression fall into the same category as being products of demonic oppression.

Paul also said:

"**For God has not given us the spirit of fear** *(refers to a disposition of the mind; the Apostle is telling the young Evangelist not to fear)*; **but of Power** *(could be said, 'the spirit of Power,' for such comes from the Holy Spirit)*, **and of love** *(again, given by the Holy Spirit)*, **and of a sound mind** *('spirit of self-control,' all made possible by the Holy Spirit, Who demands that we ever keep our Faith in the Cross [Rom. 8:1-2, 11, 13])*" **(II Tim. 1:7).**

WHAT IS THE ANSWER FOR
DEMONIC OPPRESSION?

The answer is, *"Christ and Him Crucified"* (I Cor. 1:23; 2:2).

In fact, the Cross of Christ is the answer for everything, meaning that every single thing we receive from God comes to us from the Lord Jesus Christ by means of the Cross. In other words, it is the Cross that makes it possible for all of these good and wonderful things to be given to us.

A PERSONAL EXPERIENCE

I know what demonic oppression is. And, now I know the cause and, thank God, I also know the cure.

I was ministering at Family Worship Center sometime back on a Sunday Morning. I was dealing with this very subject of demon possession and demon oppression. Then, all of a sudden it dawned on me, even while I was preaching, that I had not suffered one iota of demonic oppression from 1997 to that moment. In fact, I still haven't and that's been some twelve years at the time of this dictation.

Even though demon spirits cannot possess a Child of God, still, if the Christian doesn't know and understand God's Prescribed Order of Victory, demon spirits most definitely can oppress the Child of God and cause him terrible problems. I am persuaded that this is the cause of much sickness as well. If one is carrying a load of any nature, that load, and that's what oppression is, can wear a person down, even their immune system, opening the door for various sicknesses and diseases.

WHAT HAPPENS WHEN A BELIEVER PUTS HIS FAITH EXCLUSIVELY IN THE CROSS OF CHRIST?

The first thing, I think, which takes place is that for the first time the Believer sees who he is and sees Who Christ is. We find that when we really see ourselves as we really are, it's not a very pretty picture. And, when we see Christ as He really is, which can only be understood by the means of the Cross, our thinking changes. The Cross of Christ strips away all of man's pretensions, self-will, and self-righteousness, cutting straight to the core of the being, in which we quickly come to realize that Jesus and Him Crucified is our only hope. But, religious man doesn't like that. As someone has well said, *"The doing of religion is the most powerful narcotics there is."*

When one puts his Faith exclusively in the Cross of Christ, everything changes — Christianity becomes simpler! Living for the Lord is not tied to a body of religion, but is rather tied exclusively to Christ and what Christ did for us at the Cross. All law, rules, regulations, works, etc., are out. This does not sit well with a lot of people. It doesn't sit well with most Religious denominations. It doesn't sit well with most preachers. So, they would rather remain ignorant, which means it's not merely a situation of not knowing, but, it's a situation of not desiring to know. In other words, don't trouble me with the Truth. And willful ignorance is the worst ignorance of all. The Prophet Hosea said:

"My People are destroyed for lack of knowledge: for you have rejected knowledge, I will also reject you, that you shall be no Priest to Me: seeing you have forgotten the Law of your God, I will also forget your children" (Hos. 4:6).

Notes from THE EXPOSITOR'S STUDY BIBLE are:

('My People are destroyed for lack of knowledge,' is the cause of all the problems in the church, and the world, for that matter! The 'knowledge' spoken of is the Bible. This 'lack of knowledge' was not ignorance, but rather a willful rejection of the Law of God. They didn't know, but it was because they didn't want to know!)

HOW TO LIVE FOR GOD

As we have previously stated, almost the entirety of the Bible, all the way from Genesis 1:1 through Revelation 22:21, is given over to telling Believers how to live for God. It was to Paul that the meaning of the New Covenant was given; consequently, a full ninety percent or more of Paul's Epistles are given over to Believers and how we should live this life. The Cross of Christ has always been the pivot point, so to speak.

When we go back to the very dawn of time, actually the first page of human history, even though Adam and Eve had been driven from the Garden because of their disobedience, still, the Lord conveyed to them how, despite the Fall, they could have communion with Him and forgiveness of sins. It would be by virtue of the slain lamb characterized in Genesis, Chapter 4, which was a Symbol, a Type, if you will, of the Redeemer Who ultimately would come. So, for some 4,000 years, all the way from Adam and Eve to the coming of Christ, the Sacrificial system was at the very heart of God's dealings with man. Even though the blood of bulls and goats could not take away sins (Heb. 10:4), still, it provided a stopgap measure, one might say, until our Lord did come.

Then, one might say, all who would be Saved looked forward to the Cross, i.e., the coming of the Redeemer. Now, we look back to the Cross, but let it ever be understood, it is always the Cross. So, the Cross of Christ is not only the means by which believing sinners are made right with God but, as well, the Cross of Christ is the means by which the Believer lives for the Lord and grows in Grace. The Cross of Christ was ever meant to be the Object of one's Faith, whether in Old Testament times, or at the present. Perhaps the following short diagram will be of some help. The Believer must understand the following:

- FOCUS: the Lord Jesus Christ (Jn. 14:6).
- OBJECT OF FAITH: the Cross of Christ (Rom. 6:3-5; I Cor. 1:17, 18, 23; 2:2).
- POWER SOURCE: the Holy Spirit (Rom. 8:1-2, 11).
- RESULTS: Victory (Rom. 6:14).

The Bible Student should study minutely this little diagram that's just been given because it characterizes what the life of the Believer ought to be.

The following is the same diagram, but used in the manner in which most modern Christians are trying to live for God.

WRONG DIRECTION

- FOCUS: Works.
- OBJECT OF FAITH: One's performance.
- POWER SOURCE: Self.
- RESULTS: Defeat!

Even though the modern Church talks faith constantly, the truth is, it is not living by faith at all, but rather by works. And how do I know that?

I know it because the Cross of Christ is not being preached

in the churches, at least as it regards our Sanctification, our life, and living. As already stated, while the modern church has a modicum of knowledge regarding the Cross of Christ respecting Salvation, it has little or no knowledge at all respecting the Cross as it regards our Sanctification. As a result, it simply does not know how to live for the Lord.

If the Believer will focus on the Lord Jesus Christ, understanding, and as previously stated also, that He is the Source of all things that we receive from God and, thereby, make the Cross of Christ the Object of our Faith, understanding that it was there that all victory was won and that it was done all on our behalf, we will then find the Holy Spirit working for us, working within us, bringing about His Fruit and, as well, giving us power to live this life. That is God's Way as it has always been God's Way.

"But God forbid that I should glory *(boast)*, save in the Cross of our Lord Jesus Christ *(what the opponents of Paul sought to escape at the price of insincerity is the Apostle's only basis of exultation)*, by Whom the world is crucified unto me, and I unto the world. *(The only way we can overcome the world, and I mean the only way, is by placing our Faith exclusively in the Cross of Christ and keeping it there)*" (Gal. 6:14).

CHAPTER ELEVEN

How Were People Saved Before The Cross?

QUESTION:

HOW WERE PEOPLE SAVED BEFORE THE CROSS?

ANSWER:

They were Saved then by the same means that believing sinners are Saved presently, by looking to the Cross, of which the sacrifices were a Type.

In Old Testament times, people were Saved by looking forward to the Cross, while people are Saved now by looking backwards to the Cross. Before the Cross, believing sinners looked forward to a prophetic Jesus, while believing sinners now look backward toward a historical Jesus.

There has only been one Way of Salvation and it is for all people, both Jews and Gentiles, and that one Way is Faith in Christ and what He has done for us at the Cross.

While animal sacrifices under the Old Covenant could not take away sins (Heb. 10:4), they did serve as a Type of the One Who was to come, a Substitute, if you will, of the Lord Jesus Christ. People were Saved during Old Testament times, not so much by the sacrifices themselves, but what the sacrifices represented, namely, the Promised Redeemer.

THE FIRST PROMISE OF A REDEEMER

The first Promise of a Redeemer for the human race, strangely enough, was directed at Satan through the Serpent because of the Fall of Adam and Eve. The Lord said:

"And I will put enmity *(animosity)* between you and the woman *(presents the Lord now actually speaking to Satan, who had used the serpent; in effect, the Lord is saying to Satan, 'You used the woman to bring down the human race, and I will use the woman as an instrument to bring the Redeemer into the world, Who will save the human*

race'), **and between your seed** *(mankind which follows*
Satan) **and her Seed** *(the Lord Jesus Christ)*; **it** *(Christ)*
shall bruise your head *(the victory that Jesus won at the*
Cross [Col. 2:14-15]), **and you shall bruise His Heel** *(the*
sufferings of the Cross)" **(Gen. 3:15).**

THE SACRIFICIAL SYSTEM INSTITUTED

After the Fall with Adam and Eve driven from the Garden,
the Lord gave them a means by which they could have fellowship with Him and forgiveness of sins. It would be through
the means of the Sacrificial system, an innocent victim killed,
a lamb, which would serve as a Substitute until the coming of
the Redeemer.

In the record of the first sacrifice we have the Plan of God
for Redemption, which was given through Abel, and the plan
of Satan to hinder that process, and done so through Cain. The
Scripture says:

THE FRUIT OF THE GROUND

"**And in process of time it came to pass** *(the phrase*
used here refers to a long indefinite period), **that Cain**
brought of the fruit of the ground an offering unto the
LORD. *(This was probably the first offering that he*
brought, even though the Lord had explained to the First
Family the necessity of the Sacrificial system, that is, if
they were to have any type of communion with God and
forgiveness of sins. There is evidence that Adam, at least
for a while, offered up sacrifices. Cain knew the type
of sacrifice that the Lord would accept, but he rebelled
against that admonition, demanding that God accept the
labor of his hands, which, in fact, God could not accept.
So we have, in the persons of Cain and Abel, the first
examples of a religious man of the world and a genuine
man of Faith.)

THE FIRSTLING OF HIS FLOCK

"**And Abel, he also brought of the firstlings of his flock and of the fat thereof** *(this is what God demanded; it was a blood sacrifice of an innocent victim, a lamb, which proclaimed the fact that Abel recognized his need of a Redeemer, and that One was coming Who would redeem lost humanity; the Offering of Abel was a Type of Christ and the price that He would pay on the Cross of Calvary in order for man to be redeemed).* **And the LORD had respect unto Abel and to his offering:** *(As stated, this was a Type of Christ and the Cross, the only Offering, which God will respect. Abel's Altar is beautiful to God's Eye and repulsive to man's. Cain's altar is beautiful to man's eye and repulsive to God's. These 'altars' exist today; around the one that is Christ and His Atoning Work, few are gathered, around the other, many. God accepts the slain lamb and rejects the offered fruit; and the offering being rejected, so of necessity is the offerer.)*

AN OFFERING GOD COULD NOT ACCEPT

"**But unto Cain and to his offering He had not respect** *(let us say it again, God has no respect for any proposed way of Salvation, other than 'Jesus Christ and Him Crucified' [I Cor. 1:23; 2:2]).* **And Cain was very angry, and his countenance fell** *(that which filled Abel with peace filled Cain with wrath; the carnal mind displays its enmity against all this Truth which so gladdens and satisfies the heart of the Believer).*

THE WORD OF THE LORD

"**And the LORD said unto Cain** *(God loves Cain, just as He did Abel, and wishes to bless him also)*, **Why are you angry** *(Abel's Altar speaks of Repentance, of Faith,*

and of the Precious Blood of Christ, the Lamb of God
without blemish; Cain's altar tells of pride, unbelief, and
self-righteousness, which always elicits anger)**? and why is
your countenance fallen** *(anger, in one form or the other,
accompanies self-righteousness, for that is what plagued
Cain; God's Righteousness can only come by the Cross,
while self-righteousness is by dependence on works)*?

ACCEPTANCE

"If you do well, shall you not be accepted *(if you bring
the correct sacrifice and, thereby, place your faith)*? **and
if you do not well, sin** *(a Sin-Offering)* **lies at the door** *(a
lamb was at the door of the Tabernacle)*. **And unto you
shall be his desire, and you shall rule over him** *(the Lord
promised Cain dominion over the Earth of that day, if he
would only offer up, and place his trust in, the right sacrifice; He promises the same presently to all who trust Christ
[Mat. 5:5])*.

CAIN MURDERS ABEL

**"And Cain talked with Abel his brother: and it came
to pass, when they were in the field, that Cain rose up
against Abel his brother, and killed him** *(the first murder;
Cain's religion was too refined to kill a lamb, but not too
cultured to murder his brother; God's Way of Salvation
fills the heart with love; man's way of salvation inflames it
with hatred; 'Religion' has ever been the greatest cause of
bloodshed)*.

AM I MY BROTHER'S KEEPER?

**"And the LORD said unto Cain, Where is Abel your
brother?** *(Adam sins against God and Cain sins against
Man. In their united conduct, we have sin in all its forms,*

and that on the first page of human history.) **And he said, I know not: Am I my brother's keeper** *(he showed himself a 'liar' in saying, 'I know not'; 'wicked and profane' in thinking he could hide his sin from God; 'unjust' in denying himself to be his brother's keeper; 'obstinate and desperate' in not confessing his sin)"* **(Gen. 4:3-9)?**

As stated, the Sacrificial system ordained by God began on the first page of human history and continued unto the time of Christ, a time frame of approximately 4,000 years.

ABRAHAM

The meaning of Salvation, i.e., *"Justification by Faith,"* was first shown to Abraham. The Patriarch lived some 400 years after the Flood and some 2,000 years after Adam and Eve.

The Lord revealed Himself to Abraham, in that, from Abraham and Sarah, his wife, the Lord would bring forth an indigenous people who would have Faith in Him and who ultimately would bring the Redeemer into the world. These people would be called *"Israelites,"* after one of the names of Jacob, Abraham's grandson. It would take many centuries for all of this to come to pass, but, ultimately, it would come to fruition.

JUSTIFICATION BY FAITH

In this Revelation, the Scriptures state:

"And he *(Abraham)* **believed in the LORD** *(exercised Faith, believing what the Lord told him)***; and He** *(the Lord)* **counted it to him** *(Abraham)* **for Righteousness.** *(This is one of the single most important Scriptures in the entirety of the Word of God. In this simple term, 'Abraham believed the LORD,' we find the meaning of 'Justification by Faith.' Abraham was Saved by Grace through Faith, not by his good works. There is no other way of Salvation anywhere* *in the Bible. God demands Righteousness; however, it is the Righteousness afforded strictly by Christ and Christ Alone. Anything else is self-righteousness, and totally unacceptable to God. Directly the sinner believes God's Testimony about His Beloved Son, he is not only declared righteous, but he is made a son and an heir)"* **(Gen. 15:6).**

THE SACRIFICE

"And He *(the Lord)* **said unto him** *(Abraham)***, I am the LORD Who brought you out of Ur of the Chaldees, to give you this land to inherit it.** *(The Lord now reaffirms and, greater yet, expands the Revelation. We find from the examples of the Bible Greats, and our own experiences as well, that the Lord has to constantly reaffirm His Promises to us and, as well, to strengthen our Faith. It doesn't take much to weaken our Faith, despite our claims to the contrary.)*
"And he said, LORD God, whereby shall I know that I shall inherit it? *(Abraham asked two questions, 'What will You give me?' [15:2], and 'Whereby shall I know?' Christ is the answer to the first question; the Covenant to the second.)*

THE COVENANT

"And He *(the Lord)* **said unto him** *(to Abraham)***, Take Me an heifer of three years old, and a she goat of three years old, and a ram of three years old, and a turtledove, and a young pigeon.** *(The Covenant is founded on Grace, for five living creatures are sacrificed to establish it. Five in the Scripture is the number of Grace; and these five sacrifices set out the fullness of the great Sacrifice of Calvary [Williams].*
The 'heifer' symbolized the Priestly Office of Christ. The 'she goat' symbolized His Prophetic Office. The 'ram'

symbolized His Kingly Office. Jesus was Priest, Prophet, and King. The 'turtledove' symbolized Him being led and guided strictly by the Holy Spirit, while the 'young pigeon' symbolized Him obeying the Spirit in every capacity)" **(Gen. 15:7-9).**

Abraham built so many Altars that he actually was referred to as the *"altar builder,"* portraying the fact that his trust and Faith were in the Crucified One Who was ultimately to come.

BORN-AGAIN, BUT WITH LIMITATIONS

Before the Cross of Christ animal blood alone stood between man and eternal Hell. While it was designed by the Lord and definitely served as a stopgap measure, so to speak, still, it was woefully insufficient. It could cover sin but it could not take away sins. Paul said, and emphatically:

"For *it is* not possible that the blood of bulls and of goats should take away sins. *(The word 'impossible' is a strong one. It means there is no way forward through the blood of animals. As well, it applies to all other efforts made by man to address the problem of sin, other than the Cross)"* **(Heb. 10:4).**

If it is to be recalled, when John the Baptist introduced Christ, so to speak, his exact words were:

". . . Behold the Lamb of God *(proclaims Jesus as the Sacrifice for sin, in fact, the Sin-Offering, Whom all the multiple millions of offered lambs had represented)*, **which takes away the sin of the world** *(animal blood could only cover sin, it could not take it away; but Jesus offering Himself as the perfect Sacrifice took away the sin of the world; He not only cleansed acts of sin, but, as well, addressed the root cause [Col. 2:14-15])"* **(Jn. 1:29).**

ABRAHAM'S BOSOM

So, when Believers died before the Cross, which includes all the Old Testament Greats, they did not go to Heaven, but, rather, into a part of Hell referred to as *"Abraham's Bosom."* This is the name given to it by Jesus. In fact, all of these individuals were held captive by Satan, even though he could not hurt them in any way. In fact, Jesus said that they *"were comforted."* Actually, He gave a tremendous description of this place. Even though it's quite lengthy for us to quote the entire account, notes and all, from THE EXPOSITOR'S STUDY BIBLE, I feel it would be very profitable to read carefully this given by our Lord. He said:

A CERTAIN RICH MAN

"There was a certain rich man, who was clothed in purple and fine linen, and fared sumptuously every day *(the Jews of Jesus' day concluded that riches were the favor of God, and poverty was the curse of God; therefore, this illustration given by Christ ripped to shreds their false doctrine)*:

A CERTAIN BEGGAR

"And there was a certain beggar named Lazarus *(many claim this is a Parable not to be taken literally; however, as it is to be noticed, Jesus uses names in this illustration, meaning that it's not a Parable but actually something that really happened; consequently, it is chilling indeed!)*, which was laid at his gate, full of sores *(the rich man saw Lazarus constantly, but offered no help whatsoever; as stated, such concluded ones like Lazarus to be cursed of God, and to help such would be thwarting the Plan of God; how so much the Word of God is twisted by so many)*,

"And desiring to be fed with the crumbs which fell from the rich man's table *(probably means that this rich man felt very good with himself in even allowing 'crumbs' to be given to this beggar)*: **moreover the dogs came and licked his sores** *(proclaims the fact that this man was not only poverty stricken but, as well, was sick; he would not fit the mold of the modern prosperity gospel which, in fact, is no Gospel at all; but he definitely did fit God's mold; we should consider all of this very carefully)*.

ABRAHAM'S BOSOM

"And it came to pass, that the beggar died *(more than likely, noone cared, but the Lord cared, as we shall see)* **and was carried by the Angels into Abraham's bosom** *(Paradise; where all Believers went before the Cross; as well, Jesus also tells us here that whenever a Believer dies, his soul and spirit are escorted by Angels into the presence of God)*: **the rich man also died, and was buried** *(no Angels carried him away, for he died eternally lost; him being rich did not carry any weight as it regards his soul's Salvation)*;

HELL

"And in Hell he lift up his eyes *(Jesus here plainly proclaims the Doctrine of Eternal Hell; as well, He also proclaims the fact that the soul and the spirit immediately go to Heaven or Hell at the time of death, and that the soul and the spirit are totally conscious)*, **being in torments** *(to say the least, Hell is not a pleasant place and, as stated, it is eternal)*, **and sees Abraham afar off, and Lazarus in his bosom** *(all Believers before the Cross expressed faith in the Revelation given to Abraham by God as it regards Redemption and, in a sense, it is the same presently [Rom. 4:16])*.

TORMENTED

"And he cried and said, Father Abraham, have mercy on me *(there are no unbelievers in Hell, nor is there any Salvation there; the rich man repented, but too late)*, and send Lazarus *(he had no concern for Lazarus back on Earth, but his conscience now recalls many things, but too late)*, that he may dip the tip of his finger in water *(evidently there is no water there)*, and cool my tongue; for I am tormented in this flame *(the Bible teaches that the fires of Hell are literal; Jesus said so!)*.

COMFORT AND TORMENT

"But Abraham said, Son, remember that you in your lifetime received your good things *(in no way does it mean that this was the cause of him being lost; it merely means that he was treated very well, but showed no thankfulness for his Blessings)*, and likewise Lazarus evil things *(the rich man didn't allow his Blessings to bring him to the Lord, and Lazarus didn't allow his poverty to keep him from the Lord)*: but now he is comforted *(because he had accepted the Lord)*, and you are tormented *(the word 'now' is that which is all-important; it speaks of the time after death; will it be one of 'comfort' or 'torment'?)*.

A GREAT GULF

"And beside all of this, between us and you there is a great gulf fixed *(this is in the heart of the Earth [Mat. 12:40]; before the Cross, even though all who went to Paradise were comforted, they were still captives of Satan, with him hoping that ultimately he would get them over into the burning pit [Eph. 4:8-9]; this means that when Believers died before the Cross, due to the fact that the blood of bulls and goats could not take away sins, the sin debt remained, and Satan *still had a claim on them; so all those in Paradise were awaiting the Cross, which would deliver them)*: **so that they which would pass from hence to you cannot** *(proclaims the fact that all opportunities for Salvation are on this side of the grave; this means that the Catholic doctrine of purgatory is a 'fool's hope'; there is no such place)*; **neither can they pass to us, that would come from thence** *(but yet it was possible for those in Hell to look over and see those in Paradise, and it seems to speak to them; that place, due to the Cross, is now empty, with all liberated by Christ after the price was paid [Eph. 4:8-9])*.

A WITNESS

"Then he said, I pray you therefore, father, that you would send him *(send Lazarus)* **to my father's house** *(this is the only example of praying to a dead Saint in Scripture; let those who do so remember that prayer to all other dead Saints will avail just as much as this prayer did — nothing)*:

"For I have five brethren; that he may testify unto them *(these statements proclaim the fact that this man had a working knowledge of God and more than likely even professed Salvation before his death; but he wasn't Saved!)*, **lest they also come into this place of torment** *(he did not ask this grace for himself, for he knew that he was eternally entombed; it is easy to step into Hell, but impossible to step out)*.

THE WORD OF GOD

"Abraham said unto him, They have Moses and the Prophets; let them hear them *(doesn't mean that this event happened during the time of Moses, but that Abraham is referring to the Word of God; this tells us that at least a part of the Old Testament had then been written)*.

REPENTANCE

"And he said, Nay, father Abraham: but if one went unto them from the dead, they will repent *(the Scriptures contain all that is necessary to Salvation; a returned spirit could add nothing to them; and a man who will not listen to the Bible will not listen to a multitude if raised from the dead; in fact, a few days later, the Lord did raise a man named Lazarus from the grave, and the Pharisees went about to put him to death)*.

TODAY IS THE DAY OF SALVATION

"And he said unto him, If they hear not Moses and the *Prophets*, neither will they be persuaded, though one rose from the dead *(this illustration as given by Christ, actually happened and, in fact, presents a startling portrayal of life after death; we learn from this, and in stark reality, that the only thing that really matters in life is being right with God; there is a Heaven and there is a Hell, and every soul who has ever lived has gone or is going to one or the other; the only way to make Heaven one's eternal Home is to accept Christ; He Alone is the Door; everything else leads one to Hell, exactly as the rich man found out, and to his eternal dismay)*" (Lk. 16:19-31).

THE SALVATION OF THOSE BEFORE THE CROSS

Even though all who trusted in the Word of God before the Cross were Saved, in truth, their Salvation depended totally on the coming Cross of Christ. As stated, animal sacrifices were only a stopgap measure. The blood of animals could not take away sins. So, everything hinged on the Cross.

But the moment that Jesus died, His Soul and Spirit went down to Abraham's Bosom for the express purpose of removing them from this place and taking them with Him to Heaven.

And that He did!

Now when a Believer dies, he instantly goes to be with Christ in Heaven. Through the Cross, Jesus opened up the Way.

Concerning the death of the Saints after the Cross, Paul said:

"**For I am in a strait betwixt two** *(refers to equal pressure being exerted from both sides; Paul is speaking here of his personal desires, and not necessarily that which the Lord would desire; however, he has already made it clear his personal will is to be swallowed up in the sweet Will of God)*, **having a desire to depart, and to be with Christ; which is far better** *(the centerpiece of all of this is Christ; if one draws any other conclusions, one misses the point entirely)*" **(Phil. 1:23).**

"We read of a place that's called Heaven,
"It's made for the pure and the free;
"These Truths in God's Word He has given,
"How beautiful Heaven must be."

"In Heaven no drooping nor pining,
"No wishing for elsewhere to be;
"God's Light is forever there shining,
"How beautiful Heaven must be."

"Pure waters of life there are flowing,
"And all who will drink may be free;
"Rare jewels of splendor are glowing,
"How beautiful Heaven must be."

"The Angels so sweetly are singing,
"Up there by the beautiful sea;
"Sweet chords from their gold harps are ringing,
"How beautiful Heaven must be."

CHAPTER TWELVE

Do All Blessings Come Through The Cross?

QUESTION:

DO ALL BLESSINGS COME THROUGH THE CROSS?

ANSWER:

Yes!

God can deal with sinful man only in one way and that is by and through the Cross of Christ. It is because of Who Jesus is, the Son of the Living God, God manifest in the flesh, and what He did, which refers exclusively to the Cross. As we say over and over:

• Jesus Christ is the Source of all things we receive (Jn. 14:6).

• The Cross is the Means by which these things are given to us (Rom. 6:3-5; I Cor. 1:17-18, 21, 23; 2:2).

• Our Faith in Christ and the Cross is the means by which we receive these things given (Lk. 9:23; 14:27; Gal. 6:14).

• The Holy Spirit is the Agent in all of this, superintending every step (Rom. 8:1-2, 11; Eph. 2:13-18).

THE CROSS OF CHRIST AND
THE MODERN CHURCH

The modern church, and I speak of those who are truly Born-Again, understands the Cross of Christ as it regards Salvation; however, as it regards Sanctification, it doesn't have a clue. When we understand that ninety percent of Paul's teaching centered up on how we are to live for God, which portrays the Cross as it regards our Sanctification, then we should begin to realize how serious this omission is.

It was to Paul that the meaning of the New Covenant, which is the meaning of the Cross, was given. He said:

"Paul, an Apostle, (not of men, neither by man, but by Jesus Christ, and God the Father, Who raised Him from the dead;) *(this means Paul did not submit the authority of his Apostleship to men, neither was it conferred on him by man.)*

"**And all the Brethren who are with me, unto the Churches of Galatia** *(refers to all in that region)***:**

"**Grace** *be* **to you and Peace from God the Father** *(made possible by the Cross)***, and** *from* **our Lord Jesus Christ** *(Who made it possible)***,**

"**Who gave Himself for our sins** *(the Cross)***, that He might deliver us from this present evil world** *(the Cross alone can set the captive free)***, according to the Will of God and our Father** *(the standard of the entire process of Redemption)***:**

"**To Whom** *be* **Glory forever and ever** *(Divine Glory)***. Amen.**

NO OTHER GOSPEL

"**I marvel that you are so soon removed from Him** *(the Holy Spirit)* **Who called you into the Grace of Christ** *(made possible by the Cross)* **unto another Gospel** *(anything which doesn't have the Cross as its Object of Faith)***:**

"**Which is not another** *(presents the fact that Satan's aim is not so much to deny the Gospel, which he can little do, as to corrupt it)***; but there be some who trouble you, and would pervert the Gospel of Christ** *(once again, to make the object of Faith something other than the Cross)***.**

LET HIM BE ACCURSED

"**But though we** *(Paul and his associates)***, or an Angel from Heaven, preach any other gospel unto you than that which we have preached unto you** *(Jesus Christ and Him Crucified)***, let him be accursed** *(eternally condemned; the Holy Spirit speaks this through Paul, making this very serious)***.**

"As we said before, so say I now again *(at some time past, he had said the same thing to them, making their defection even more serious)*, If any man preach any other gospel unto you *(anything other than the Cross)* than that you have received *(which Saved your souls)*, let him be accursed *('eternally condemned,' which means the loss of the soul)*.

"For do I now persuade men, or God? *(In essence, Paul is saying, 'Do I preach man's doctrine, or God's?')* or do I seek to please men? *(This is what false apostles do.)* for if I yet pleased men, I should not be the Servant of Christ *(one cannot please both men and God at the same time)*.

THE REVELATION

"But I certify you, Brethren *(make known)*, that the Gospel which was preached of me *(the Message of the Cross)* is not after man. *(Any Message other than the Cross is definitely devised by man.)*

"For I neither received it of man *(Paul had not learned this great Truth from human teachers)*, neither was I taught *it (he denies instruction from other men)*, but by the Revelation of Jesus Christ. *(Revelation is the mighty Act of God whereby the Holy Spirit discloses to the human mind that which could not be understood without Divine Intervention)*" **(Gal. 1:1-12)**.

Having been given the Revelation of the New Covenant, in essence, what it meant, the Apostle, even as we have stated, plainly warns all preachers that they must preach what he has preached.

Why was he so adamant?

The Apostle knew, and beyond the shadow of a doubt, that what he had received from the Lord was, in effect, *"the Gospel."* He tells us in I Corinthians as to exactly what the Gospel is. Let's see what he said:

THE DEFINITION OF THE GOSPEL

The Apostle said:

"**For Christ sent me not to baptize** *(presents to us a Cardinal Truth)*, **but to preach the Gospel** *(the manner in which one may be Saved from sin)*: **not with wisdom of words** *(intellectualism is not the Gospel)*, **lest the Cross of Christ should be made of none effect.** *(This tells us in no uncertain terms that the Cross of Christ must always be the emphasis of the Message. In other words, the Message of the Cross is the Gospel)*" **(I Cor. 1:17).**

If it is correct that the Cross of Christ is, in fact, the Gospel, then this means that most of the modern church is little preaching the Gospel.

THE MASTERBUILDER OF THE CHURCH

The reason we give all of this information concerning the Gospel, concerning the Church, is to establish the fact of what the Gospel actually is. Pure and simple, the Gospel is the Cross of Christ. What Jesus did at the Cross actually presents the New Covenant. Inasmuch as this great Revelation was given to the Apostle Paul, and considering that Paul *"preached the Cross,"* and of that no one can deny, this establishes the fact that everything must come through the Cross of Christ.

The Apostle went on to say:

"**Who then is Paul, and who is Apollos** *(the idea is these men, though used greatly by God, were still mere men)*, **but Ministers by whom you believed** *(better translated, 'through whom you believed')* **even as the Lord gave to every man?** *(Whatever Gifts each Preacher had came from the Lord, and was not due to their own abilities or merit.)*

"**I have planted** *(refers to Paul being the founder of the*

Church per se unto Christ), **Apollos watered** *(the strength-ening of the Faith of wavering Churches)*; **but God gave the increase** *(pertains to souls and their Spiritual Growth)*.

"**So then neither is he who plants anything, neither he who waters** *(the Planter and the Waterer are nothing by comparison to the Lord)*; **but God Who gives the increase.** *(Man by his own ability cannot bring about the increase, no matter how much he plants or waters, spiritually speaking.)*

"**Now he who plants and he who waters are one** *(literally means in the Greek, 'one thing')*: **and every man shall receive his own reward according to his own labor.** *(Paul did not say, 'according to his own success,' but rather 'labor.' God hasn't called us to be successful, but He has called us to be Faithful.)*

LABORERS TOGETHER WITH GOD

"**For we are laborers together with God** *(pertains to labor in the harvest)*: **you are God's husbandry** *(God's Field, God's tilled Land)*, ***you are* God's building** *(Vineyard)*.

"**According to the Grace of God which is given unto me, as a wise masterbuilder** *(in essence, Paul, under Christ, founded the Church)*, **I have laid the foundation** *(Jesus Christ and Him Crucified)*, **and another builds thereon** *(speaks of all Preachers who followed thereafter, even unto this very moment, and have built upon this Foundation)*. **But let every man take heed how he builds thereupon.** *(All must preach the same Doctrine Paul preached, in essence, 'Jesus Christ and Him Crucified.')*

FOUNDATION

"**For other foundation can no man lay than that is laid** *(anything other than the Cross is another foundation* *and, therefore, unacceptable to the Lord)*, **which is Jesus Christ.** *(Who He is, God manifest in the flesh, and What He did, Redemption through the Cross)*" **(I Cor. 3:5-11).**

The Cross of Christ is the meaning of the New Covenant. Concerning that, Paul also said:

THE EVERLASTING COVENANT

"Now the God of Peace *(proclaims that Peace has been made between God and fallen man, and done so through what Jesus did on the Cross on man's behalf)*, **that brought again from the dead our Lord Jesus** *(presents the only mention of the Resurrection of Christ in this Epistle to the Hebrews)*, **that Great Shepherd of the sheep** *(presents the One Who died for us, and Whom God raised from the dead)*, **through the Blood of the Everlasting Covenant** *(points to the Cross and proclaims the fact that this Covenant, being perfect, is Eternal)*" **(Heb. 13:20).**

Inasmuch as we have established the fact that the Cross of Christ is the meaning of the New Covenant, let us again state that every single thing that man receives from the Lord is made possible by the Cross.

THERE IS A BLESSING IN THE CROSS

Not only is there Salvation in the Cross, not only is the Baptism with the Holy Spirit in the Cross, not only is there Sanctification in the Cross, but, as well, every other type of Blessing is in the Cross, be it material, physical, financial, etc.

While preaching in Family Worship Center one Sunday morning sometime ago, the Spirit of the Lord began to move in a mighty way during the Message. I began to state to the people, as the Holy Spirit poured it through my heart, *"If you need a bigger house, there is a bigger house in the Cross; if you* *need a raise in pay, there is a raise in pay in the Cross; if you need Divine Healing, there is Divine Healing in the Cross; whatever you need is found in the Cross."* **The Spirit of God swept the place as those words were given to the people.**

From that one message the Lord began to bless people in our Church with particular needs being met that, heretofore, they did not see how such was possible. They truly found that there was a Blessing in the Cross, and a Blessing of unprecedented proportions. Paul also said:

> **"But God forbid that I should glory** *(boast)***, save in the Cross of our Lord Jesus Christ** *(what the opponents of Paul sought to escape at the price of insincerity is the Apostle's only basis of exultation)***, by Whom the world is Crucified unto me, and I unto the world.** *(The only way we can overcome the world, and I mean the only way, is by placing our Faith exclusively in the Cross of Christ and keeping it there)***" (Gal. 6:14).**

MOSES KNEW THERE WAS A BLESSING IN THE CROSS

The Scripture says:

> **"So Moses brought Israel from the Red Sea, and they went out into the wilderness of Shur; and they went three days in the wilderness, and found no water.** *(God tests Faith in order to strengthen and enrich it.)*
>
> **"And when they came to Marah, they could not drink of the waters of Marah, for they were bitter: therefore the name of it was called Marah.** *(Marah means 'bitter.' Pink says: 'While the wilderness may and will make manifest the weakness of God's Saints and, as well, our failures, this is only to magnify the Power and Mercy of Him Who brought us into the place of testing. Further, and we must understand, God always has in view our ultimate*

good.' The bitter waters of Marah typify life and its disap-
pointments.)

"**And the people murmured against Moses, saying,**
What shall we drink? *(Three days before, the children of*
Israel were rejoicing on the shores of the Red Sea. Now,
some 72 hours later, they are 'murmuring against Moses.'
Such presents a lack of Faith. 'Tests' brought upon us by
the Lord portray what is in us. Regrettably, it doesn't take
much to bring out the unbelief.)

THE CROSS

"**And he cried unto the LORD** *(Moses set the exam-*
ple; there is no help outside of the Lord, but man, even
the Church, seems to find difficulty in believing this); **and**
the LORD showed him a Tree *(the 'Tree' is a type of the*
Cross [Acts 5:30; 10:39; 13:29; Gal. 3:13; I Pet. 2:24]),
which when he had cast into the waters, the waters were
made sweet *(we must put the Cross into every difficulty and*
problem of life, which alone holds the answer; only by this
means can the bitter waters be made 'sweet'): **there He**
(God) **made for them a Statute and an Ordinance, and**
there He proved them *(tested them! We must understand*
that God doesn't give victory to men, only to Christ; His
Victory becomes ours, as we are properly in Him [Jn. 14:20;
Rom. 6:3-5]),

I AM THE LORD WHO HEALS YOU

"**And said, If you will diligently hearken to the Voice**
of the LORD your God, and will do that which is right
in His Sight, and will give ear to His Commandments,
and keep all His Statutes, I will put none of these diseases
upon you, which I have brought upon the Egyptians:
for I am the LORD Who heals you. *(It is demanded that*
all these 'Statutes' and 'Ordinances' be perfectly kept;

however, no man can boast of such; Christ has perfectly kept all the Commandments and, as our Substitute, kept them perpetually. Looking to Him, we can claim this blessing. As well, the 'healing' promised here has to do not only with physical diseases but, as well, of emotional and spiritual diseases.

"The Cross is to be put into the bitter waters of these problems, whatever they might be. They can then be made sweet. The name 'LORD,' in the Hebrew, as used here, is 'Jehovah-Ropheka,' which means 'Jehovah, the Healer.' Jehovah has proven Himself as the Deliverer of Israel, and now He proclaims Himself as their 'Healer')" (Ex. 15:22-26).

HOW DO WE OBTAIN THESE BLESSINGS WHICH ARE IN THE CROSS?

We do it simply by exercising Faith in Christ and what He did for us at the Cross, understanding that the Cross is the Means by which these Blessings are given to us.

DAVID UNDERSTOOD THE BLESSING OF THE CROSS AND HOW IT COMES TO US

David wrote the 23rd Psalm from the position of the sheep which looked to the Shepherd for all things.

Jesus proclaimed the fact that He was the Shepherd. He said:

"I am the Good Shepherd *(speaks of Jesus dying for the Sheep; the 'Good Shepherd' dies for the Sheep, the 'Great Shepherd' lives for the Sheep [Heb. 13:20], and the 'Chief Shepherd' comes for the Sheep [I Pet. 5:4]):* **the Good Shepherd gives His Life for the Sheep** *(the Cross: His 'Life,' if given for the Sheep, would guarantee 'Eternal Life'; the 'Cross' is ever the Central Point of Christianity)"* **(Jn. 10:11).**

So David says this about the Shepherd:

"The LORD is My Shepherd; I shall not want. *(Even though this beautiful Psalm applied to David, and to all Believers as well, more than all it applied to Christ.*

"Williams says, 'Only one voice sang this Psalm in perfect tune. It was the Voice of Jesus. When walking through the dark valley of His earthly Life, Jehovah was His Shepherd. There is no suggestion of sin in the Psalm. Its great theme is not so much what Jehovah gives, or does, as what or Who He is.

"And yet, at the same time, as Christ presents Himself as the Sheep, He is also presented as the Great Shepherd of His People, for He was raised from the dead in order to be such [Heb. 13:20].)

GREEN PASTURES

"He makes Me to lie down in green pastures *(any other voice that is followed will lead only to barren pastures)***: He leads Me beside the still waters.** *(The 23rd Psalm makes it abundantly clear that the church is not the Saviour, neither is religious hierarchy the Saviour, neither are rules and regulations the Saviour, only the Lord is. We can follow Him, or we can follow other things; we cannot follow both.)*

HE ALONE CAN RESTORE THE SOUL

"He restores My soul *(when the sheep skin their foreheads foraging for grass, the shepherd will pour oil over the wounds)***: He leads Me in the paths of Righteousness for His Name's sake.** *(At times the lamb will leave the appointed path, even doing so several times, being retrieved each time by the shepherd. But, if it leaves too many times, the shepherd, upon retrieving it from the rocky crevices, will* *take his staff and break one of the legs. He then carefully 'sets' the leg, and then lays the lamb on his shoulder close to his heart. He carries it until the wound is healed. That is a symbol of chastisement [Heb. 12:5-11]).*

I WILL FEAR NO EVIL

"Yes, though I walk through the valley of the shadow of death, I will fear no evil *(the powers of darkness, constituting powerful attacks by Satan)***: for You are with Me; Your rod and Your staff they comfort Me.** *(The ideal position for the 'lamb' is to allow the shepherd to fight for him. In fact, the only fight we are told to fight is the 'good fight of Faith' [I Tim. 6:12].*

"What a comfort it is to know that the 'rod' and 'staff' are constantly beating back the powers of darkness on our behalf.)

GOODNESS AND MERCY

"You prepare a table before Me in the presence of My enemies *(and these 'enemies' cannot touch this 'prepared table')***: You anoint My head with oil** *(a Type of the Holy Spirit)***; My cup runs over** *(a figure of speech that refers to abundance).*

"Surely goodness and mercy shall follow Me all the days of My life *('goodness' gives us green pastures and still waters; 'mercy' retrieves us when we foolishly leave the 'paths of righteousness')***: and I will dwell in the House of the LORD forever.** *(As long as the Lord is our Shepherd, we can expect all of this, 'all the days of our lives')***" (Ps. 23:1-6).**

CHAPTER THIRTEEN

What Does It Mean For One To Place One's Faith In The Cross Of Christ?

QUESTION:

WHAT DOES IT MEAN FOR ONE TO PLACE ONE'S FAITH IN THE CROSS OF CHRIST?

ANSWER:

It means for one to place their faith exclusively in Christ and what He did for us at the Cross, exclusive of everything else.

There is nothing physical about placing one's faith in the Cross of Christ. It is simply a matter of Believing.

BELIEVING WHAT?

We are to understand and, therefore, believe that every single thing that comes to anyone from God comes by the means of Christ and what Christ has done for us at the Cross. This means that Salvation comes to the sinner because of what Jesus did at the Cross. It means that every single Blessing received by the Believer from the Lord was all made possible by the Cross. In other words, anything that anyone has ever received from the Lord is because Jesus offered Himself as a Sacrifice on Calvary's Cross, which paid the sin debt, making it possible for God to deal directly with human beings, at least those who believe.

BEFORE THE CROSS

Before the Cross of Christ the way to God was closed except under certain particular circumstances.

THE SACRIFICIAL SYSTEM

Adam and Eve fell because of disobedience, meaning, they did what the Lord told them not to do. The Scripture says:

"And the LORD God took the man, and put him into

the Garden of Eden to dress it and to keep it.

"And the LORD God commanded the man, saying, Of every tree of the Garden you may freely eat *(as stated, before the Fall, man was vegetarian)*:

"But of the Tree of the Knowledge of Good and Evil, you shall not eat of it *(as for the 'evil,' that was obvious; however, it is the 'good' on this tree that deceives much of the world; the 'good' speaks of religion; the definition of religion pertains to a system devised by men in order to bring about Salvation, to reach God, or to better oneself in some way; because it is devised by man, it is unacceptable to God; God's answer to the dilemma of the human race is 'Jesus Christ and Him Crucified' [I Cor. 1:23])*: **for in the day that you eat thereof you shall surely die** *(speaks of spiritual death, which is separation from God; let it be understood that the Tree of the Knowledge of Good and Evil was not the cause of Adam's Fall; it was a failure to heed and obey the Word of God, which is the cause of every single failure; spiritual death ultimately brought on physical death, and has, in fact, filled the world with death, all because of the Fall)*" **(Gen. 2:15-17).**

THE DISOBEDIENCE

Despite what the Lord had said to Adam, now we come to the disobedience, i.e., *"the Fall."* The Scripture says:

"And when the woman saw that the tree was good for food *(presents the lust of the eyes)*, and that is was pleasant to the eyes *(the lust of the flesh)*, and a tree to be desired to make one wise *(the pride of life)*, she took of the fruit thereof, and did eat *(constitutes the Fall)*, and gave also unto her husband with her; and he did eat *(refers to the fact that evidently Adam was an observer to all these proceedings; some claim that he ate of the forbidden fruit which she offered him out of love for her; however, no one *ever sins out of love; Eve submitted to the temptation out of deception, but 'Adam was not deceived' [I Tim. 2:14]; he fell because of unbelief; he simply didn't believe what God had said about the situation; contrast this Verse with Lk. 4:1-13; both present the three temptations, 'the lust of the flesh,' 'the lust of the eyes,' and 'the pride of life'; the first man falls, the Second Man conquers)"* **(Gen. 3:6).**

EXPULSION FROM THE GARDEN

Due to the fact that man is now fallen, he must be driven from the Garden, which is explained in the following Scripture:

"And the LORD God said, Behold, the man is become as one of Us, to know good and evil *(the Lord knew evil, not by personal experience, but rather through Omniscience; man now knows evil by becoming evil, which is the fountainhead of all sorrow in the world; the pronoun 'Us' signifies the Godhead, 'God the Father, God the Son, and God the Holy Spirit')***: and now, lest he put forth his hand, and take also of the Tree of Life, and eat, and live forever** *(this would have been the worst thing of all, to have an Adolf Hitler to live forever, etc.)***:**
"Therefore the LORD God sent him forth from the Garden of Eden *(in effect, this was an act of mercy; man is expelled from the Garden lest by eating the Tree of Life he should perpetuate his misery; but God's Love for him, though fallen and guilty, is so strong that He accompanies him into exile; as well, through Jesus Christ, God's only Son, Who will be given in Sacrifice, the Lord will show Adam, and all who would follow him, how to come back into Paradise; regrettably, there is no record that Adam and Eve placed any faith in the Lord; unfortunately, untold billions have followed suit)***, to till the ground from whence he was taken** *(refers to a place of toil, not to a place of torment).*

THE FLAMING SWORD

"So He *(God)* drove out the man *(implies the idea of force and displeasure)*; and He placed at the east of the Garden of Eden Cherubims *(these Cherubims signified the Holiness of God, which man had now forfeited)*, and a flaming sword which turned every way, to keep the way of the Tree of Life *(the 'flaming sword' was emblematic of the Divine Glory in its attitude toward sin)*" (Gen. 3:22-24).

THE SACRIFICIAL SYSTEM

From the Fourth Chapter of Genesis we know of the Sacrificial system, which was instituted by the Lord so that Adam and Eve and all who followed them could have access to the Lord and, as well, forgiveness of sins. This was a slain lamb, which would be symbolic of the Lord Jesus Christ Who ultimately would come. It must be remembered that no one could approach God except through the sacrifice.

Some 2,500 years after the Garden of Eden, the Lord gave His Law to Moses, which governed every aspect of Jewish life. In the midst of the Law was the Sacrificial system, which comprised the core of the Law, one might say.

The truth is, man could not keep the law no matter how hard he tried, so, his only recourse was the sacrifice. To be sure, in the Lord Jesus Christ, it is our only recourse presently as well.

THE TABERNACLE

The Lord, as well, gave to Moses the diagram, as it regards the Tabernacle, in which He was to dwell between the Mercy Seat and the Cherubim. It was referred to as the *"Holy of Holies."* Not even the Priests were allowed into the Holy of Holies, with the exception of the High Priest, and he could only go in once a year, which was on the Great Day of Atonement.

In all of this we see how that sin had separated man from God, and how that man could approach God only on the basis of the Cross of Calvary, one might say. Even before Jesus came, the offering up of the sacrificial lambs always pointed to Christ Who was to come. As we've said it before, let us say it again.

The only thing standing between mankind and eternal Hell is the Cross of Christ.

When Jesus came, of course, He fulfilled the entirety of the Law, and in every respect, meaning that the Temple, along with the Sacrificial system, etc., were no more.

EVERYTHING IS IN CHRIST AND THE CROSS

Now, it should be understood, the only way that mankind can approach God is by virtue of the Cross of Christ. This means that everything we receive from the Lord, as well, is all made possible by the Cross.

THE TORN VEIL

When Jesus died on the Cross, atoning for all sin, past, present, and future, at least for all who will believe, this opened up the way to God for sinful man, which had not heretofore been possible. It is all due to the fact that Jesus has atoned for all sin and did so by His Death on Calvary's Cross. Sin is what blocked the access to God, but now, with all sin atoned the way is open.

Even though there were many rooms attached to the Temple, there were two main rooms where all the activity occurred. The first one was *"The Holy Place."* In that room were the ten tables of Showbread, ten Golden Lampstands, along with the Altar of Incense. The ten tables of bread were on the right side of the room with the Golden Lampstands on the left. The Altar of Incense sat immediately in front of the

Veil, which hid the Holy of Holies. This was where God was supposed to dwell, which was between the Mercy Seat and the Cherubim, both on the Ark of the Covenant. However, the Ark was lost during the time of Jeremiah so the Holy of Holies in the Temple during the time of Christ was empty. Nevertheless, the Veil still hung between the Holy Place and the Holy of Holies. Josephus, the Jewish historian, said that it was 30 feet tall and 4 inches thick. He went on to say that four yoke of oxen could not pull it apart.

But, when Jesus died, the Scripture says, *"Jesus, when He had cried again with a loud Voice, yielded up the ghost. And, behold, the Veil of the Temple was rent in twain from the top to the bottom . . ."* (Mat. 27:50-51).

The Veil being torn from the top to the bottom proclaims the fact that man could not have done such, even had he been able to do so. So, the Veil was torn by God, meaning that the Way to the very Throne of God was now open, and all because of what Jesus had done on the Cross.

IT IS THE CROSS ALONE

One never matures beyond the Cross! Williams said, *"The whole of the Christian life from beginning to end, day by day, moment by moment, is simply learning what it means to live by Grace through Faith alone in Christ Alone."*[1]

Most Christians do not understand the Cross, because they do not understand the Bible. As we have attempted to state in the answer to this question, when one actually understands the Word of God as one should, one finds that the Cross is prevalent from the first page of human history and goes into eternity future. In fact, Paul labeled it as *"The Everlasting Covenant"* (Heb. 13:20).

As you have read this answer, we have brought you through the Bible by the Way of the Cross, which surely causes one to see that it is the Cross alone that has made it possible for the Salvation of the sinner and Sanctification for the Saint.

WHAT IS THE ALTERNATIVE TO
THE CROSS OF JESUS CHRIST?

There is only one alternative and that is to fall back on one's own personal resources. We should take inventory if we are going to do that. What type of resources do we have? How stable is our strength? What merit do I have? What do I personally have to offer a Holy and Just God?

If the Believer doesn't place his faith exclusively in Christ and what Christ has done at the Cross, then his only other recourse is himself, and, please understand, that particular direction is defeated before it even begins. It is foolish indeed! In fact, Satan must laugh at our pitiful efforts to try to substitute our foolishness in the place of God's Way — and His Way is the Cross of Christ.

TURNING TO THE CROSS MEANS THAT
EVERYTHING ELSE MUST BE ABANDONED

And, that's where the difficult part comes in. We like to hold on to our pet schemes. Religious men are very adept at making up new rules and regulations. The Church, in fact, stumbles from one fad to the other. One day it's casting demons out of Christians and the next day it is falling at the foot of the Purpose Driven Life. As soon as one fad comes to the fore, another one is waiting in the wings. None of them work, and simply because they cannot work, because if it's not the Cross, no matter how good it may seem to be on the surface, it is something devised by man and is a waste of time. Paul said:

"**For they who are after the flesh do mind the things of the flesh** *(refers to Believers trying to live for the Lord by means other than Faith in the Cross of Christ)*; **but they who are after the Spirit the things of the Spirit** *(those who place their Faith in Christ and the Cross, do so exclusively; they are doing what the Spirit desires, which alone can bring*

Victory)" **(Rom. 8:5).**

One's faith placed in something other than the Cross of Christ constitutes the *"flesh,"* and Paul also said, *"So then they that are in the flesh cannot please God"* (Rom. 8:8).

The flesh, as the Holy Spirit through Paul used the word, pertains to that which is indicative to human beings, in other words, our talent, education, ability, intellect, motivation, etc. While these things within themselves aren't wrong, the truth is, they are woefully inadequate for the task. Besides that, the Holy Spirit will not work with anything that originates with man, and anything that originates with the flesh is of man and man exclusively.

Some 3,000 years ago, Solomon said, *"There is a way that seems right unto a man, but the end thereof are the ways of death"* (Prov. 16:25).

Quoting from THE EXPOSITOR'S STUDY BIBLE, this same Proverb is quoted in 14:12. It is given thusly by the Holy Spirit by design. The entirety of the problems of the human family is because of wrong direction. The only *"true way"* is *"Jesus Christ and Him Crucified"* (I Cor. 1:14-18, 21, 23; 2:2).

WALKING AFTER THE SPIRIT

If we are to please the Lord and be recipients of His many benefits, we must *"walk after the Spirit."* How do we do that?

We must place our faith exclusively in Christ and the Cross, and I mean exclusively.

The Holy Spirit works exclusively within the parameters of the Finished Work of Christ. In fact, the Holy Spirit refers to this as a *"Law."* He said:

"For the Law of the Spirit of Life in Christ Jesus has made me free from the Law of Sin and Death" (Rom. 8:2).

Inasmuch as the Holy Spirit works exclusively within the parameters of the Finished Work of Christ, in other words, the Cross, this means that our faith, and let us say it again, must be in Christ and the Cross exclusively.

As we've already stated, when one places one's faith entirely in the Cross of Christ, everything else must go.

While we continue to love our Church, we have now come to the understanding that the Church didn't die on the Cross for us. While we continue to love preachers, we must understand that no human being died on that Cross except the Lord Jesus Christ.

FAITH

Faith is the key!
Paul said:

"**Therefore being justified by Faith** *(this is the only way one can be justified; refers to Faith in Christ and what He did at the Cross)***, we have peace with God** *(justifying peace)* **through our Lord Jesus Christ** *(what He did at the Cross)***:**

"**By Whom also we have access by Faith into this Grace** *(we have access to the Goodness of God by Faith in Christ)* **wherein we stand** *(wherein alone we can stand)***, and rejoice in hope** *(a hope that is guaranteed)* **of the Glory of God** *(our Faith in Christ always brings Glory to God; anything else brings glory to self, which God can never accept)***" (Rom. 5:1-2).**

One can say the following, I think, and be theologically sound:

Faith in Christ and what He did at the Cross is the only Faith that God will accept. Faith in anything else, irrespective as to what it is, is actually in self, which God will never recognize.

So, while placing one's faith exclusively in Christ and the Cross, which is God's Way, is very simple of understanding, the doing of such is something else altogether.

THE WORDS OF OUR LORD

Jesus said:

"**And He said to** *them* **all, If any man will come after Me** *(the criteria for Discipleship)***, let him deny himself** *(not asceticism as many think, but rather that one denies one's own willpower, self-will, strength, and ability, depending totally on Christ)***, and take up his cross** *(the benefits of the Cross, looking exclusively to what Jesus did there to meet our every need)* **daily** *(this is so important, our looking to the Cross; that we must renew our Faith in what Christ has done for us, even on a daily basis, for Satan will ever try to move us away from the Cross as the Object of our Faith, which always spells disaster)***, and follow Me** *(Christ can be followed only by the Believer looking to the Cross, understanding what it accomplished, and by that means alone [Rom. 6:3-5, 11, 14; 8:1-2, 11; I Cor. 1:17-18, 21, 23; 2:2; Gal. 6:14; Col. 2:14-15])*.

"**For whosoever will save his life shall lose it** *(try to live one's life outside of Christ and the Cross)***: but whosoever will lose his life for My sake, the same shall save it** *(when we place our faith entirely in Christ and the Cross, looking exclusively to Him, we have just found 'more abundant life' [Jn. 10:10])*" **(Lk. 9:23-24).**

Then Jesus said:

"**And whosoever does not bear his Cross** *(this doesn't speak of suffering as most think, but rather ever making the Cross of Christ the Object of our Faith; we are Saved and we are victorious not by suffering, although that sometimes will happen, or any other similar things, but rather by our Faith, but always with the Cross of Christ as the Object of that Faith)***, and come after Me** *(one can follow Christ only by Faith in what He has done for us at the Cross; He* *recognizes nothing else)*, **cannot be My Disciple** *(the statement is emphatic! If it's not Faith in the Cross of Christ, then it's faith that God will not recognize, which means that such people are refused)*" **(Lk. 14:27).**

CHAPTER FOURTEEN

What Happens To The Believer When His Faith Is Placed In The Cross?

QUESTION:

WHAT HAPPENS TO THE BELIEVER WHEN HIS FAITH IS PLACED IN THE CROSS?

ANSWER:

He is now functioning in God's Divine Order and if Faith remains in the Cross of Christ exclusively, he or she will now experience all that for which Jesus died.

Doesn't it make sense, considering the price that Jesus paid on the Cross of Calvary that He would want us to have all that for which He died? I think the answer to that is obvious! But sadly, most Believers are living far beneath their Spiritual Privileges in Christ and it is because of not understanding the Cross of Christ as it refers to our Sanctification, i.e., how we live for God.

AN ILLUSTRATION

The following illustration is an actual happening and has been used by preachers all over the world and rightly so. Even though it is well known, still, it perfectly illustrates the tenor of that which we are addressing.

A young man and his young wife resided in the country of Ireland. At the turn of the Twentieth Century there were many problems in that beautiful little country and this young couple longed to immigrate to the United States. They saved all the money they could and finally got enough to purchase the least expensive ticket on an ocean liner.

About a day out of New York, after having been on the high seas for well over a week, one of the ship's pursers happened to walk by their little cabin. The door was open and he stopped to chat for a few minutes.

He noticed some crumbs on the bed and the young man, noticing the purser's observation, made mention that they had just eaten their lunch.

"What do you mean, you have just eaten your lunch?" the purser asked!

The young man replied, *"We only had money for the least expensive ticket for our passage and had none left over at all for food."* So, he then said, *"We packed all the food that we could, but I'll admit it's getting very stale."*

The purser looked at him and said, *"Did I hear you correctly? Are you saying that you brought your food with you?"*

"Yes," the young man replied!

The purser said, *"Did you not know that your ticket included all the meals?"* He then went on to say, *"Young man, there are several restaurants on this ship and your ticket paid for you going to these restaurants as much as you liked and eating as much as you desired."*

The young man, along with his wife, stared at the purser for a few moments and then said, *"You mean to say that my ticket paid for all the meals, as well?"*

"That's exactly what I'm saying," the purser answered!

The young man seemed to say to himself more than to the purser, *"And to think, we have been eating this stale food for this entire trip when we could have had three meals a day."*

"That's exactly what I'm saying!" the purser added.

This perfectly describes most modern Christians. We are eating stale bread when we could have so very, very much more!

THE FIRST THING THAT HAPPENS TO THE CHILD OF GOD WHEN THEY PLACE THEIR FAITH EXCLUSIVELY IN THE CROSS

Paul is an excellent example.

In the giving to the great Apostle the meaning of the New Covenant, the Lord showed the Apostle the condition of the entirety of the world, which included both Jews and Gentiles. They were both placed on the same level, lost, undone without God, and in dire need of the Redeemer, Who is the Lord Jesus Christ.

The First Chapter was devoted to the Gentiles with Chapters 2 and 3 devoted to the Jews. Admittedly, the Jewish people did not at all relish the idea of being put down on the lower level of the Gentiles, but, that's where the Holy Spirit placed them, and despite their knowledge of the Lord. All of mankind, in fact, was placed in a position of being unable to save themselves.

THE CROSS OF CHRIST, THE ANSWER TO THE DILEMMA

In Chapters 4 and 5 of Romans, the Holy Spirit proclaims to Paul the answer to the fallen sons of Adam's lost race.

There was no way that Salvation could be earned; it could only be received in one way and that was by Faith. This meant that merit was out, hence, the Jews being placed on the same level with the Gentiles and, as well, works were out. The answer was clear and clean:

"**Therefore being Justified by Faith** *(this is the only way one can be justified; refers to Faith in Christ and what He did at the Cross)*, **we have peace with God** *(justifying peace)* **through our Lord Jesus Christ** *(what He did at the Cross)*:

"**By Whom also we have access by Faith into this Grace** *(we have access to the Goodness of God by Faith in Christ)* **wherein we stand** *(wherein alone we can stand)*, **and rejoice in hope** *(a hope that is guaranteed)* **of the Glory of God.** *(Our Faith in Christ always brings Glory to God; anything else brings glory to self, which God can never accept)*" **(Rom. 5:1-2).**

HOW TO LIVE FOR GOD!

The Sixth Chapter of Romans provides this information. However, due to the fact that we have already given the information contained in Romans 6 in the answer to another question, let us use the great statement given in the Second Chapter of Colossians, which actually goes into a little more detail as it regards the Believer who has now placed his or her faith exclusively in the Cross of Christ. The great Apostle said:

DON'T BE BEGUILED WITH ENTICING WORDS

"**And this I say** *(points directly to the false teachers)*, **lest any man should beguile you with enticing words** *(refers to being deceived by subtle reasoning)*.

"**For though I be absent in the flesh, yet am I with you in the spirit** *(refers to Paul's human spirit)*, **joying and beholding your order, and the steadfastness of your Faith in Christ** *(speaks of 'holding rank,' and refers to maintaining one's Faith in the Cross)*.

"**As you have therefore received Christ Jesus the Lord** *(refers to the manner of one's Salvation, which is Christ and Him Crucified)*, *so* **walk** *you* **in Him** *(behavior is to be ordered in the sphere of Christ and the Cross)*:

"**Rooted and built up in Him** *(pertains to a proper foundation)*, **and stablished in the Faith** *(in Christ and the Cross)*, **as you have been taught** *(refers to the Colossians coming in the right way, but some of them considering the false message of the Gnostics)*, **abounding therein with thanksgiving.** *(This refers to the fact that the Gospel of the Cross, which had brought them to Christ, had also brought them untold benefits.)*

THE TRADITION OF MEN

"**Beware lest any man spoil you through philosophy and vain deceit** *(anything that pulls the Believer away from the Cross is not of God)*, **after the tradition of men** *(anything that is not of the Cross is of men)*, **after the rudiments of the world, and not after Christ.** *(If it's truly after Christ, then it's after the Cross.)*

"For in Him *(Christ)* **dwells all the fullness of the Godhead bodily.** *(This is Godhead as to essence. Christ is the completion and the fullness of Deity, and in Him the Believer is complete.)*

COMPLETE IN HIM

"And you are complete in Him *(the satisfaction of every spiritual want is found in Christ, made possible by the Cross)*, **which is the Head of all principality and power** *(His Headship extends not only over the Church, which voluntarily serves Him, but over all forces that are opposed to Him, as well [Phil. 2:10-11]):*

"In Whom also you are circumcised with the Circumcision made without hands *(that which is brought about by the Cross [Rom. 6:3-5])*, **in putting off the body of the sins of the flesh by the Circumcision of Christ** *(refers to the old carnal nature that is defeated by the Believer placing his Faith totally in the Cross, which gives the Holy Spirit latitude to work):*

THE CRUCIFIXION OF CHRIST

"Buried with Him in Baptism *(does not refer to Water Baptism, but rather to the Believer baptized into the death of Christ, which refers to the Crucifixion and Christ as our Substitute [Rom. 6:3-4])*, **wherein also you are risen with** *Him* **through the Faith of the operation of God, Who has raised Him from the dead.** *(This does not refer to our future physical Resurrection, but to that spiritual Resurrection from a sinful state into Divine Life. We died with Him, we are buried with Him, and we rose with Him [Rom. 6:3-5], and herein lies the secret to all Spiritual Victory.)*

"And you, being dead in your sins and the uncircumcision of your flesh *(speaks of spiritual death [i.e.,* *'separation from God'], which sin does!)*, **has He quick-ened together with Him** *(refers to being made spiritually alive, which is done through being 'Born-Again')*, **having forgiven you all trespasses** *(the Cross made it possible for all manner of sins to be forgiven and taken away)*;

THE BROKEN LAW WAS ADDRESSED
AT THE CROSS

"Blotting out the handwriting of Ordinances that was against us *(pertains to the Law of Moses, which was God's Standard of Righteousness that man could not reach)*, **which was contrary to us** *(Law is against us, simply because we are unable to keep its precepts, no matter how hard we try)*, **and took it out of the way** *(refers to the penalty of the Law being removed)*, **nailing it to His Cross** *(the Law with its decrees was abolished in Christ's Death, as if Crucified with Him)*;

SATAN AND ALL POWERS
OF DARKNESS DEFEATED

"*And* having spoiled principalities and powers *(Satan and all of his henchmen were defeated at the Cross by Christ Atoning for all sins; sin was the legal right Satan had to hold man in captivity; with all sin atoned, he has no more legal right to hold anyone in bondage)*, **He** *(Christ)* **made a show of them openly** *(what Jesus did at the Cross was in the face of the whole universe)*, **triumphing over them in it.** *(The triumph is complete and it was all done for us, meaning we can walk in power and perpetual Victory due to the Cross.)*

NO MORE RULES AND REGULATIONS

"Let no man therefore judge you in meat, or in drink,

or in respect of an holy day, or of the new moon, or of the Sabbath *Days (the moment we add any rule or regulation to the Finished Work of Christ, we have just abrogated the Grace of God)*:

"**Which are a shadow of things to come** *(the Law, with all of its observances, was only meant to point to the One Who was to come, Namely Christ)*; **but the Body** *(Church)* **is of Christ** *(refers to 'substance and reality,' as opposed to shadow)*" **(Col. 2:4-17).**

UNDERSTANDING THE DEATH OF CHRIST

1. The moment the Believer places his faith exclusively in the Cross of Christ, he begins to understand the Crucifixion of Christ, and that understanding will continue to be enlarged all the days of his or her life.

2. The Believer will see that everything that comes from the Lord to us comes by the Means of the Cross, and no other way. In fact, the Holy Spirit will not allow it to come any other way (Rom. 8:2; Eph. 2:13-18).

3. The Believer will begin to see then how the Holy Spirit works exclusively in the framework of the Finished Work of Christ. In other words, it is the Cross of Christ that gives the Holy Spirit the legal means to do all that He does. As well, that is found in Romans 8:2.

EVERYTHING ELSE MUST BE LAID ASIDE

Once the Believer sees the Victory of the Cross and places his or her faith accordingly, he will then begin to realize that everything else must be laid aside with the Cross of Christ exclusively the Object of Faith. That's what Paul was talking about when he said, *"Let no man judge you in meat, or in drink, or in respect of an holy day. . . ."* On paper this may seem very simple, but such a Believer will then find the flesh beginning to come to the fore in some of his friends and relatives. In other words, they will not be happy at all with what is taking place. The *"doing"* of religion is the most powerful narcotic there is and when people are told that this avails them nothing with the Lord, with everything being rather in the Cross, that's when the problem begins.

SATAN WILL NOW BEGIN TO FIGHT HARDER

Upon first hearing this Message and believing it and, thereby, engaging oneself in that which is God's Prescribed Order of Victory, the Evil One, knowing that we have now found God's Way, will begin to oppose the Child of God in every capacity. While we will deal with this in another answer, suffice to say, all temptation, opposition, and oppression may very well increase, at least for a period of time, and will, no doubt, do so. It is Satan's efforts to discourage such a Believer in order that such a one would simply quit. But, in the midst of the opposition, such a Believer will find himself growing in Grace and the Knowledge of the Lord (II Pet. 3:18).

A PERSONAL EXPERIENCE

I have been on both sides of this proverbial fence, so to speak. To be sure, God forbid that I would have to function again in the confines of *"law,"* i.e., *"religious law."* God forbid that I would ever have to go in that direction again. Again, proverbially speaking, that side of the fence constitutes nothing but failure and defeat, with the sin nature ruling the individual.

THE VICTORY SIDE

Victory is found only in the Cross of Christ. The Cross is where the demands of the broken law were fully met in Christ and, as well, with all sin atoned, Satan was totally defeated. On this side, proverbially speaking, there is, as the song says, *"Victory over sin and purity within."* While a person can be Saved and not understand the Cross of Christ, as it regards daily life and living, one most definitely cannot walk in victory over the world, the flesh, and the Devil without the Cross of Christ being the Object of our Faith. As stated, I've been on both sides of this fence and I do not want any more of the other side. I'll take the side of the Cross, for there Grace abounds and the Holy Spirit works. This is the key to all Victory, all life, and all living. This is what Jesus was talking about when He said:

"I am come that they might have life, and that they might have it more abundantly" (Jn. 10:10).

CHAPTER FIFTEEN

Did God Forsake Jesus On The Cross?

QUESTION:

DID GOD FORSAKE JESUS ON THE CROSS?

ANSWER:

No! at least not in the way that some claim.

THE CRUCIFIXION

We quote from **THE EXPOSITOR'S STUDY BIBLE:**

"**And they bring Him unto the place Golgotha, which is, being interpreted, The place of a skull** *(two meanings:*
• *Some claim this is the place where Adam was buried, and his skull later found; however, there is no evidence whatsoever of this tradition.*
• *Others think the interpretation simply means that the rock face of the hill resembles a skull, which is probably the correct interpretation).*
"**And they gave Him to drink wine mingled with myrrh** *(referred to a strong narcotic made of sour wine and mingled with bitter herbs; it was supposed to dull the sense of pain; some think that Christ was offered the drink twice, but there is some indication that it was offered three times):* **but He received** *it* **not** *(He would not seek alleviation of the agonies of the Crucifixion by any drug potion, which might render Him insensible; He would bear the full burden consciously).*
"**And when they had crucified Him** *(referred to them nailing Him to the Cross),* **they parted His garments, casting lots upon them, what every man should take** *(His garments, with the exception of the seamless Robe, were divided among the soldiers; not wanting to tear the seamless Robe apart, they cast lots with the winner taking ownership of the garment [Ps. 22:18]).*

THE KING OF THE JEWS

"And it was the third hour *(9 a.m. in the morning, the time of the morning Sacrifice)*, and they crucified Him.

"And the superscription of His accusation was written over *(over the Cross)*, **THE KING OF THE JEWS** *(out of anger, no doubt, toward the Jews, Pilate wrote the title himself [Jn. 19:19]; the Chief Priests were visibly angry over this, and strongly requested that it be changed to read, 'He said, I am King of the Jews'; Pilate answered by saying, 'What I have written I have written' [Jn. 19:21-22]; so, Who, and what Jesus really was, were fitly placed over His Head on the Cross)*.

TWO THIEVES

"And with Him they crucified two thieves *(robbers)*; the one on His right hand, and the other on His left.

"And the Scripture was fulfilled, which said, And He was numbered with the transgressors *(Isa. 53:12 — He took the place of the transgressors; so His Death, its manner, and with whom He died, were fitting!)*.

THE TAUNTS

"And they who passed by railed on Him *(Ps. 22:7-8 — 'they' referred to the religious leaders of Israel)*, **wagging their heads, and saying, Ah, You Who destroyed the Temple, and build *it* in three days** *(they were referring to the statement He did make, recorded in Jn. 2:19-21, which referred to His Body the Temple, its Death, and Resurrection in three days; He wasn't talking about the Temple in Jerusalem)*,

"Save Yourself, and come down from the Cross *(this jest was the harder to endure since it appealed to a consciousness of power held back only by the self-restraint of a Sacrificed Will; had He saved Himself, no one else could have been Saved)*.

"**Likewise also the Chief Priests mocking said among themselves with the Scribes, He Saved others; Himself He cannot save** *(they could not deny the fact that He Saved others, but they attempted to turn that fact against Him, by alleging that He performed these miracles by the power of Satan, rather than by the Power of God)*.

"**Let Christ the King of Israel descend now from the Cross** *(said in mockery)*, **that we may see and believe** *(they lied!; He rose from the dead after the third day, and they still didn't believe)*. **And they who were crucified with Him reviled Him** *(while both did revile Him, one shortly thereafter repented and was Saved, which Mark did not mention)*.

THE DEATH OF JESUS

"**And when the sixth hour was come** *(12 noon)*, **there was darkness over the whole land until the ninth hour** *(until 3 p.m.; as it was now the Passover time, the moon was full so that it could not have been caused by an eclipse; for when the moon is full, it cannot intervene between the Earth and the Sun; how far this darkness extended, we aren't told; we do know that it went as far as Egypt toward the south, and as far as Bithynia toward the north; it was at this time that He became the Burnt-Offering, and the Sin-Offering of Lev. 1:4)*.

THE TIME OF HIS DEATH

"**And at the ninth hour** *(3 p.m.)* **Jesus cried with a loud voice** *(proving that He did not die from physical weakness, but that He purposely laid down His Own Life [Jn. 10:17-18])*, **saying Eloi, Eloi, lama sabachthani? which is, being interpreted, My God, My God, why have**

You forsaken Me? *(During this three hour period when darkness covered that part of the world, if not the whole Earth, He bore the sin penalty of mankind, on which the Heavenly Father could not look [Hab. 1:13; 1 Pet. 2:24])"* **(Mk. 15:22-34).**

Momentarily, the picture will change.

THE PROPHET HABAKKUK

Some 600 years before Christ, the Prophet Habakkuk said concerning God: *"You are of purer eyes than to behold evil, and cannot look on iniquity"* **(Hab. 1:13).**

FATHER

Luke then recorded:

"And when Jesus had cried with a loud voice *(proclaims the fact that He did not die from weakness; actually, they did not take His Life, He gave it up freely [Jn. 10:17-18])***, He said, Father, into Your hands I commend My Spirit** *(proclaims the last words He uttered)***: and having said thus, He gave up the ghost.** *(He didn't die until the Holy Spirit told Him He could die [Heb. 9:14])"* **(Lk. 23:46).**

GOD — FATHER

If it is to be noticed, during the three hours from 12 noon till 3 p.m. when Jesus was bearing the sin penalty of mankind, which He did by the giving of Himself in Sacrifice, He referred to His Father as *"God"***; however, the moment He came to die,** *"He said, Father, into Your hands I commend My Spirit: and having said thus, He gave up the ghost."*
This doesn't have Jesus dying as a sinner on the Cross and going to Hell, as the Word of Faith doctrine claims, but rather

commending His Spirit to His Father. That settles the argument!

SIMON PETER

Concerning the Crucifixion of Christ, Peter said:

"**For even hereunto were you called** *(called to act Christlike, irrespective)***: because Christ also suffered for us** *(Peter reminds these slaves that Christ also suffered unjustly, for He, the Just One, died on behalf of unjust ones)***, leaving us an example, that we should follow His steps** *(we are to reproduce Christ in our lives, which we can only do by the Help, Guidance, Leading, and Power of the Holy Spirit [Jn. 16:7-16])***:**

SINLESS

"**Who did no sin** *(Christ was the only sinless human being Who ever lived)***, neither was guile found in His mouth** *(He never sinned by speaking hypocritically or falsely, not even one time)***:**
"**Who, when He was reviled, reviled not again** *(He did not respond in kind)***; when He suffered, He threatened not** *(when He suffered unjustly, He did not call down wrath from Heaven, which He definitely could have done)***; but committed *Himself* to Him Who Judges Righteously** *(He committed His defense to God, which we, as well, should do)***:**

THE BEARING OF OUR SINS

"**Who His Own Self bear our sins in His Own Body on the tree** *(gave Himself in Sacrifice on the Cross, taking the full penalty for our sins, which was physical death; it was not Christ's suffering that redeemed us, although that definitely was a part of what happened, but rather the price*

He paid by the giving of Himself), **that we, being dead to sins, should live unto Righteousness** *(we are 'dead to sins' by virtue of us being 'in Christ' when He died on the Cross, which is done by our exhibiting Faith in Christ [Rom. 6:3-5]; and we were raised with Him in 'newness of life,' which guarantees us a perfect, spotless Righteousness)*: **by Whose stripes you were healed.** *(This refers to the healing of our souls, and the healing of our physical body as well. The Atonement included everything man lost in the Fall, but we only have the Firstfruits now, with the balance coming at the Resurrection [Rom. 8:23]).*

OUR SHEPHERD

"For you were as sheep going astray *(we were like a flock without a shepherd)*; **but are now returned unto the Shepherd and Bishop of your souls** *(refers to the Lord Jesus Christ; He Alone is the True 'Shepherd,' and He Alone is the True 'Bishop' of our souls; if we allow man to take His Place, we spiritually wreck ourselves; man can only serve as an under-shepherd)*" **(I Pet. 2:21-25).**

PSALM 22

When Jesus uttered the Words, *"My God, My God, why have You forsaken Me?"*, He was quoting the first Verse of the 22nd Psalm.

Even though the following notes taken from THE EXPOSITOR'S STUDY BIBLE have already been used in the answer to another question in this Volume, still, considering what we are addressing, please permit us the latitude of quoting it again.

The stark reality of Psalm 22 portrays the Crucifixion of the Lord Jesus Christ. The Gospels narrate the fact of the Crucifixion; this Psalm, the feelings of the Crucified.

Jesus cried this Word while hanging on the Cross (Mat. 27:46). This portrayal glorifies Him as the Sin-Offering.

THE SINLESS MAN

It presents a sinless Man, the Lord Jesus Christ, forsaken by God, but only in the sense that God allowed Him to die. Such a fact is unique in history and will never need to be repeated. This sinless Man — Himself God manifest in the flesh — was made to be a Sin-Offering, in effect, the penalty of sin, which in this case was physical death (II Cor. 5:21), and, thereby, pierced with the sword of Divine Wrath (Zech. 13:7). In that judgment God dealt infinitely with sin and, in so dealing with it in the Person of His Beloved Son, showed His wrath against sin and His love for the sinner. Thus, He vindicated Himself and, as well, redeemed man. God revealed Himself at Calvary as in no other place or way.

THE SIN-OFFERING

What the depth of horror was to which the sinless soul of Jesus sank under the Wrath of God as the Sin-Offering is unfathomable for men or Angels; therefore, our efforts to explain these sufferings will, of necessity, fall short of that which He really experienced.

As we have stated, Jesus was placed on the Cross at 9 a.m. (Mk. 15:25). From 12 noon until 3 p.m., the latter being the time when Jesus died and also the time of the evening Sacrifice, darkness covered the land for that three-hour period — the period when Jesus was bearing the sin penalty of the world (Mat. 27:45). During that three-hour period, the Lord would not answer the prayers of Christ nor help Him in any way; however, at the moment He died, the sin penalty was paid (Mat. 27:51), and the Lord could and, in fact, most definitely did answer His prayers from that moment on (Jn. 19:30; Lk. 23:46).

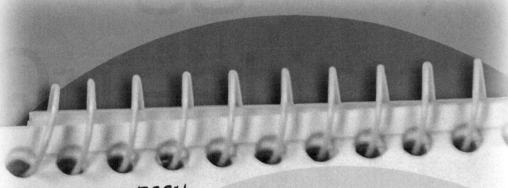

CHAPTER SIXTEEN

Can The Cross Of Christ Work With Humanistic Psychology?

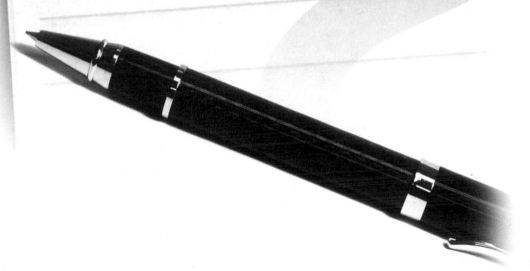

QUESTION:

CAN THE CROSS OF CHRIST WORK WITH HUMANISTIC PSYCHOLOGY?

ANSWER:

No!

The Cross of Christ is God's Prescribed Order of Life and Living. Psychology is the religion of humanism. The former is totally of God, while the latter is totally of man. It is impossible to meld the two. If one embraces the Cross of Christ, all humanistic psychology must go. If one embraces humanistic psychology, the Word of God must be abandoned. Unfortunately, the modern church has attempted to wed the two. Such is impossible, and for all the obvious reasons!

DOES THE BIBLE HOLD ALL THE ANSWERS FOR LIFE AND LIVING?

Some in the church claim that it doesn't. Some claim that modern man is facing problems and difficulties that are not addressed in the Bible and, therefore, must have both the Bible and psychology in order for the need to be met. Such borders on blasphemy!

The idea that the Holy Spirit, Who Authored the Word of God and Who is God, doesn't fully understand man, modern or otherwise, is ludicrous indeed!

THE HOLY SPIRIT THROUGH SIMON PETER SAID . . .

"Grace and Peace be multiplied unto you through the knowledge of God, and of Jesus our Lord (*this is both Sanctifying Grace and Sanctifying Peace, all made available by the Cross*),

"According as His Divine Power has given unto us all things (*the Lord with large-handed generosity has given us all things)* **that** *pertain* **unto Life and godliness** *(pertains to the fact that the Lord Jesus has given us everything we need regarding life and living)*, **through the knowledge of Him Who has called us to Glory and Virtue** *(the 'knowledge' addressed here speaks of what Christ did at the Cross, which alone can provide 'Glory and Virtue')*:

EXCEEDING GREAT AND PRECIOUS PROMISES

"**Whereby are given unto us exceeding great and Precious Promises** *(pertains to the Word of God, which alone holds the answer to every life problem)*: **that by these** *(Promises)* **you might be partakers of the Divine Nature** *(the Divine Nature implanted in the inner being of the believing sinner becomes the source of our new life and actions; it comes to everyone at the moment of being 'Born-Again')*, **having escaped the corruption that is in the world through lust.** *(This presents the Salvation experience of the sinner, and the Sanctification experience of the Saint)*" **(II Pet. 1:2-4).**

Now, either the Lord has *"given unto us all things that pertain unto Life and godliness,"* or else the Holy Spirit through Peter lied! If that is the case, then we should turn to the pitiful prattle of poor fallen man who has given us humanistic psychology!

However, I happen to believe, and with all of my heart, that the Holy Spirit gave us exactly what He said, and that is *"all things that pertain unto Life and godliness."*

Either He did or didn't! I happen to believe He did.

WHAT IS THE ANSWER TO THE PERVERSIONS AND ABERRATIONS OF MAN?

The answer and, in fact, the only answer, is *"Jesus Christ and Him Crucified"* (I Cor. 1:23).

So, the first question that comes to mind is, *"How can the*

Cross of Christ be the answer for the terrible bondages of darkness such as alcoholism, child molestation, homosexuality, drug addiction, etc.?"

The Cross of Christ is the answer according to the following:

• The individual, whoever the person might be, has to accept Christ as his or her personal Saviour. This is not optional, but rather an absolute necessity.

• Once the person accepts Christ as their personal Saviour, or if they are already a Believer, they must place their Faith totally and completely in the Cross of Christ. In other words, understanding that everything we receive from the Lord comes to us from Christ with the Cross as the Means, the Cross of Christ must be the Object of one's Faith, and the Cross of Christ Alone as the Object of one's Faith. As conversion is an absolute necessity, likewise, the Cross of Christ as the Object of one's Faith is also an absolute necessity (Rom. 8:1-2, 11; I Cor. 1:17-18, 23; 2:2; Gal. 6:14).

• With the Believer's Faith exclusively in the Cross of Christ, the Holy Spirit, Who is God and Who works exclusively within the parameters of the Finished Work of Christ, will immediately begin to help such a person. And we must remember, what is impossible for us is fully possible for Him, as God the Holy Spirit can do anything (Rom. 8:1-2, 11; Gal., Chpt. 5).

While the steps we have given are absolutely Biblically correct, this doesn't mean that Satan will cease all activity against such a person. In fact, he may increase his pressure against the individual and, no doubt, will, attempting to discourage such a person so that they throw over their walk with God. He knows that the Cross of Christ is the answer, so, the Believer in question might very well have to face a greater onslaught than ever, but only for a short period of time. Ultimately, if the Believer doesn't waver and doesn't quit, total and complete Victory will be his. The Scripture says:

"**For sin shall not have dominion over you** *(the sin nature will not have dominion over us if we as Believers* *continue to exercise Faith in the Cross of Christ; otherwise, the sin nature most definitely will have dominion over the Believer)*: **for you are not under the Law** *(means that if we try to live this life by any type of religious law, no matter how good that religious law might be in its own right, we will conclude by the sin nature having dominion over us)*, **but under Grace** *(the Grace of God flows to the Believer on an unending basis only as long as the Believer exercises Faith in Christ and what He did at the Cross; Grace is merely the Goodness of God exercised by and through the Holy Spirit, and given to undeserving Saints)*" **(Rom. 6:14).**

THE PSYCHOLOGICAL WAY

"For My people have committed two evils; they have forsaken Me the Fountain of Living Waters, and hewed them out cisterns, broken cisterns, that can hold no water" (Jer. 2:13).

William Kirk Kilpatrick says, *"True Christianity does not mix well at all with psychology. When you try to mix them, you end up with a watered-down Christianity instead of a Christianized psychology.*

"But the process is subtle and is rarely noticed. It is not a frontal attack on Christianity. It is not even a case of the wolf at the door. Actually the wolf is already in the fold, dressed in sheep's clothing. From the way it was petted and fed by some of the shepherds, one would think it was the prized sheep."[1]

Jacob Needleman says, *"Modern psychiatry arose out of the vision that man must change himself and not depend for help on an imaginary God. Over half a century ago (mainly through the insights of Freud and through the energies of those he influenced), the human psyche was wrested from the faltering hands of organized religion and was situated in the world of nature as a subject for scientific study."*

Incidentally, Freud opened his office in Vienna, the first devoted to psychotherapy, well over a hundred years ago.

Martin Gross, in his book, *"The Psychological Society"*, says,

"When educated man lost faith in formal religion, he required a substitute belief that would be as reputable in the 21st Century as Christianity was in the 20th Century, or at least the first half of the 20th Century. Psychology and psychiatry have now assumed that special role."[2]

Modern day psychotherapy has its roots in atheism, evolution, and humanism. Psychology pretends to have a cure for troubled souls. It is taught in atheistic universities, oftentimes by atheistic professors. This same subject, with the same foundations and influences, is accepted today as an integral part of the Christian curriculum in most Bible Colleges and Seminaries. There aren't, we might quickly add, two kinds of psychotherapy. There is only one. And, as Paul Vitz says, *"It is deeply anti-Christian."*

AMERICA'S PROBLEM IS THAT SHE ACCEPTS A LIE

Someone once said, *"America's problem is not ignorance; America's problem is that she accepts a lie."*

Now, the problem with our preachers may once have been ignorance, but this is no longer the case. I am now concerned that what they accept (psychotherapy) is not truth — it is a lie. In fact, the church has become so psychologized that most preachers lace their sermons with psychology each and every week, hardly realizing this is what they are doing.

I maintain that psychotherapy is not scientific, that it is not even an *"art,"* as claimed. It is a lie, pure and simple, and has no basis in scientific or Biblical fact. When Bible Colleges offer it, they are offering a bold fabrication. When Seminaries teach it, they are teaching a lie. When would-be preachers immerse themselves in it, they immerse themselves in falsehood. When individuals accept a Doctorate in this nefarious shamanism, they are receiving a certificate without scientific validity.

I say that preachers of the Gospel, so-called, attempting to meld psychotherapy with the Word of God, will help no one. They will deliver only confusion. People will be led away from the true aid available through the Word of God.

The two, psychology and the Word of God, are as immiscible and as antagonistic as oil and water.

THE BIBLE AND PSYCHOLOGY

When it was suggested that modern day psychology is not found in the Bible, one preacher stated that neither is the automobile, the airplane, nor the computer. We do not, he reasoned, resist utilization of these tools in our lives, so why should we resist the tool of psychology (or any other self-help method or technique)?

My answer is this:

Admittedly, the Bible has nothing to say about the automobile, computer, airplane, or a host of other crafts developed since it was written. The Bible does not claim to be a handbook on engineering, science, or whatever; however, whatever it does say on these subjects is absolutely correct.

These extraneous subjects, we might quickly add, are not man's problems. Man can be an expert scientist, a qualified engineer, or a host of other things — and still be a moral and spiritual wreck. However, the Bible does claim to be a handbook on the *"human condition"* — and does come right out and claim to hold all the answers to this particular human area.

Simon Peter said so, which we quoted at the first part of this article (II Pet. 1:3-4).

DIFFERENCES IN THE BIBLE AND PSYCHOLOGY

• The Bible is the Word of God (Jn. 1:1). The *"bible"* for psychology is man's opinion, which changes almost on a daily basis.

• The Bible holds all answers relative to human behavior with untold millions attesting to that fact (II Pet. 1:3). Psychology claims to hold all answers relative to human behavior, but offers no examples whatsoever.

• The Bible says man is an eternal soul (Jn. 3:16). Psychology has its roots in evolution.

• The Bible says man is a sinner (Rom. 3:23). Psychology says man is a victim.

• The Bible says that man's problem is an evil heart (Jer. 17:9). Psychology says man's problem is his environment.

• The Bible says man is inherently evil (Jer. 17:9). Psychology says man is inherently good.

• The Bible treats the core of man's problem, which is an evil heart (Jer. 17:14). Psychology treats only man's symptoms.

• The Bible says that Jesus Christ is the answer (Mat. 11:28-30). Psychology says that psychotherapy is the answer.

• The Bible says that we must deny self (Mat. 16:24). Psychology says we should love self.

• The Bible directs us to the Spirit of God (Zech.4:6). Psychology directs us to the flesh.

• The Bible directs us to faith in God (Mk. 11:22). Psychology directs us to self-effort.

• The Bible directs us to Repentance (Acts 28:20). Psychology directs us to remorse.

• The Bible directs us to Restoration (Gal. 6:1). Psychology directs us to referral.

• The Bible directs us to the Cross of Christ (Rom. 6:3-5). Psychology directs us to the psychologist.

• The Bible directs us to a relationship with Christ (Jn. 3:16). Psychology directs us to idolatry.

• The Bible directs us to personal responsibility (Rev. 22:17). Psychology directs us to irresponsibility.

• The Bible directs us to free will (Rev. 22:17). Psychology directs us to determinism (causes other than oneself).

• The Bible deals with a *"cure of souls"* (Mat. 11:28-30). Psychology deals with a *"cure of minds."*

• The Bible says God's Truth is unchangeable (Ps. 119:89). Psychology says truth is determined by majority and culture.

• The Bible says it is sufficient (II Pet. 1:3). Psychology says the Bible is insufficient.

• The Bible leads to love for God and man (Mat. 22:37-39). Psychology leads to love for self.

HUMANISM

Psychology is actually the religion of humanism. Humanism puts man in the center of all things. Hence, psychology puts man in the center of all things. Conversely, the Bible puts Christ in the center as the only answer for man. Psychology (psychotherapy) and the Bible, therefore, are total opposites and cannot be reconciled.

HOW IS THE CROSS OF CHRIST THE ANSWER FOR MAN'S DILEMMA?

First of all, let it be understood, there are no magical qualities about the Cross, i.e., what Jesus did there. As well, when we speak of the Cross, we aren't speaking of a wooden beam, but rather what Jesus accomplished there, which Paul referred to as *"The Everlasting Covenant."* This means that its effectiveness will never cease and, as well, its Covenant will never have to be amended, because it is perfect, and because it is all in Christ. So, if there are no magical qualities about the Cross, how can it be the answer for man's dilemma?

For man to be delivered there must be a power greater than the power of darkness to set him free. Those of us who believe the Bible know that the Power of God is sufficient for whatever the need might be; however, the first thing that the Believer must understand is the following:

• Everything the Lord does on this Earth is done through the Power, Person, Office, and Ministry of the Holy Spirit. The Word of the Lord came to the Prophet Zechariah with him saying, *"Not by might, nor by power, but by My Spirit, says the LORD, of Hosts"* (Zech. 4:6). *"Not by (human) might, nor by (human) power, but by My Spirit,"* presents God's Method of accomplishing His Work. Everything that has ever been done on this Earth, as it regards the Godhead, has been done by the Holy Spirit with the exception of Christ and His Crucifixion; however, the Holy Spirit even superintended that from beginning to end (Lk. 4:18-19).

If it is claimed to be for the Lord, whatever is being done must be done by the Moving, Operation, Power, and Person of the Holy Spirit through Believers. Otherwise, it will not be recognized by God; in fact, it will be constituted as a *"work of the flesh"* (Rom. 8:1).

"Says the LORD of Hosts" in Zechariah 4:6 presents God's Supreme Personal Power over everything in the material and Spiritual universe. All is organized under His Command. As well, the word *"Hosts,"* as used here is associated with warfare and relates to the word *"armies."* In other words, Jehovah is the *"Lord of Armies."*

• Knowing it is the Holy Spirit Who does the doing, one might say, the next thing is that we should learn how the Holy Spirit works.

THE MANNER OF THE HOLY SPIRIT

The Holy Spirit works exclusively within the parameters, one might say, of the Finished Work of Christ. In other words, what Jesus did at the Cross gives the Holy Spirit the legal right to do all that He does. The main thing is that at the moment of conversion the Holy Spirit comes into the heart and life of the new Believer, there to abide forever (Jn. 14:16-17). Paul said:

> "Know you not that you are the Temple of God *(where the Holy Spirit abides)*, and *that* the Spirit of God dwells in you? *(That makes the Born-Again Believer His permanent Home)*" (I Cor. 3:16).

However, the mere fact of the Holy Spirit abiding permanently within our hearts and lives does not guarantee victory.

Many Christians think that whatever the Holy Spirit does, it's just an automatic procedure. It isn't!

If the Holy Spirit just automatically worked within our lives, there would never be another failure on the part of another

Christian, which should be obvious, but we all know that isn't true. So, that means the Holy Spirit requires something on our part.

What does He require?

THE CROSS OF CHRIST MUST BE THE OBJECT OF THE BELIEVER'S FAITH

The Cross is where every Victory was brought about by our Lord giving Himself in Sacrifice, which atoned for all sin. As we have previously stated, sin is that which gives the Evil One the legal right to hold man in bondage. It is the *"Law of Sin and Death"* (Rom. 7:21, 23; 8:2). With all sin atoned, which Jesus did at the Cross, and at the Cross alone, the legal right that Satan had to hold men in bondage was removed. So, if that is the case, as many would ask, *"Why is it that most of the world is still under satanic bondage?"*

THE REASON FOR SATANIC BONDAGE DESPITE THE CROSS

First of all, let us state that untold millions have been set free from every bondage of darkness from the time of the Cross to this present moment. As well, millions are being set free presently, and wondrously so! But, that still leaves every unsaved person in the world and, regrettably, most of Christendom.

Unsaved mankind remains in bondage simply because they will not accept what our Lord has done at Calvary's Cross. Thank God for the millions who did accept and are accepting presently, but, at the same time, the far, far greater majority will not accept the Lord. So, in a sense, they are giving the Evil One their consent to keep them in bondage, which he readily does!

WHY ARE MOST CHRISTIANS PRESENTLY IN BONDAGE IN ONE WAY OR THE OTHER?

Every person who is genuinely Saved is so by virtue of their

Faith in Christ and what He did for them at the Cross, as it regards Salvation. However, they have no Faith whatsoever in the Cross of Christ regarding Sanctification or how we are to live for God on a daily basis. Not understanding the Cross of Christ as it regards Sanctification, invariably such a Believer will place his or her Faith in something other than the Cross, which greatly hinders the Holy Spirit. As we have stated previously, it takes *"power"* to live a godly, consecrated life. That Power is resident within the Holy Spirit. True, He desires to give that Power to us (Acts 1:8); however, He does so on one premise, and that is our Faith be placed exclusively in Christ and what Christ did for us at the Cross in order for us to live a godly, dedicated life.

HOW IS THE POWER TRANSFERRED FROM THE HOLY SPIRIT TO THE BELIEVER?

Paul said:

"For the preaching *(Word)* of the Cross is to them who perish foolishness *(Spiritual things cannot be discerned by unredeemed people, but that doesn't matter; the Cross must be preached just the same, even as we shall see)*; but unto us who are Saved it is the Power of God. *(The Cross is the Power of God simply because it was there that the total sin debt was paid, giving the Holy Spirit, in Whom the Power resides, latitude to work mightily within our lives)*" (I Cor. 1:18).

As we gave you in the notes quoted from THE EXPOSITOR'S STUDY BIBLE regarding this Scripture, let us say it again:

HOW IS THE MESSAGE OF THE CROSS CONSTITUTED AS THE POWER OF GOD?

As it regards the wooden beam on which Jesus died, there is no power whatsoever. So, when we speak of the *"Cross,"* we aren't speaking of the wooden beam, but rather what Jesus there accomplished. In fact, were it possible that the actual Cross could be found in Jerusalem on which Jesus died, it would contain no more power than any other piece of wood. As well, the actual fact of dying, at least within itself, carried no power. Concerning that, the Scripture says:

"For though He was Crucified through weakness *(Christ purposely did not use His Power)*, yet He lived by the Power of God *(was Resurrected; we have this power at our disposal as well [Rom. 8:11])*. For we also are weak in Him *(regarding our personal strength and ability)*, but we shall live with Him by the Power of God toward you. *(This refers to our everyday life and living, which we do by constant Faith in the Cross. This gives the Holy Spirit latitude to work mightily in our lives)*" **(II Cor. 13:4).**

In this Verse the Scripture plainly says that Christ *"was Crucified through weakness."* To be sure, it was a contrived weakness, for at any time He could have called twelve legions of Angels to His Side to carry out any work He so desired. But, had He done so, mankind would have been forever lost.

So, the wooden beam itself carried no power and neither did His Death per se. The Truth is, the Power is in the Holy Spirit.

What Jesus did at the Cross, however, made it possible for the Holy Spirit to come into our hearts and lives and abide forever and, as well, to use His Power on our behalf.

HOW IS THE POWER OF THE HOLY SPIRIT GIVEN TO US?

First of all, let me repeat what we've already stated:

Most Believers think the Holy Spirit just does what He does automatically. That is not the case at all. Were that the case, no Christian would ever fail, would ever sin, would ever go in the wrong direction, would ever do anything wrong. But, we know that's not the case, don't we?

The Holy Spirit, Who resides within our hearts and lives, does so permanently and, as God, can do anything; however, for many and varied reasons, He has to have our cooperation. To be sure, He most definitely could work independently of such cooperation, but that He will not do, and for our good.

He doesn't demand much of us, but He does demand one thing and that is that our Faith rest exclusively in Christ and what Christ did for us at the Cross as it regards our daily life and living and, in fact, everything else, as well.

And that's where Satan fights us so hard. Satan will do everything within his power to keep the Message of the Cross from coming to us, or if it does come to us, that we register unbelief, or that we get discouraged and quit. He doesn't care too very much where our faith is, just so it's not in Christ and the Cross.

UNBELIEF

Many Christians, perhaps most, have the mistaken idea that, while the Cross is necessary for Salvation, thereafter, or so they think, it is of no more use. Nothing could be further from the truth. The very reason that the majority of the church world has opted for humanistic psychology is because it simply doesn't believe that what Jesus did at the Cross is the answer to all victory within our lives. Not believing that, they have embraced humanistic psychology, which, in effect, is actually of Satan.

Even many who have not turned in that direction still think the Cross is of no more consequence after Salvation.

So, where do they go? What do they do?

I suppose if most of them were pushed into giving an answer, they would claim that they go to the Holy Spirit. However, the Holy Spirit works exclusively within the parameters of the Cross of Christ, i.e., *"the Finished Work of Christ."* In fact, He, as stated, will not work outside of those parameters.

THE LAW OF THE SPIRIT OF
LIFE IN CHRIST JESUS

Actually, the great Truth that the Holy Spirit works exclusively within the Cross of Christ, meaning that it is the Cross that has given him the legal means to do all that He does, is so ironclad, so guaranteed, so positive, that it is referred to as a *"Law,"* meaning that He will, in no uncertain terms, function in this manner and this manner alone.

Paul said:

"There is **therefore now no condemnation** *(guilt)* **to them which are in Christ Jesus** *(refers back to Rom. 6:3-5 and our being baptized into His Death, which speaks of the Crucifixion),* **who walk not after the flesh** *(depending on one's personal strength and ability or great religious efforts in order to overcome sin),* **but after the Spirit** *(the Holy Spirit works exclusively within the legal confines of the Finished Work of Christ; our Faith in that Finished Work, i.e., 'the Cross,' guarantees the help of the Holy Spirit, which guarantees Victory).*

"For the Law *(that which we are about to give is a Law of God, devised by the Godhead in eternity past [I Pet. 1:18-20]; this Law, in fact, is 'God's Prescribed Order of Victory')* **of the Spirit** *(Holy Spirit, i.e., 'the way the Spirit works')* **of Life** *(all life comes from Christ, but through the Holy Spirit [Jn. 16:13-14])* **in Christ Jesus** *(any time Paul uses this term or one of its derivatives, he is, without fail, referring to what Christ did at the Cross, which makes this 'life' possible)* **has made me free** *(given me total Victory)* **from the Law of Sin and Death.** *(These are the two most powerful Laws in the Universe; the 'Law of the Spirit of Life in Christ Jesus' alone is stronger than the 'Law of Sin and Death'; this means that if the Believer attempts to live for God by any manner other than Faith in Christ and the Cross, he is doomed to failure)"* **(Rom. 8:1-2).**

Plainly and clearly in Romans 8:2, we are told how the Holy Spirit works. The three words, *"In Christ Jesus,"* pertain to Christ and what He did at the Cross. So, if one claims they are going to the Holy Spirit, He, without fail, will lead them right back to the Cross of Christ. Let us say it again:

THE ONLY THING STANDING BETWEEN MANKIND AND ETERNAL HELL IS THE CROSS OF CHRIST

That being the case, we should realize how important all of this is. That's why the Apostle Paul said:

"But we preach Christ Crucified *(this is the Foundation of the Word of God and, thereby, of Salvation)*, unto the Jews a stumblingblock *(the Cross was the stumblingblock)*, and unto the Greeks foolishness *(both found it difficult to accept as God a dead Man hanging on a Cross, for such Christ was to them)*" (I Cor. 1:23).

THE ONLY MEANS OF VICTORY FOR THE CHILD OF GOD IS THE CROSS OF CHRIST

Listen again to Paul for he plainly tells us that all Victory is in the Cross of Christ and no other place. He said:

"And I, Brethren, when I came to you, came not with excellency of speech or of wisdom *(means that he depended not on oratorical abilities, nor did he delve into philosophy, which was all the rage of that particular day)*, declaring unto you the Testimony of God *(which is Christ and Him Crucified)*.

"For I determined not to know any thing among you *(with purpose and design, Paul did not resort to the knowledge or philosophy of the world regarding the preaching of the Gospel)*, save Jesus Christ, and Him Crucified *(that and that alone is the Message, which will save the sinner, set*

the captive free, and give the Believer perpetual Victory)"
(I Cor. 2:1-2).

Now, how much clearer could it be?!
What Paul said here, and did so in many other places in his
fourteen Epistles, as well, leaves no room for humanistic psychology, or anything else for that matter. It is *"Jesus Christ and
Him Crucified,"* and it is *"Jesus Christ and Him Crucified Alone."*
Paul was one of the most educated men used of God as an
instrument regarding the writing of the Sacred Text. As stated,
he wrote fourteen Epistles, which is almost half the New Testament. He was the Master Builder of the Church.
I think it can be safely said that no one else in the world of
his day knew or understood the Law of Moses as did this man.
Also, it is believed by many Scholars that Paul also attended
the great University in Tarsus, his home town, which in his day
was one of the most noted universities in the world. He made
any number of statements, which portrays to us the fact not
only of his religious education, but also, his secular education.
Despite all of that, he told the Church at Corinth, as well
as you and me, *"For I determined not to know anything among
you save Jesus Christ, and Him Crucified."*
One must understand that the city of Corinth was noted in
two particular ways, actually, the two great efforts of Satan,
philosophy and vice.
Philosophy is the search for truth and, of course, it is obvious as to what vice is.
It would have been the popular thing for Paul to have shown
his knowledge of the philosophic directions of that particular
day, with which he was well versed; however, he threw aside
that temptation and did what the Holy Spirit told him to do,
"preach Christ Crucified."
Why?
Jesus Christ and what He did at the Cross on behalf of sinners is the only cure for hurting souls. It is the only cause of a
consecrated life. It is the only means of victory in our daily walk.

Paul had come from Athens to Corinth, the latter, one of the most wicked cities in the world. It has been ventured by some that when Paul left Athens, he had not been exactly pleased with the direction the effort had taken.

While he had some small response in Athens, it evidently was not what he expected.

While what Paul preached at Athens, as recorded in Acts Seventeen, was excellent, to say the least, still, he did not there preach the Cross. On the journey to Corinth, he very well could have been troubled in mind and spirit. Knowing that Corinth was, as well, a city of philosophy exactly as Athens, he may have wondered as to how in the world these people could be reached. His efforts in Athens had not been met with great success. How could it be any greater in Corinth?

If, in fact, those were some of the thoughts in his mind, I believe the Spirit of God spoke to him and stated as it regarded Corinth, *"Preach the Cross!"* The Spirit of God may have continued, *"And if it will work in Corinth, it will work anywhere."* And to be sure, it most definitely did work in Corinth. That's the reason he said, *"For I determined not to know anything among you, save Jesus Christ and Him Crucified."*

Paul did not journey to Corinth and give those Corinthians some psychological gibberish, as is being done so often presently, but he gave them the Message that could set them free and, in fact, the only Message that could set them free, *"Jesus Christ and Him Crucified."*

Let me hurriedly state, while nearly 2,000 years have come and gone from that day until now, still, man's problem is identical today as it was then, sin. The solution today is the same now as it was then, *"Jesus Christ and Him Crucified."*

IN CLOSING . . .

No, humanistic psychology has no place in the Gospel, as the Gospel has no place in humanistic psychology.

One of the largest churches in America, a Seeker Sensitive

devotee, took a poll the other day of its members. And, I might quickly add, it is very doubtful that there is a single soul in that church who is truly Born-Again.

At any rate, having immersed themselves in the Purpose Driven Life Seeker Sensitive scenario, the leaders of that particular church wanted to see how their members were faring. They sent a very detailed questionnaire to every member and, due to the fact that it was to remain anonymous, in other words, no one would know who said what; they were more apt to get the Truth.

They did not so much like what they got.

They found, and I read the account for myself, that the far greater number of the members of that church was involved in adultery, homosexuality, alcoholism, gambling, drug addiction, child molestation, in other words, just about every vice of which one could think.

I'll have to say something for the leaders in that they were honest. They stated, *"It is obvious that the Seeker Sensitive method is not working, so we are going to have to rethink our approach."*

No, it's not working and, no; it will never work, because it's not the Gospel. Pure and simple, it is nothing but humanistic psychology in a religious dress.

> *"What can wash away my sin? Nothing but the Blood*
> *of Jesus;*
> *"What can make me whole again? Nothing but the Blood*
> *of Jesus."*

> *"For my pardon this I see, Nothing but the Blood of Jesus;*
> *"For my cleansing this my plea, Nothing but the Blood*
> *of Jesus."*

> *"Nothing can for sin atone, Nothing but the Blood of Jesus;*
> *"Naught of good that I have done, Nothing but the Blood*
> *of Jesus."*

"This is all my hope and peace, Nothing but the Blood of Jesus;
"This is all my righteousness, Nothing but the Blood of Jesus."

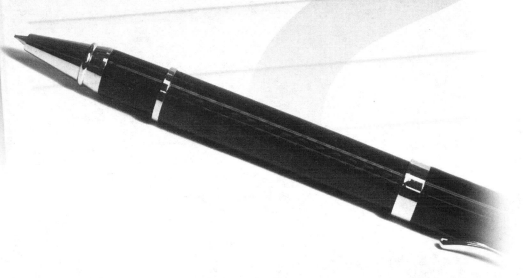

CHAPTER SEVENTEEN

What Is Meant By The Term, "The Object Of One's Faith"?

QUESTION:

WHAT IS MEANT BY THE TERM, "THE OBJECT OF ONE'S FAITH"?

ANSWER:

The phrase, *"The object of one's Faith,"* refers to where one's Faith is placed and why one's Faith is placed there!
First of all, let's look at Faith itself.

FAITH

In order to lay a foundation, I want to copy the first six Verses of the Eleventh Chapter of Hebrews. As most know, this is the great Faith Chapter of the Bible. The first six Verses lay the foundation. They tell us:
• What Faith is!
• The foundation on which it is placed, which is the Sacrifice of Christ.
• And that Faith alone pleases God.

"Now Faith is the substance *(the title deed)* of things hoped for *(a declaration of the action of Faith)*, the evidence of things not seen. *(Faith is not based upon the senses, which yield uncertainty, but rather on the Word of God.)*
"For by it *(by Faith, and as we shall see, it is Faith in the Cross)* the Elders obtained a good report *(the approval of the Lord)*.
"Through Faith we understand that the worlds were framed by the Word of God *(refers to Creation, along with everything that goes with Creation)*, so that things which are seen were not made of things which do appear. *(God began with nothing, thereby, speaking into existence the things needed to create the universe.)*

THE SACRIFICE

"**By Faith Abel offered unto God a more excellent sacrifice than Cain** *(immediately proclaims the fact that the Object of our Faith must be 'Jesus Christ and Him Crucified' [I Cor. 2:2])*, **by which he obtained witness that he was Righteous** *(proclaims the fact that Righteousness comes exclusively from Christ, and is obtained by the Cross being the Object of our Faith)*, **God testifying of his gifts** *(referring to the fact that the sacrifice of the lamb which represented Christ was accepted by God; at the dawn of time it was 'the Cross,' and it is still 'the Cross')*: **and by it he being dead yet speaks** *(speaks of that alone God will accept)*.

THAT WHICH PLEASES GOD

"**By Faith Enoch was translated that he should not see death** *(refers to God transferring Enoch to Heaven in his physical body while he was yet alive)*; **and was not found, because God had translated him** *(refers to his translation being well-known at that time)*: **for before his translation he had this Testimony, that he pleased God.** *(He pleased God because he placed his Faith exclusively in Christ and the Cross.)*

"**But without Faith** *(in Christ and the Cross; anytime Faith is mentioned, always and without exception, its root meaning is that its Object is Christ and the Cross; otherwise, it is faith God will not accept)* ***it is*** **impossible to please Him** *(Faith in anything other than Christ and the Cross greatly displeases the Lord)*: **for he who comes to God must believe that He is** *(places Faith as the foundation and principle of the manner in which God deals with the human race)*, **and** *that* **He** *(God)* **is a rewarder of them who diligently seek Him** *(seek Him on the premise of Christ and Him Crucified)*" **(Heb. 11:1-6).**

FAITH, NOT WORKS

Proper Faith always produces good works, but good works will never produce proper Faith. This is where the church so often runs aground. All too often Believers attempt to work for their Righteousness. Such cannot be done. It only leads to self-righteousness. For Faith to be that which God honors, it must have the Cross of Christ as its Object, and the Cross alone as its Object. As it regards Faith and works, Paul said:

"What shall we say then that Abraham our father, as pertaining to the flesh, has found? *(having stated that the Old Testament teaches that God justifies the sinner on the Faith principle as opposed to the merit principle, the Holy Spirit now brings forward Abraham.)*
"For if Abraham were justified by works *(which he wasn't)*, he has *whereof* to glory; but not before God *(the boasting of Salvation by works, which God will not accept)*.

WHAT DOES THE BIBLE SAY?

"For what says the Scripture? Abraham believed God, and it was counted unto him for Righteousness *(Gen. 15:6 — if one properly understands this Verse, he properly understands the Bible; Abraham gained Righteousness by simple Faith in God, Who would send a Redeemer into the world [Jn. 8:56])*.
"Now to him who works *(tries to earn Salvation or Righteousness)* is the reward *(Righteousness)* not reckoned of Grace *(the Grace of God)*, but of debt *(claiming that God owes us something, which He doesn't!)*.
"But to him who works not *(doesn't trust in works for Salvation or Righteousness)*, but believes on Him Who Justifies the ungodly *(through Christ and the Cross)*, his faith is counted for Righteousness *(God awards Righteousness only on the basis of Faith in Christ and His*

Finished Work)" **(Rom. 4:1-5).**

THE FAITH PRINCIPLE

As it regards the Lord, He has constructed everything on the premise of Faith. That's at least one of the reasons that America and Canada have been so blessed. Capitalism, which is the economic system of these two nations, and such is the same for several others, is built on the principle of Faith. If honesty is joined with Faith, it presents the greatest economic system on the face of the Earth.

That's the very reason that Communism or Socialism will not work. Those twin evils rule out faith and, thereby, rule out the incentive.

The truth is, man was created by God as a faith creature. That means that every human being on the face of the Earth has faith. Even the scientist, who boasts that he will accept nothing unless he can prove it, works tirelessly in the laboratory, trying to bring forth that which he desires. Whether he realizes it or not, he is functioning on the faith principle. Even the atheist has faith. To be sure, it's not in God, just as most faith is not in God; nevertheless, he has faith. It is faith in himself, etc.

However, none of this is faith that God will recognize. He recognizes only one element of faith and that is trust and confidence placed exclusively in Christ and what Christ has done for us at the Cross.

THE CHURCH AND FAITH

This, the Cross of Christ exclusively as the Object of our Faith, is the dividing line in the Church.

Every attack that Satan formulates against the Child of God, irrespective as to whether it's in the economic realm, the physical, the domestical, or the Spiritual, is for but one purpose and that is to destroy our Faith or at least seriously weaken it.

Most of all, Satan seeks to divert our faith to that which, while very religious, still is not the correct object. This is the great battleground for Believers.

As we've already stated, most of the modern church is attempting to earn Righteousness by the premise of works. By that manner it cannot be done and, as also stated, such always leads to self-righteousness. Righteousness can be given to the worst sinner who ever lived, and given instantly, if that person will evidence true Faith in Christ and what He did for us at the Cross. That's what the Text meant when it said of Abraham that, *"He believed God, and it was accounted unto him for Righteousness."*

So, why is Christian man loath to simply follow the outline designed by the Lord? What the Lord has given us, Faith in Christ and the Cross, which guarantees a spotless Righteousness, can be easily brought about by any Believer, yet, it is rejected by most!

FAITH PLUS

I had a preacher to say to me the other day, *"Oh, yes, Brother Swaggart, we must have Faith in the Cross, but there are other things that must be done as well."* In other words, it's Faith plus works. This is something God will not accept.

Why?

He will not accept it because it insults, and grossly so, His Son, and our Saviour, the Lord Jesus Christ, and what He did for us at the Cross. The idea is this:

THERE IS NOTHING MAN CAN DO THAT GOD WILL ACCEPT

As it regards Righteousness, man cannot produce anything that the Lord will accept, irrespective if it's the godliest man on the face of the Earth. If it's not Righteousness that begins with Him, then it is self-righteousness.

From the dawn of time man has attempted to invent another god, and sadly so, the church from its inception has tried to invent another sacrifice. There is only one God, manifested in Three Persons, *"God the Father, God the Son, and God the Holy Spirit."* And there is only one Sacrifice and that is Jesus Christ and what He did for us at the Cross. That and that alone must be the Object of our Faith.

So, the Object of our Faith must always be the Cross of Christ, and the Cross of Christ alone, or else it is faith that God will not recognize.

And yet, most of the modern church has as the object of its faith, all types of religious things, things we might quickly add, which within themselves, are right and correct, but they are never meant to be the object of our faith. Listen again to Paul.

OBJECTS OF FAITH OTHER THAN
THE CROSS OF CHRIST

The church at Corinth had drifted, as do many churches, into objects of faith other than the Cross of Christ. In this particular case, it was Water Baptism, and more particularly, who had done the baptizing. In answer to this, the Apostle said:

"**Now** *(implies the transition from thanksgiving to reproof)* **I beseech you** *(I beg you)*, **Brethren, by the Name of our Lord Jesus Christ** *(proclaims the Lord as the Head of the Church)*, **that you all speak the same thing** *(demands unity with respect to the Person of Christ, and what He has done to redeem us through the Cross)*, **and *that* there be no divisions among you** *(as it regards Christ and the Cross)*; **but *that* you be perfectly joined together in the same mind and in the same judgment** *(presents that which can only be done by the Cross ever being the Object of one's Faith, which then gives the Holy Spirit the latitude to bring about these things in our lives)*.

CONTENTION

"**For it has been declared unto me of you, my Breth-ren, by them** *which are of the House* **of Chloe** *(Paul wisely and kindly mentions his authority for these reports)*, **that there are contentions among you.** *(We will see that these contentions centered on disagreements concerning the Cross.)*

"**Now this I say, that every one of you says** *(refers to a self-assertive manner)*, **I am of Paul; and I of Apollos; and I of Cephus** *(Simon Peter)* **and I of Christ.** *(In effect, this latter group was saying they didn't need any preachers at all, which is wrong.)*

"**Is Christ divided?** *(Is there a Baptist Christ, a Pente-costal Christ, or a Holiness Christ? The answer is a solid 'no.')* **Was Paul crucified for you?** *(The Apostle rebukes the partisanship, which attached itself to his own name.)* **or were you baptized in the name of Paul?** *(This proclaims the idea that he had never attempted to draw away Disciples after himself, but rather to Christ.)*

WATER BAPTISM

"**I thank God that I baptized none of you, but Crispus and Gaius** *(if Water Baptism were essential to Salvation, as some claim, I hardly think Paul would have blatantly announced that he had only baptized these few, as he did here)*;

"**Lest any should say that I had baptized in my own name** *(nothing must be done to draw away allegiance from Christ)*.

"**And I baptized also the household of Stephanas: besides, I know not whether I baptized any other** *(informs us that the inspiration of the Apostles in writing the Scrip-tures involved none of the mechanical infallibility ascribed to them by popular dogma)*.

LEST THE CROSS OF CHRIST SHOULD
BE MADE OF NONE EFFECT

The Apostle now says:

"**For Christ sent me not to baptize** *(presents to us a Cardinal Truth)*, **but to preach the Gospel** *(the manner in which one may be Saved from sin)*: **not with wisdom of words** *(intellectualism is not the Gospel)*, **lest the Cross of Christ should be made of none effect.** *(This tells us in no uncertain terms that the Cross of Christ must always be the emphasis of the Message, i.e., 'the Object of our Faith.')*"
(**I Cor. 1:10-17**).

Was the Apostle demeaning Water Baptism? No! And, we can say the same thing about the Lord's Supper. While such is a viable Biblical Doctrine, it must not be the object of our Faith. The same can be said for manifestations, as real as they may be. Neither must we make the Purpose Driven Life the object of our faith, or the confession message, or the Government of Twelve, etc. Again we state it, and do so unequivocally, it is the Cross of Christ and the Cross of Christ alone, which must be the Object of our Faith.

WHY THE CROSS?

The Cross of Christ must be the Object of our Faith and must ever be the Object of our Faith.
Why?
It is there where Jesus paid the price for our Redemption and satisfied the demands of a thrice-Holy God by the giving of Himself as a Perfect Sacrifice in the shedding of His Life's Blood.
Going back to the Old Testament for the foundation of all of this, we find that there was one place designated by the Lord where sacrifices were to be offered. Likewise, there is one Cross. Moses wrote:

ONE PLACE OF SACRIFICE

"And the LORD spoke unto Moses, saying *(if is to be noticed, over and over again this phrase is used, signifying that all was of God and nothing at all of man; in other words, Moses must not deviate from what the Lord had told him; this is a lesson that religious man finds very difficult to obey)*,

"Speak unto Aaron, and unto his sons, and unto all the Children of Israel, and say unto them; This is the thing which the LORD has commanded, saying,

"What man soever there be of the house of Israel, who kills an ox, or lamb, or goat, in the camp, or who kills it out of the camp *(should have been translated 'sacrifices,' in the place of 'kills')*,

"And brings it not unto the door of the Tabernacle of the congregation, to offer an Offering unto the LORD before the Tabernacle of the LORD; blood shall be imputed unto that man; he has shed blood; and that man shall be cut off from among his people *(Mackintosh says, 'A man might say, Can I not offer a sacrifice in one place as well as another? The answer is, Life belongs to God, and His claim thereto must be recognized in the place where He has appointed — before the Tabernacle of the Lord. That was the only meeting-place between God and man. To offer elsewhere proved that the heart did not want God.*

" *'The moral of this is plain. There is one place where God has appointed to meet the sinner, and that is the Cross — the antitype of the Brazen Altar. There and there alone has God's claims upon the life been duly recognized. To reject this meeting-place is to bring down judgment on oneself — it is to trample underfoot the just claims of God, and to arrogate to oneself a right to life which all have forfeited.')*

"To the end that the Children of Israel may bring their Sacrifices, which they offer in the open field *(which they have been offering in the open field)*, **even that they may bring them unto the LORD, unto the door of the Tabernacle of the congregation, unto the Priest, and offer them for Peace Offerings unto the LORD** *(in essence, some three times the warning is given concerning the offering up of sacrifices in places except the Tabernacle, or Temple, that is, when the Temple would be built [Verses 4, 7, 10]).*

SPRINKLING THE BLOOD

"**And the Priest shall sprinkle the blood upon the Altar of the LORD at the door of the Tabernacle of the congregation, and burn the fat for a sweet savour unto the LORD.** *(Expositors say, 'The Blood of Christ is the foundation of everything. It is the ground of God's Righteousness in justifying an ungodly sinner who believes on the Name of the Son of God; and it is the ground of the sinner's confidence in drawing near to a Holy God, Who is of purer eyes than to behold evil. God would be just in the condemnation of the sinner; but through the Death of Christ, He can be just and the Justifier of him who believes — a just God and a Saviour.*

"*'The Righteousness of God is His consistency with Himself — His acting in harmony with His revealed character. Hence, were it not for the Cross, His consistency with Himself would, of necessity, demand the death and judgment of the sinner; but in the Cross, that death and judgment were borne by the sinner's surety, so that the same Divine consistency is perfectly maintained, while a Holy God justifies an ungodly sinner through Faith. It is all through the Blood of Jesus — nothing less, nothing more, and nothing different')*" **(Lev. 17:1-6).**

Moses continues:

"**For the life of the flesh is in the blood** *(it should be* *translated 'for the soul of the flesh is in the blood'; the Hebrew word here rendered 'life' occurs twice more in this very Verse, and is properly translated 'soul')*: **and I have given it to you upon the Altar to make an Atonement for your souls: for it is the blood** *(the Blood of Christ)* **that makes an Atonement for the soul.** *(This latter phrase plainly and purely tells us that the Death of Christ on the Cross, which was brought about by the shedding of His Precious Blood, which means that in the shedding of His Blood, His Life poured out, is not only the means of Salvation, but, in fact, is the only means of Salvation.*

"The expositor says, 'When man duly takes his place as one possessing no title whatsoever to life — when he fully recognizes God's claims upon him, then the Divine record is, 'I have given you the life to make an Atonement for your soul.' Yes, Atonement is God's gift to man; and be it carefully noted that this Atonement is in the Blood, and only in the Blood, and we speak of the Blood of Christ. It is not the Blood and something else. The Word is most explicit. It attributes Atonement exclusively to the Blood' [Heb. 9:22; Eph. 1:7; Col. 1:14; I Jn. 1:6; Rev., Chpt. 12])" **(Lev. 17:11).**

THE CROSS OF CHRIST IS THE FOUNDATION OF ALL BIBLE DOCTRINE

The Cross was not an afterthought with God. It was not something that just merely happened. In fact, the Cross of Christ, the manner in which Jesus would give Himself as a Sacrifice, was decided by the Godhead even before the foundation of the world. Even though we have given the following in the answer of another question, because of the vast significance of this Truth, please allow us the liberty of giving it again. Peter wrote:

"Forasmuch as you know that you were not redeemed with corruptible things, as silver and gold *(presents the* *fact that the most precious commodities [silver and gold] could not redeem fallen man)*, **from your vain conversation** *(vain lifestyle)* **received** **by tradition from your fathers** *(speaks of original sin that is passed on from father to child at conception)*;

   "But with the Precious Blood of Christ *(presents the payment, which proclaims the poured out Life of Christ on behalf of sinners)*, **as of a Lamb without blemish and without spot** *(speaks of the lambs offered as substitutes in the Old Jewish economy; the Death of Christ was not an execution or assassination, but rather a Sacrifice; the Offering of Himself presented a Perfect Sacrifice, for He was Perfect in every respect [Ex. 12:5])*:

BEFORE THE FOUNDATION OF THE WORLD

   "Who verily was foreordained before the foundation of the world *(refers to the fact that God, in His Omniscience, knew He would create man, man would Fall, and man would be redeemed by Christ going to the Cross; this was all done before the Universe was created; this means the Cross of Christ is the Foundation Doctrine of all Doctrine, referring to the fact that all Doctrine must be built upon that Foundation, or else it is specious)*, **but was manifest in these last times for you** *(refers to the invisible God Who, in the Person of the Son, was made visible to human eyesight by assuming a human body and human limitations)*"
(I Pet. 1:18-20).

WOULD NOT DEATH IN ANY FORM HAVE SUFFICED?

   No!
   It had to be a Cross, which is referred to several times as a *"tree."*
   When Jesus died on the Cross, He had to atone for every sin, even the vilest of sins. That's the reason that His shed Blood

can atone for all sins (I Jn. 1:7).

Going back to the Old Testament, we see all of this in Type. Moses wrote:

THE WORST SINS

"And if a man has committed a sin worthy of death, and he be to be put to death, and you hang him on a tree:

"His body shall not remain all night upon the tree, but you shall in any wise bury him that day; (for he who is hanged is accursed of God;) that your land be not defiled, which the LORD your God gives you for an inheritance. *(This is the reason that the religious leaders of Israel demanded that Jesus be put on the Cross [Mat. 27:23]. They knew that one put on the tree was accursed of God, and so they reasoned that the people would then think, were He really the Messiah, God would never allow Him to be put on a Cross. They did not realize that the Lord had foretold the event of the Cross some 1500 years earlier, as it concerned the brazen serpent on the pole [Num. 21:8-9]. It was necessary that Jesus go to the Cross, in order that He might atone for all the sins of mankind, at least for all who will believe [Jn. 3:16]. So, Jesus was made a curse on the Cross, not because of His sins, for He had none, but for the sin of the whole world, and for all time [Jn. 1:29; Gal. 3:13])"* **(Deut. 21:22-23).**

So, to fulfill Old Testament typology, Jesus couldn't die by being thrust through with a spear or even stoned to death, but must, in fact, be crucified.

WHAT HAPPENED AT THE CROSS?

1. He satisfied the demands of the broken Law. Paul wrote:

"Christ has redeemed us from the curse of the Law

(He did so on the Cross), **being made a curse for us** *(He took the penalty of the Law, which was death)*: **for it is written, Cursed is everyone who hangs on a tree"** **(Gal. 3:13).**

2. **Christ atoned for all sin, past, present, and future, at least for all who will believe (Jn. 3:16).**

3. **His sacrificial Death made it possible for believing sinners to be Justified by Faith. Paul said:**

"That the blessing of Abraham *(Justification by Faith)* **might come on the Gentiles through Jesus Christ** *(through what He did at the Cross)* **. . ." (Gal. 3:14).**

4. **Atoning for all sin, which means that He satisfied the sin debt that was owed to God the Father, which made it possible for Believers to:**

"Receive the Promise of the Spirit through Faith. *(All sin was atoned at the Cross, which lifted the sin debt from believing man, making it possible for the Holy Spirit to come into the life of the Believer and abide there forever [Jn. 14:16-17])"* **(Gal 3:14).**

5. **By atoning for all sin, sin being the legal right that Satan had to hold man captive, Jesus defeated Satan, all fallen Angels and demon spirits, meaning that Satan now, upon the Faith of the Believer, has no more right to hold the Believer in bondage. Paul said,** *"And having spoiled principalities and powers, He made a show of them openly, triumphing over them in it"* **(Col. 2:15).**

REDEMPTION WAS COMPLETED AT CALVARY

While the Ascension, the Resurrection, and the Exaltation of Christ were of supreme significance, still, these great happenings were the result of the Atonement, and not the cause.

When Jesus said:

"It is finished, Father into Your Hands I commend My Spirit" (Jn. 19:30; Lk. 23:46). At that moment, the Atonement was complete.

When He died, the Scripture says:

"And the Veil of the Temple was rent in the midst. *(Probably referred to the approximate time He died, about 3 p.m.; this 'Veil' separated the Holy Place in the Temple from the Holy of Holies, where God was supposed to dwell; the Veil being torn apart, in effect, stated that God had accepted the Sacrifice, and now the way was open for sinful man to come to God and be cleansed; but he would have to come by the Way of Christ and the Cross; there is no other way of Salvation [Jn. 14:6])"* (Lk. 23:45).

That is the reason that the Cross of Christ must ever be the Object of our Faith. That is the reason that our Faith being placed in the Cross of Christ is the only Faith that God will recognize. While everything the Lord did was of supreme significance, yet, it was His sacrificial giving of Himself in Sacrifice, i.e., *"the Cross,"* which is the foundation of it all.

"You did leave Your Throne and Your Kingly Crown,
"When You came to Earth for me;
"But in Bethlehem's home there was found no room,
"For Your Holy Nativity.
"Oh come to my heart, Lord Jesus,
"There is room in my heart for Thee."

"Heaven's arches rang when the Angels sang,
"Proclaiming Your Royal Decree;
"But in lowly Birth did You come to Earth,
"And in great humility.
"Oh come to my heart, Lord Jesus,
"There is room in my heart for Thee."

"The foxes found rest, and the birds their nest,
"In the shade of the forest tree;
"But Your Couch was the sod, Oh Thou Son of God,
"In the deserts of Galilee.
"Oh come to my heart, Lord Jesus,
"There is room in my heart for Thee."

"You came, Oh Lord, with the Living Word,
"That should set Your People free;
"But with mocking scorn, and with crown of thorn,
"They bore You to Calvary.
"Oh come to my heart, Lord Jesus,
"There is room in my heart for Thee."

"When Heaven's arches shall ring and her choir shall sing,
"At Your Coming to Victory,
"Let Your Voice call me Home saying 'Yet there is room,
"'There is room at My Side for thee!'
"And my heart shall rejoice, Lord Jesus,
"When You come and call for me."

CHAPTER EIGHTEEN

What Does It Mean To Preach The Cross?

QUESTION:

WHAT DOES IT MEAN TO PREACH THE CROSS?

ANSWER:

It means that the emphasis must always be on the Cross of Christ.

Let me explain!

First of all, it doesn't mean that the preacher has to preach about the Cross every time he preaches. That's not the idea at all!

Paul said, *"For the preaching of the Cross is to them who perish foolishness, but to we who are Saved, it is the Power of God"* (I Cor. 1:18).

On the other side of the coin, scores of people hear their Pastor mention the Cross occasionally and they think that he's preaching the Cross. While he certainly might be, chances are, he isn't!

WHAT DOES IT MEAN TO PREACH THE CROSS?

1. The preacher or Bible teacher must have a thorough understanding of what the Cross actually means. He must understand that Christ is the Source of all things given to us from God (Jn. 1-2, 14, 29; 3:16; 20:6).

2. Next, he must understand that the Cross of Christ is the Means by which all of these things are given, whatever they might be (Rom. 6:3-5; I Cor. 1:17-18, 23; 2:2; Gal. 6:14).

3. As well, the Cross of Christ as the Object of our Faith is the way everything is received.

4. And last, he must understand that the Holy Spirit superintends all of this. In other words, he must understand that the Cross of Christ provides the legal means for the Holy Spirit to do all that He does (Rom. 8:1-2, 11).

All of this means that nothing else must be the object of one's Faith. The Finished Work of Christ needs no help.

In all of this, the preacher must understand that the Cross

of Christ, being the manner in which the Holy Spirit works, means that everything, and we mean everything, comes from the Lord Jesus Christ with the Cross as the Means.

THE PREACHER MUST UNDERSTAND THE MEANING OF THE CROSS OF CHRIST AS IT REFERS TO SALVATION AND SANCTIFICATION

Most preachers have at least a modicum of understanding as it regards the Cross of Christ respecting Salvation; however, the preachers who understand the Cross of Christ respecting Sanctification are few and far between. Quite a few preachers, and rightly so, mention the Cross as it regards Salvation and, because they do such, many times those hearing them think they are preaching the Cross. To be sure, what is preached in this respect is Scriptural and good and should be continued; however, what Paul was talking about as it regards *"preaching the Cross"* mostly referred to Sanctification.

ENCOUNTERS

Devotees to the cell groups, who also conduct what is referred to as *"encounters,"* claim to be preaching the Cross as well. They aren't!

Their understanding of the Cross functions more in the realm of superstition, or that which is mystical, more than anything else.

Mostly, they try to picture the sufferings of Christ on the Cross, which is supposed to cause some type of reaction on the part of those who are being indoctrinated. In these meetings some, at times, have physically embraced a replica of the Cross, thinking that provides some type of help. Others write all their sins and failures on a piece of paper, tear the paper into pieces, and throw it at the foot of the Cross, etc.

To be frank, this is not that much different in the Eyes of God than some in the Philippines who, I have heard, actually cause themselves to be nailed to the cross, suffering the pain of such, etc.

None of this is what Paul referred to as *"preaching the Cross."* As stated, it is more superstition than anything else.

We must understand that a wooden replica of the Cross of Christ, or any such thing, is worthless as far as Faith is concerned. That's not what the Scriptures are referring to. As we've said before, if by chance the actual Cross on which Jesus died was found in Jerusalem, it would not be worth any more than another piece of wood. When Paul talks about the Cross, he's not speaking of the wooden beam or any such thing, He's speaking of what Jesus did there and the benefits which are provided for us because of the great price that He paid. So, those who practice the encounter sessions, so-called, are not preaching the Cross of Christ, are not proclaiming the Cross of Christ, with what they are doing being basically nothing that God will honor or recognize.

A WAY OF LIFE

What we are speaking of, as it regards preaching the Cross, is that which one believes more so than what one does.

The following has been given in another one of our questions and answers; however, quite possibly as a diagram it will help one to understand what we are saying.

• FOCUS: The Lord Jesus Christ (Jn. 1:1-2, 14, 29; 14:6; Col. 2:10).

• OBJECT OF FAITH: The Cross of Christ (Rom. 6:3-10; I Cor. 1:17-18, 21, 23; 2:2; Col. 2:14-15).

• POWER SOURCE: The Holy Spirit (Rom. 8:1-2, 11).

• RESULTS: Victory (Rom. 6:14).

PREACHING THE CROSS VERSUS PREACHING PSYCHOLOGY

The modern church, even as we have addressed in another

question and answer, has embraced humanistic psychology in totality. In fact, the church has so very much embraced such that, any more, almost every sermon heard from behind most pulpits is laced with humanistic psychology, even though at times the preacher is unaware of such. But, when the Cross of Christ is preached as the answer and solution for every single problem that faces mankind, this means an end to humanistic psychology. Now, the preacher should understand, if he is to preach the Cross, he not only will not preach psychology, but will be unalterably opposed to this nefarious system. That might cause him a problem with the denomination with which he is associated, that is if he, in fact, is associated with such. Due to the fact that virtually every religious denomination in America and Canada has embraced humanistic psychology, this could very easily put him at odds with the leadership in these respective denominations. As a result, he had best be prepared to be frowned upon, or even possibly disfellowshipped. In regard to this, Paul said:

"For do I now persuade men, or God? *(In essence, Paul is saying, 'Do I preach man's doctrine, or God's?')* or do I seek to please men? *(This is what false apostles do.)* For if I yet please men, I should not be the Servant of Christ. *(One cannot please both men and God at the same time)*" (Gal. 1:10).

THE BLESSINGS OF PREACHING THE CROSS

The Cross of Christ is the Gospel that Paul preached. Inasmuch as the meaning of the New Covenant was given to this man by the Lord Jesus Christ, and inasmuch as the meaning of the New Covenant is, in effect, the meaning of the Cross, then we should understand how important this is. As previously asked, *"Do we want to please God or men?"* I think the answer to that should be overly obvious!

Paul also said:

"For I determined not to know any thing among you *(with purpose and design, Paul did not resort to the knowledge or philosophy of the world regarding the preaching of the Gospel)***, save Jesus Christ, and Him Crucified** *(that and that alone is the Message, which will save the sinner, set the captive free, and give the Believer perpetual Victory)*" **(I Cor. 2:2).**

I think by now it should be obvious, this is not something that is new. It may seem to be new since it has been so long since it's been preached, but in reality, it is the story of the Bible. It is the Word of God!

"You have said You are the Vine, Lord,
"And that I'm a branch in Thee,
"But I do not know the reason,
"Why I should so barren be."

"Bearing Fruit is my deep longing,
"More Your Life to manifest,
"To Your Throne to bring more glory,
"That Your Will may be expressed."

"But I fail to understand, Lord,
"What it means — 'Abide in Me,'
"For the more I seek 'abiding,'
"More I feel I'm not in Thee."

"How I feel I'm not abiding;
"Though I pray and strongly will,
"Yet from me You seem distant,
"And my life is barren still."

"Yet You are the Vine, You said it,
"And I am a branch in Thee;
"When I take You as my Saviour,

"Then this fact is wrought in me."

"Now I'm in You and need not,
"Seek into Yourself to come,
"For I'm joined to You already,
"With Your Flesh and Bones I'm one."

"Not to 'go in' is the secret,
"But that I'm 'already in!'
"That I ne're may leave, I'd ask Thee,
"Not how I may get within."

"I am in, already in Thee!
"What a place to which I'm brought!
"There's no need for pleading or struggling,
"God Himself the work has wrought."

"Since I'm in, why ask to enter?
"Oh how ignorant I've been!
"Now with praise and much rejoicing,
"For Your Word, I dwell therein."

"Now in You I rest completely,
"With myself I gladly part;
"You are Life and You are Power,
"All in all to me You Art."

CHAPTER NINETEEN

Can A Believer Live A
Victorious Life If He Doesn't
Understand The Cross
Respecting Sanctification?

QUESTION:

CAN A BELIEVER LIVE A VICTORIOUS LIFE IF HE DOESN'T UNDERSTAND THE CROSS RESPECTING SANCTIFICATION?

ANSWER:

No!

The person asking the question went on to say, *"I know quite a number of people who do not understand the Cross of Christ respecting Sanctification, and they live a victorious life."*

OUTWARD APPEARANCE

First of all, we as Believers can never look at another Believer, no matter what seems to be on the outside, and know what is actually going on in such a person's heart and life. Only the Lord can do that. Furthermore, if a Believer can live a victorious life without understanding the Cross of Christ respecting Sanctification, then the statement given by Paul carries no meaning. He said, *"For if Righteousness come by the Law, then Christ is dead in vain"* (Gal. 2:21).

Righteousness can come only one way and that is by the Believer exercising Faith in Christ and what Christ has done for us at the Cross, which then automatically gives us a perfect, spotless Righteousness. If we attempt to obtain it in any other manner, it is constituted as *"Law"* or *"works," and always ends in self-righteousness.*

WHAT EVERY BELIEVER OUGHT TO KNOW

Please understand, a person can be Saved, baptized with the Holy Spirit, used of the Lord respecting Gifts, and, in fact, used of God mightily, without understanding the Cross as it refers to Sanctification. In fact, there are no perfect people, Cross or otherwise. There is only a Perfect Christ, Who has a Perfect Redemption, which is given to us upon Faith.

Many Believers do not understand the manner in which the Lord uses people. First of all, and as stated, there are no perfect people. They simply don't exist! This in no way is meant to condone sin in any fashion. It is meant, however, to see the situation as it really is. No matter how much the Lord is using a person, with His use of them being real and genuine, if that Believer, whomever he or she might be, doesn't understand God's Prescribed Order of Victory, i.e., *"of life and living,"* such a person, despite being used by the Lord, cannot live a victorious life. Let me use the Apostle Paul, who would be the greatest example of all.

PAUL

The Ninth Chapter of Acts records the miraculous conversion of Paul, which took place on the Road to Damascus. Three days after his conversion, Ananias, at the behest of the Lord, went to where Paul was staying and said to him, *"Brother Saul, the Lord, even Jesus, Who appeared unto you in the way as you came, has sent me, that you might receive your sight, and be filled with the Holy Spirit"* (Acts 9:17).

So, Paul was Saved and then three days later baptized with the Holy Spirit and then he immediately began to *"preach Christ in the Synagogues."*

Now, at this time and for a period probably of several years, Paul knew nothing about the Cross of Christ as it refers to Sanctification, or any other manner either. In fact, all of the Apostles, plus Paul, during that intervening time preached the Resurrection more than anything else. The Apostles had been eyewitnesses of Christ being raised from the dead and, by and large, this is what they preached. They knew nothing about the New Covenant, what it meant, and simply because the Lord had not yet given that information. In fact, He would give the meaning of the New Covenant to Paul (Gal. 1:12). Now, as stated, how long it was after Jesus ascended until this information was given to Paul, we aren't told.

We do know the following: It is believed that Paul was Saved in the year A.D. 35. In approximately A.D. 44, Barnabas, no doubt, led by the Lord went to Tarsus, *"for to seek Saul"* (Acts 11:25). After Barnabas found him, the Scripture says, *"He brought him unto Antioch. And it came to pass, that a whole year they assembled themselves with the church, and taught much people"* (Acts 11:26).

It is almost guaranteed that by this time, a time frame of some nine years after Paul was Saved, the Apostle had by now been given the great meaning of the New Covenant. In fact, even though the Scripture does not pointedly say, I personally believe that Paul received this Revelation when *"he was caught up into Paradise, and heard unspeakable words, which is not lawful for a man to utter"* (II Cor. 12:4). He related this account in approximately A.D. 60; however, this was some fourteen years after he had experienced this tremendous phenomenon (II Cor. 12:1-2). This means that this Revelation was given to him a short time before Barnabas found him in Tarsus and then brought him to Antioch.

Now, we must understand, all of these dates are speculative at best, yet, I think we can say without fear of contradiction that it was at least several years after Paul was Saved before this great Revelation of the New Covenant was given to him.

At any rate, during this period of time, ever how long it was, even though the great Apostle was ministering, and constantly, still, he did not know how to live a victorious life, no matter how hard he tried. He stated:

SPIRITUAL FAILURE

"For I was alive without the Law once *(Paul is referring to himself personally and his conversion to Christ; the Law, he states, had nothing to do with that conversion; neither did it have anything to do with his life in Christ)*: but when the Commandment came *(having just been*

Saved, and not understanding the Cross of Christ, he tried to live for God by keeping the Commandments through his own strength and power; in his defense, no one else at that time understood the Cross; in fact, the meaning of the Cross, which is actually the meaning of the New Covenant, would be given to Paul), **sin revived** *(the sin nature will always, without exception, revive under such circumstances, which results in failure)*, **and I died.** *(He was not meaning that he physically died, as would be obvious, but that he died to the Commandment; in other words, he failed to obey no matter how hard he tried; let all Believers understand that if the Apostle Paul couldn't live for God in this manner, at least successfully, neither can you!)*" **(Rom. 7:9).**

PAUL FOUND THAT HIS WILLPOWER WAS NOT ENOUGH

The great Apostle went on to say:

"For I know that in me (that is, in my flesh,) dwells no good thing *(speaks of man's own ability, or rather the lack thereof in comparison to the Holy Spirit, at least when it comes to spiritual things)*: **for to will is present with me** *(Paul is speaking here of his willpower; regrettably, most modern Christians are trying to live for God by means of willpower, thinking falsely that since they have come to Christ, they are now free to say 'no' to sin; that is the wrong way to look at the situation; the Believer cannot live for God by the strength of willpower; while the will is definitely important, it alone is not enough; the Believer must exercise Faith in Christ and the Cross, and do so constantly; then he will have the ability and strength to say 'yes' to Christ, which automatically says, 'no' to the things of the world)*; **but *how* to perform that which is good I find not** *(outside of the Cross, it is impossible to find a way to do good).*

"**For the good that I would I do not** *(if I depend on self,* *and not the Cross)*: **but the evil which I would not** *(don't want to do)*, **that I do** *(which is exactly what every Believer will do no matter how hard he tries to do otherwise, if he tries to live this life outside of the Cross [Gal. 2:20-21])*" **(Rom. 7:18-19).**

Now, if Paul couldn't live a victorious life outside of the Cross, again I ask, *"How can we do such?"*

A MODERN EXPERIENCE

Back in the mid 1950's, if I remember the period of time correctly, a particular Preacher was drawing some of the largest crowds in the world and, in fact, seeing a tremendous work for God accomplished. Many were being healed and many were being Saved.

At a point in time, the dear brother was found to be having a problem with alcohol.

Now, many would say, as a result of this revelation, that he was a hypocrite and that his Ministry was not valid. None of that is correct!

His Ministry was valid. God was using him, and greatly so; however, he was trying to live for the Lord without under-standing the Cross of Christ relative to Sanctification. In other words, he simply did not know how the Holy Spirit worked. So, he tried to beat this thing himself, but, as untold millions have found out, it cannot be done that way. There can be victory, but only God's Way, which is the Cross of Christ, which then gives the Holy Spirit latitude to work in one's life.

The tragedy then, as by and large is the tragedy now, was that very few preachers knew and understood the Message of the Cross as it regarded Sanctification. Respecting Salvation, yes! Sanctification, no!

Frances and I sat across the table in a restaurant with Brother Gordon Lindsay, who was editor of the very influential *"Voice of Healing"* Magazine. He knew this brother intimately.

I asked him as to the reason for the failure. Frances and I, in those days just beginning in Evangelistic work were, as well, totally ignorant of this which we now teach you.

Brother Lindsay said to me, *"Brother Swaggart, I simply don't know what happened."* And there are untold numbers at this very moment, and I speak of preachers, who are struggling with problems in their lives, which, to say the least, is a monumental hindrance to them. Some will be found out and will suffer tremendous reproach. Some will simply quit preaching, because they lack understanding concerning these things.

A PRESENT EXPERIENCE

I'm thinking now of a Preacher of the Gospel who is at the present time building a great church in a respective southern city, but, until he heard the Message of the Cross, he had simply quit. He couldn't overcome particular problems within his life, and no matter how hard he tried. I heard him state, as he preached here at Family Worship Center just a short time ago, *"Everybody told me what I had to do, but no one told me how to do it."* The reason they didn't tell him how to do it is because they did not know how themselves.

There came an hour that he lost everything and, above all, lost his way with God. Reduced to working as a janitor, through a Latino that God used, this dear brother heard the Message of the Cross and his whole world changed. As stated, he is now building a great Church, and for the Glory of God.

If a Believer could successfully live for the Lord outside of God's provision, which is the Cross of Christ, then our Lord would not have had to come to this sin-cursed world and die on a cruel tree. But, He had to do such, simply because without that, the fallen sons of Adam's lost race would never find their way home.

A PERSONAL EXPERIENCE

I know what it is to be on both sides of this fence, proverbially speaking. And, please believe me, to try to live this life without knowing what I now know, which the Lord has given to me and which I'm doing my best to give it to others, simply wouldn't be worth living.

Paul said:

"**I am Crucified with Christ** *(as the Foundation of all Victory; Paul, here, takes us back to Rom. 6:3-5)*: **nevertheless I live** *(have new life)*; **yet not I** *(not by my own strength and ability)*, **but Christ lives in me** *(by virtue of me dying with Him on the Cross, and being raised with Him in Newness of Life)*: **and the life which I now live in the flesh** *(my daily walk before God)* **I live by the Faith of the Son of God** *(the Cross is ever the Object of my Faith)*, **Who loved me, and gave Himself for me** *(which is the only way that I could be Saved)*" **(Gal. 2:20).**

Several things are said in this one statement. They are:
• **In a very abbreviated form, the Holy Spirit here through Paul tells us how to live for God.**
• **The three words,** *"yet not I,"* **are some of the most important ever. The Apostle is simply telling us that he (we), within himself (ourselves), could not successfully live this life.**
• **If it is to be noticed, the great Apostle begins with the Cross (***"Crucified with Christ"***) and ends with the Cross (***"Who loved me, and gave Himself for me"***).**

"**I do not frustrate the Grace of God** *(if we make anything other than the Cross of Christ the Object of our Faith, we frustrate the Grace of God, which means we stop its action, and the Holy Spirit will no longer help us)*: **for if Righteousness** *come* **by the Law** *(any type of Law)*, **then Christ is dead in vain.** *(If I can successfully live for the Lord by any means other than Faith in Christ and the Cross, then the Death of Christ was a waste)*" **Gal. 2:21).**

FRUSTRATING THE GRACE OF GOD

1. Let us state that the Grace of God is simply the Goodness of God given to undeserving people.

2. We must ever understand that all Grace is made possible to us by virtue of the Cross of Christ, and no other way.

3. The Believer can keep the Grace of God, i.e., *"the Goodness of God,"* coming to him in an uninterrupted flow as long as his Faith is anchored in Christ and the Cross. The moment our Faith is placed somewhere else, this *"frustrates the Grace of God,"* with all of its attendant problems.

This means that every Believer in the world at this present time and, in fact, it has always been that way, who doesn't place his Faith exclusively in Christ and the Cross as it regards living for God, succeeds in doing nothing but *"frustrating the Grace of God."* This means that most of the help which can be given to us by the Holy Spirit is stopped. Regrettably, that's where most modern Believers are.

FALLING FROM GRACE

Paul also stated:

"**Christ is become of no effect unto you** *(this is a chilling statement, and refers to anyone who makes anything other than Christ and the Cross the Object of his Faith)*, **whosoever of you are Justified by the Law** *(seek to be Justified by the Law)*; **you are fallen from Grace** *(fallen from the position of Grace, which means the Believer is trusting in something other than the Cross; it actually means, 'to apostatize')*" (Gal. 5:4).

What does it mean to fall from Grace?

Once again, it means that such a Believer is placing his faith in something other than Christ and the Cross. Considering that the far greater majority of the modern church knows absolutely nothing about the Cross of Christ as it regards our Sanctification, in other words, how we live for God, this means that most modern Christians are living in a state of being fallen from Grace.

Are these Christians, which include almost all, aware of their situation?

No!

A HOMEBORN SLAVE

Christians in this state know that something is wrong, but they don't really know what it is.

The great Prophet Jeremiah said, *"Is Israel a servant? is he a homeborn slave? why is he spoiled?"* (Jer. 2:14). Notes on this Scripture are from THE EXPOSITOR'S STUDY BIBLE.

> *"Israel was a son, not a slave, yet they were about to become slaves! In fact, Israel had become a 'servant,' i.e., slave, to the heathenistic gods. As a result, they would soon become a slave to a foreign power.*
>
> *"The question, 'Is he a homeborn slave?', is interesting indeed! It has reference to an animal in a zoo. An animal was made by God to be free and unfettered. However, if born in a zoo and knowing nothing but the confines of such, it is a slave without really knowing it. Such was Israel, and such are so many modern Believers!*
>
> *"But there is freedom in Christ, and freedom only in Christ.*

LIVING THE RESURRECTION LIFE

Paul said:

> **"For if we have been planted together** *(with Christ)* **in the likeness of His Death** *(Paul proclaims the Cross as the instrument through which all Blessings come; consequently,*

the Cross must ever be the Object of our Faith, which gives the Holy Spirit latitude to work within our lives), **we shall be also** *in the likeness of His* **Resurrection** *(we can have the 'likeness of His Resurrection,' i.e., 'live this Resurrection Life,' only as long as we understand the 'likeness of His Death,' which refers to the Cross as the means by which all of this is done)*" **(Rom. 6:5).**

Many years ago when Frances and I were travelling from church to church in meetings, I would hear preachers mention the *"Resurrection Life."* Much of the time when such was said, it was a denigration of the Cross. In other words, they were stating that they wanted nothing to do with the Cross, because they were *"Resurrection People."* To be frank, they were influenced by the Word of Faith people, so-called, who openly denigrate the Cross.

It is certainly proper and right for the Believer to desire to live the Resurrection Life and, in fact, that's exactly what we should do; however, to live this Resurrection Life, which means a life of Victory, and perpetual Victory at that, we must understand that everything is predicated on the Cross of Christ. In other words, it is the Cross which makes all of this possible.

No, again we state, no matter who the Believer is and no matter what it looks like outwardly, no one can live a victorious life in Christ and not understand the Cross of Christ as it refers to our Sanctification. In fact, this is the entire gist of Paul's fourteen Epistles. This is at least a great part of the meaning of the New Covenant.

> *"Free from the Law, Oh happy condition,*
> *"Jesus has bled, and there is remission;*
> *"Cursed by the law and bruised by the fall,*
> *"Grace has redeemed us once for all."*
>
> *"Now are we free, there's no condemnation,*
> *"Jesus provides a perfect Salvation;*

"Come unto Me, Oh hear His sweet Call,
"Come, and He saves us once for all."

"Children of God, Oh glorious calling,
"Surely His Grace will keep us from falling;
"Passing from death to life at His Call,
"Blessed Salvation once for all."

CHAPTER TWENTY

Why Do You Say,
"The Story Of The Bible Is
The Story Of Jesus Christ
And Him Crucified?"

QUESTION:

WHY DO YOU SAY, "THE STORY OF THE BIBLE IS THE STORY OF JESUS CHRIST AND HIM CRUCIFIED?"

ANSWER:

Many state that the story of the Bible is the Creation of man, the Fall of man, and the Redemption of man. That is true. The Creation and Fall of man occupy the first three Chapters of the Bible. All the balance of the Word of God is taken up with man's Redemption, which, in brief, is *"Jesus Christ and Him Crucified."* Everything we will give respecting the addressing of this particular question has already been given in other answers; however, even though repetition is unavoidable, still, the chronological order in which this answer is given will help us, hopefully, to have a better grasp of the story of the Bible. In fact, properly understanding the answer to this question will give us, I think, a better understanding of the Word of God all around and, to be sure, there is nothing in the world more important than that.

When one begins to understand that the simple phrase, *"Jesus Christ and Him Crucified,"* pertains to the bedrock of the Salvation of the sinner and, as well, the Sanctification of the Saint, then one begins to understand just how important this phrase is. As well, understanding that the simple phrase, *"Jesus Christ and Him Crucified,"* addresses in totality the need of mankind and, as well, addresses itself to the revolution of Lucifer against God (Eph. 1:9-10; Col. 2:15), then one begins to understand just how important this phrase actually is.

THE INTRODUCTION OF THE SACRIFICIAL SYSTEM

When Adam and Eve fell, they were driven out of the Garden of Eden lest they eat of the Tree of Life and, thereby, live forever. The idea of an Adolf Hitler, a Joseph Stalin, etc., living forever presents itself as unthinkable. Concerning their expulsion from the Garden, the Bible says:

"And the LORD God said, Behold, the man is become as one of Us, to know good and evil *(the Lord knew evil, not by personal experience, but rather through Omniscience; man now knows evil by becoming evil, which is the fountainhead of all sorrow in the world; the pronoun 'Us' signifies the Godhead, 'God the Father, God the Son, and God the Holy Spirit')*: and now, lest he put forth his hand, and take also of the Tree of Life, and eat, and live forever:

EXPULSION FROM THE GARDEN

"Therefore the LORD God sent him forth from the Garden of Eden *(in effect, this was an act of mercy; man is expelled from the Garden, lest by eating the Tree of Life he should perpetuate his misery; but God's Love for him, though fallen and guilty, is so strong that He accompanies him into exile; as well, through Jesus Christ, God's only Son, Who will be given in Sacrifice, the Lord will show Adam, and all who would follow him, how to come back into Paradise; regrettably, there is no record that Adam and Eve placed any faith in the Lord; unfortunately, untold billions have followed suit)*, to till the ground from whence he was taken *(refers to a place of toil, not to a place of torment)*.

"So He *(God)* drove out the man *(implies the idea of force and displeasure)*; and He placed at the east of the Garden of Eden Cherubims *(these Cherubims signified the Holiness of God, which man had now forfeited)*, and a flaming sword which turned every way, to keep the way of the Tree of Life. *(The 'flaming sword' was emblematic of the Divine Glory in its attitude toward sin)*" (Gen. 3:22-24).

As we've stated, the following has already been given in the addressing of another question in this Volume; however, due to its vast significance, please allow the repetition. In fact, the Fourth Chapter of Genesis lays the groundwork for all that will follow, even unto this present hour. We have in this Chapter: The introduction of the Sacrificial system, which symbolizes *"Jesus Christ and Him Crucified"*; the opposition against that system, as it regards the murder of Abel by his brother Cain; the lack of faith registered by Eve, which again plagues the entirety of the human race; and, the Promise of God renewed in the birth of Seth, the son of Adam and Eve, who would be in the lineage of Christ.

THE BIRTHS OF CAIN AND ABEL

"And Adam knew Eve his wife *(is the Biblical connotation of the union of husband and wife in respect to the sex act)*; and she conceived, and bore Cain *(the first child born to this union, and would conclude exactly as the Lord said it would, with 'sorrow')*, and said, I have gotten a man from the LORD *(by Eve using the title 'LORD,' which means 'Covenant God,' and which refers to the 'Seed of the woman,' [Gen. 3:15], she thought Cain was the Promised One; she evidently didn't realize that it was impossible for fallen man to bring forth the Promised Redeemer. Unfortunately, the modern church continues to have problems in believing this)*.

VANITY

"And she again bore his brother Abel *('Abel' means 'vanity'; Cain being the oldest, this shows that Eve by now had become disillusioned with her firstborn, undoubtedly seeing traits in him, which she knew could not be of the Promised Seed; she was losing faith in God)*. And Abel was a keeper of sheep, but Cain was a tiller of the ground *(both were honorable professions)*.

THE FRUIT OF THE GROUND

"And in process of time it came to pass *(the phrase used here refers to a long indefinite period)*, that Cain brought of the fruit of the ground an offering unto the LORD.** *(This was probably the first offering that he brought, even though the Lord had explained to the First Family the necessity of the Sacrificial system, that is, if they were to have any type of communion with God and forgiveness of sins. There is evidence that Adam, at least for a while, offered up sacrifices.*

"Cain knew the type of Sacrifice that the Lord would accept, but he rebelled against that admonition, demanding that God accept the labor of his hand, which, in fact, God could not accept. So we have, in the persons of Cain and Abel, the first examples of a religious man of the world and a genuine man of Faith.)

THE OFFERED LAMB

"And Abel, he also brought of the firstlings of his flock and of the fat thereof *(this is what God demanded; it was a blood sacrifice of an innocent victim, a lamb, which proclaimed the fact that Abel recognized his need of a Redeemer, and that One was coming Who would redeem lost humanity; the Offering of Abel was a Type of Christ and the price that He would pay on the Cross of Calvary in order for man to be redeemed).* And the LORD had respect unto Abel and to his offering:** *(As stated, this was a Type of Christ and the Cross, the only Offering which God will respect. Abel's Altar is beautiful to God's Eye and repulsive to man's. Cain's altar is beautiful to man's eye and repulsive to God's. These 'altars' exist today; around the one that is Christ and His atoning work, few are gathered, around the other, many. God accepts the slain lamb and rejects the offered fruit; and the offering being rejected, so* *of necessity is the offerer.)*

NO RESPECT FOR ANY OFFERING
EXCEPT THE CROSS

"**But unto Cain and to his offering He had not respect** *(let us say it again, God has no respect for any proposed way of Salvation, other than 'Jesus Christ and Him Crucified' [I Cor. 1:23; 2:2])*. **And Cain was very angry, and his countenance fell** *(that which filled Abel with peace filled Cain with wrath; the carnal mind displays its enmity against all this Truth which so gladdens and satisfies the heart of the Believer)*.

"**And the LORD said unto Cain** *(God loves Cain, just as He did Abel, and wishes to bless him also)*, **Why are you angry** *(Abel's Altar speaks of Repentance, of Faith, and of the Precious Blood of Christ, the Lamb of God without blemish; Cain's altar tells of pride, unbelief, and self-righteousness, which always elicits anger)*? **And why is your countenance fallen** *(anger, in one form or the other, accompanies self-righteousness, for that is what plagued Cain; God's Righteousness can only come by the Cross, while self-righteousness is by dependence on works)*?

ACCEPTANCE AND REJECTION

"**If you do well, shall you not be accepted** *(if you bring the correct sacrifice, and thereby place your Faith)*? **And if you do not well, sin** *(a Sin-Offering)* **lies at the door** *(a lamb was at the door of the Tabernacle)*. **And unto you shall be his desire, and you shall rule over him** *(the Lord promised Cain dominion over the Earth of that day, if he would only offer up, and place his trust in, the right sacrifice; He promises the same presently to all who trust Christ [Mat. 5:5])*.

OPPOSITION TO THE WAY OF GOD

"**And Cain talked with Abel his brother: and it came to pass, when they were in the field, that Cain rose up against Abel his brother, and killed him** *(the first murder; Cain's religion was too refined to kill a lamb, but not too cultured to murder his brother; God's Way of Salvation fills the heart with love; man's way of salvation inflames it with hatred; 'Religion' has ever been the greatest cause of bloodshed).*

"**And the LORD said unto Cain, Where is Abel your brother?** *(Adam sins against God and Cain sins against man. In their united conduct, we have sin in all its forms, and that on the first page of human history.)* **And he said, I know not: Am I my brother's keeper?** *(He showed himself a 'liar' in saying, 'I know not'; 'wicked and profane' in thinking he could hide his sin from God; 'unjust' in denying himself to be his brother's keeper; 'obstinate and desperate' in not confessing his sin).*

THE BLOOD

"**And He** *(God)* **said, What have you done** *(this concerns man's sins, the fruit of his sinful nature)*? **The voice of your brother's blood cries unto Me from the ground.** *(There is some Scriptural evidence that Cain cut his brother's throat. Thus, with the first shedding of human blood, that ominous thought sprang up, divinely bestowed, that the Earth will grant no peace to the one who has wantonly stained her fair face with the life-stream of man.)*

THE CURSE

"**And now are you cursed from the Earth** *(Cain repudiated the Cross, murdered his brother, and is now cursed by*

God; this is the first curse leveled by God against a human being), **which has opened her mouth to receive your brother's blood from your hand** *(was the beginning of what has proven to be a saturation; from then until now, the Earth has been soaked with the blood of innocent victims)*;

"**When you till the ground, it shall not henceforth yield unto you her strength** *(presents the fact that Cain had polluted man's habitation, and now, when he tilled the soil, it would resist him as an enemy)*; **a fugitive and a vagabond shall you be in the Earth** *(presents the search, not of a better lot, but under the compulsion of an evil conscience)*.

"**And Cain said unto the LORD, My punishment is greater than I can bear** *(Cain did not see the enormity of his sin, but the severity of his punishment; in other words, there was no repentance)*.

A FUGITIVE AND A VAGABOND

"**Behold, You have driven me out this day from the face of the Earth** *(Adam's sin brought expulsion from the inner circle, Cain's from the outer)*; **and from Your face shall I be hid** *(to be hidden from the Face of God is to be not regarded by God, and not protected by His Guardian care)*; **and I shall be a fugitive and a vagabond in the Earth** *(a wanderer)*; **and it shall come to pass, that everyone who finds me shall** *(seek to)* **kill me.** *(This reference by Cain to other individuals proves that in the some one hundred plus years since Adam and Eve were created, the first parents had other children. By this time, there could very well have been several thousands of people on the Earth, and, no doubt, were.)*

"**And the LORD said unto him, Therefore whosoever kills Cain, vengeance shall be taken on him sevenfold** *(Cain was allowed to live in order that he might be a perpetual warning to others that the blood of their fellowman* *must not be spilled; however, very few heeded, as few presently heed).* **And the LORD set a mark upon Cain, lest any finding him should kill him** *(we aren't told what the mark was, but evidently, all knew).*

THE PRESENCE OF THE LORD

"And Cain went out from the Presence of the LORD *(those in rebellion against God do not at all desire His Presence, and for all the obvious reasons)*, **and dwelt in the land of Nod, on the east of Eden** *('Nod' means 'wandering'; the majority of the human race 'wander,' because they don't know God, and, therefore, have no peace).*

"And Cain knew his wife *(Biblical terminology for conception)*; **and she conceived, and bore Enoch: and he built a city** *(actually means 'was building' or 'began to build'; the idea is, it was not finished; and so it has been, and is, with the human race; nothing is ever quite finished with the unredeemed, simply because what is built doesn't satisfy)*, **and called the name of the city, after the name of his son, Enoch** *(carries the idea, due to the meaning of the name Enoch, that this city would be a place of education and learning — but it was education and learning without God).*

THE HUMAN RACE

"And unto Enoch was born Irad: and Irad begat *(fathered)* **Mehujael: and Mehujael begat Methusael: and Methusael begat Lamech** *(all of this was three hundred or more years after the creation of Adam and Eve).*

"And Lamech took unto him two wives: the name of the one was Adah, and the name of the other Zillah *(the first instance of polygamy recorded in the Bible).*

"And Adah bore Jabal: he was the father of such as dwell in tents, and of such as have cattle.

THE BEGINNING OF MUSIC ON EARTH

"And his brother's name was Jubal: he was the father of all such as handled the harp and organ *(it seems that Jubal was the originator of musical instruments; man's ear is now filled with other sounds than those, which issue from Calvary, and his eye is filled with other objects than a Crucified Christ)*.

"And Zillah, she also bore Tubal-cain, an instructor of every artificer in brass and iron: and the sister of Tubal-cain was Naamah *(Tubal-cain was the first one to begin to work with metals; the name of 'Cain' was probably added to show that these were 'Cainites'; 'Naamah' means 'beautiful')*.

THE FIRST POEM IN HUMAN HISTORY

"And Lamech said unto his wives, Adah and Zillah, Hear my voice; you wives of Lamech, hearken unto my speech: for I have slain a man to my wounding, and a young man to my hurt.

"If Cain shall be avenged sevenfold, truly Lamech seventy and sevenfold. *(This is the first recorded poem in human history. Like so much poetry ever since, it glorifies immorality and murder, and denies coming wrath. Man has attempted to deny Judgment ever since; nevertheless, Judgment one day is coming [Rev. 20:11-15])*.

THE SPIRITUAL SEED RENEWED

"And Adam knew his wife again; and she bore a son, and called his name Seth *(after dealing with Cain's line in the beginnings of corruption of violence, Moses goes back some years to the birth of 'Seth'; the Holy Spirit will single out 'Seth,' because he was in the lineage of Christ; the name 'Seth' means 'appointed substitute')*: **For God, said she, has**

appointed me another seed instead of Abel, whom Cain killed. *(When 'Cain' was born, Eve said, 'I have gotten a man from the LORD,' indicating that she believed in the Covenant of Gen. 3:15. Now she uses the term 'God,' in effect, stating that she has lost faith in the Covenant. As stated, this 'seed' would be the one through whom Christ would come, but because of faithlessness, Eve did not know or believe this.)*

"**And to Seth, to him also there was born a son; and he called his name Enos** *(the name 'Enos' means 'sickly, mortal, decaying man'; the awful results of the Fall are now beginning to sink in)*: **then began men to call upon the Name of the LORD** *(probably refers to contempt; quite possibly the family of Cain, knowing that Seth had now taken the place of Abel, as it regards the 'firstborn' or 'appointed one,' contemptuously refers to them as the 'God people,' or the 'Lord people')*" **(Gen., Chpt. 4).**

THE EVIL

From the time of Adam and Eve to the time of the Flood, a period of about 1,600 years, mankind sank into such a vortex of evil that the Scripture says:

"**And it came to pass, when men began to multiply on the face of the Earth, and daughters were born unto them** *(the events of this Chapter probably begin at about the time of Enoch, which was about a thousand years before the Flood. There were, no doubt, several millions of people on the face of the Earth at that time. The Verse just quoted is not meant to imply that the births of baby girls were more than that of baby boys, but is rather meant to set up the narrative for that which is about to be said)*,

THE SONS OF GOD

"**That the sons of God saw the daughters of men that**

they were fair; and they took them wives of all which they chose *(the 'sons of God' portrayed here refer to fallen Angels, which had thrown in their lot with Lucifer, who led a revolution against God some time in eternity past; in order to spoil the human lineage through which the Messiah would ultimately come, they would seek to corrupt that lineage, and to do so by marrying the 'daughters of men,' thereby, producing a mongrel race, so to speak, of which at least some of these offspring turned out to be 'giants'; at any rate, all who were the result of such a union were tainted; the term 'sons of God' in the Old Testament, at least as it is used here, is never used of human beings, but always of Angels, whether righteous or fallen [Job 1:6; 2:1]; in his short Epistle Jude mentions these particular 'angels.' He said that they 'kept not their first estate, but left their own habitation'; he then said what their sin was: 'going after strange flesh.' Concerning this, Jude also said that God 'has reserved [them] in everlasting chains unto darkness unto the Judgment of the great day' [Jude, Verses 6-7]).*

THE WARNING OF GOD

"And the LORD said, My Spirit *(Holy Spirit)* **shall not always strive with man** *(the Lord is speaking here of the man, Adam, and not mankind in general)***, for that he also is flesh** *(refers to the fact that even though the first man was created personally by God, he still was flesh, and because of the Fall must ultimately die)***: yet his days shall be an hundred and twenty years.** *(from the time of this announcement, Adam was to be given one hundred and twenty years to repent; there is no evidence that he did; many think that this one hundred and twenty years referred to the time limit to repent before the Flood; however, it has nothing to do with the Flood, as we will later prove).*

GIANTS

"There were giants in the Earth in those days *(as a result of the union of the fallen Angels with the 'daughters of men')*; and also after that *('those days' speak of the time before the Flood, while 'also after that' speaks of the time after the Flood; in fact, Goliath, who was killed by David, was one of those specimens)*, when the sons of God came in unto the daughters of men, and they bore children to them, the same became mighty men which were of old, men of renown *(these terms, 'mighty men, men of renown' shoot down the hypotheses of these terms referring merely to the lineage of Seth and the lineage of Cain).*

ONLY EVIL CONTINUALLY

"And God saw that the wickedness of man was great in the Earth *(these 'men of renown,' the giants, were developing more and more ways of wickedness)*, and that every imagination of the thoughts of his heart was only evil continually *(due to this infestation, the evil began with the very thought processes, and incorporated every human being; this was a continuous action of evil which never let up, and constantly grew more degrading).*

THE RESPONSE OF THE LORD

"And it repented the LORD that He had made man on the Earth *(God does not change as it regards His Nature; however, the fact that the Lord repents presents the truth that God, in consistency with His Immutability, assumes a changed position in respect to changed man)*, and it grieved Him at His Heart *(this is not merely an anthropomorphic statement, as some claim, but a true statement regarding the Nature of God; sin grieves the Lord!).*

"And the LORD said, I will destroy man whom I

have created from the face of the Earth *(the wickedness of man had become so great, if God had not done this, man would ultimately have destroyed himself, although it would have taken much longer. Sin has to be judged, and inevitably will be judged)*; both man and beast, and the creeping thing, and the fowls of the air; for it repents Me that I have made them *(the animal kingdom was made for man, and if man is destroyed, there is no more purpose or reason for the animal kingdom; so it must be destroyed, as well)*" (Gen. 6:1-7).

NOAH'S SACRIFICE

As stated, the Flood happened some sixteen hundred years after the Fall of Adam and Eve. After the Flood, the Scripture says:

"And Noah built an Altar unto the LORD; and took of every clean beast, and of every clean fowl, and offered Burnt Offerings on the Altar *(Civilization, as it sprang from the sons of Noah, has its foundation in the Cross of Christ, i.e., 'the Altar')*.

"And the LORD smelled a sweet savor *(the burning of the Sacrifice was sweet unto the Lord, because it spoke of the Coming Redeemer, Who would lift man out of this morass of evil)*; and the LORD said in His Heart, I will not again curse the ground any more for man's sake *(the 'curse' of which God speaks here refers to the fact that He will not again visit the Earth with a flood)*; for the imagination of man's heart is evil from his youth; neither will I again smite any more every living thing, as I have done *(it means that God will take into consideration the results of the Fall, over which man at the time has no control; however, there is a remedy, which is the Altar, i.e., 'the Cross')*.

"While the Earth remained, seedtime and harvest, and cold and heat, and summer and winter, and day and night shall not cease *(the Promise is given here that the seasons of the year will continue forever, because the Earth will remain forever)*" **(Gen. 8:20-22).**

ONLY TWO

From the time of the Fall to the time of Noah, but not including that Patriarch, the Bible only records two men who were Saved, Abel and Enoch **(Gen. 5:21-24).** There may very well have been more simply because we do know that the understanding of the Sacrificial system continued until Noah; however, it is positive that there were very few, if any more at all. In fact, there is no record whatsoever that Adam and Eve found their way back to the Lord although that way had been shown to them.

NOAH'S DRUNKENNESS

Even though the only people left on the face of the Earth at that time were Noah and his three sons and their wives, still, the Promise of God regarding a coming Redeemer still held true, but with an amazing turn. Concerning all of this, the Scripture says:

"And Noah began to be an husbandman, and he planted a vineyard:

"And he drank of the wine, and was drunken; and he was uncovered within his tent. *(This is the first mention of wine in the Bible, or any type of intoxicating beverage. Inasmuch as the first mention of intoxicating beverage in the Bible reveals such a shameful episode, we cannot help but garner from this illustration, as given by the Holy Spirit concerning Noah, the warning against alcohol taught here.)*

"And Ham, the father of Canaan, saw the nakedness of his father, and told his two brethren without *(sin is like leaven; it always spreads; Noah not only gets drunk, but now pulls off his clothes, and does so intentionally; there is a form of insanity about sin.)*

THE COVERING

"**And Shem and Japheth took a garment, and laid it upon both their shoulders, and went backward, and covered the nakedness of their father; and their faces were backward, and they saw not their father's nakedness** *(a lack of love exposes sin, while the Love of God covers sin, but without condoning it)*.

"**And Noah awoke from his wine, and knew what his younger son had done unto him** *(there are some Scholars who believe that either Ham or Canaan, and more likely Canaan, committed an act of homosexuality on the Patriarch; while there is no concrete proof of such, there is definitely some indication in that direction)*.

THE CURSE ON CANAAN

"**And he said, Cursed be Canaan; a servant of servants shall he be unto his brethren.** *(What was this curse? It had absolutely nothing to do with the skin of some people being black. In fact, all the descendants of Ham and Canaan were not black; some where white, and we speak of those who occupied the land of Canaan. The evidence is, it was only upon those, and because they opposed Israel, hence, the statement being 'Cursed be Canaan'*

"*Even then, Canaanites who place their Faith in God could escape it. Rahab, a Canaanite and a harlot, is an excellent example. She placed her Faith in God and after a period of purification, was brought into Israel's camp. She married an Israelite, and became and ancestress of David, and even the greater Son of David, the Lord Jesus Christ [Josh. 6:25; Mat. 1:5; Heb. 11:31])*.

THE ENLARGEMENT OF JAPHETH

"**And he said, Blessed be the LORD God of Shem**

(through Shem would come the Jewish people, who would give the world the Word of God and, as well, would bring forth the Messiah, the Saviour of the world); **and Canaan shall be his servant** *(the Canaanites in Israel were defeated by David, and became the servants of Israel).*

"God shall enlarge Japheth, and he shall dwell in the tents of Shem *(Israel, the descendants of Shem, would reject Christ, while the descendants of Japheth would accept Him, which means that the Blessing intended for Shem, i.e., Israel, would instead go to the descendants of Japheth, i.e., the Gentiles)*; **and Canaan shall be his servant.** *(The descendants of Canaan continue unto this hour [2009], in a sense, to be the servants of Japheth. For instance, the descendants of Canaan, wherever they might be, in a sense, answer to the United States, which part of the population are descendants of Japheth)*" **(Gen. 9:20-27).**

As stated, the 'blessing,' which was intended for Shem and, in fact, did come through Shem, Who was the Lord Jesus Christ, Who would give Himself as a ransom for many, would be rejected by Shem, i.e., *"Israel,"* but would be accepted by the descendants of Japheth. In fact, the church is almost totally Gentile, who are descendants of Japheth. So, the blessing that was intended for Shem has instead come to the descendants of Japheth, hence, the Word saying, *"God shall enlarge Japheth, and he shall dwell in the tents of Shem,"* meaning that he would dwell in the blessings of Shem. As also stated, Shem, referring to Israel as the descendants of Shem, forfeited the blessing, and it was because they rejected the Lord Jesus Christ, their Messiah. This Prophecy given by Noah, which we have quoted and given about twenty-four hundred years before Christ, would come to pass exactly as stated. Once again, that Prophecy centered up on the coming of the Redeemer, the Lord Jesus Christ, Who would give Himself as a Sacrifice, and do so on the Cross of Calvary, shedding His Life's Blood in order that we might be Saved.

ABRAHAM, THE ALTAR BUILDER

There are precious few in Biblical history who could equal Abraham. The first thing said of him by the Lord concerned, even though given in Shadow, the coming of the Redeemer. The Scripture says, and I continue to quote from THE EXPOSITOR'S STUDY BIBLE:

"Now the LORD had said unto Abram *(referring to the Revelation which had been given to the Patriarch a short time before; Genesis Chapter Twelve is very important, for it records the first steps of this great Believer in the path of Faith)*, Get thee out of your country *(separation)*, and from your kindred *(separation)*, and from your father's house *(separation)*, and to a land that I will show you *(refers to the fact that Abraham had no choice in the matter; he was to receive his orders from the Lord, and go where those orders led him)*:

YOU SHALL BE A BLESSING

"And I will make of you a great Nation *(the Nation which God made of Abraham has changed the world, and exists even unto this hour; in fact, this Nation 'Israel' still has a great part to play, which will take place in the coming Kingdom Age)*, and I will bless you, and make your name great *(according to Scripture, 'to bless' means 'to increase,' the builders of the Tower of Babel sought to 'make us a name,' whereas God took this man, who forsook all, and 'made his name great')*; and you shall be a blessing: *(Concerns itself with the greatest blessing of all. It is the glory of Abraham's Faith. God would give this man the meaning of Salvation, which is 'Justification by Faith,' which would come about through the Lord Jesus Christ, and what Christ would do on the Cross. Concerning this, Jesus said of Abraham, 'Your father Abraham rejoiced to see My day: and he saw it, and was glad' [Jn. 8:56].)*

IN YOU ALL THE FAMILIES OF THE EARTH
SHALL BE BLESSED

"And I will bless them who bless you *(to bless Israel, or any Believer, for that matter, guarantees the Blessings of God)***, and curse him who curses you** *(to curse Israel, or any Believer, guarantees that one will be cursed by God)***: and in you shall all families of the Earth be blessed.** *(It speaks of Israel, which sprang from the loins of Abraham and the womb of Sarah, giving the world the Word of God and, more particularly, bringing the Messiah into the world. Through Christ, every family in the world who desires blessing from God can have that Blessing, i.e., 'Justification by Faith')***"** **(Gen. 12:1-3).**

THE ALTAR

"And the LORD appeared unto Abraham *(though the hostile Canaanite was in the land, the Lord was there as well)***, and said, Unto your seed will I give this land** *(the 'seed' through Isaac, and not Ishmael; Satan has contested this Promise from the very beginning, with the struggle continuing even unto this hour, as it regards Israel and the Palestinians)***: and there built he an Altar unto the LORD, Who appeared unto him.** *(The 'Altar' and its Sacrifice represented the Lord Jesus Christ, and the price He would pay on the Cross in order to redeem humanity. The Promises of God to Abraham, as are all the Promises of God, are built upon the foundation of the 'Altar,' i.e., 'the Cross.')*

"And he removed from thence unto a mountain on the east of Beth-el, and pitched his tent, having Beth-el on the west, and Hai on the east *('Beth-el' means 'House of God,' while 'Hai' means 'the heap of ruins')***: and there he built an Altar unto the LORD, and called upon the**

Name of the LORD. *(The 'Altar' and the 'tent' give us the two great features of Abraham's character. He was a worshipper of God, hence, the Cross, and a stranger in the world, hence, the tent. Our prayers are based upon our Faith in Christ and what Christ has done for us at the Cross, of which the Altar was a Type)*" **(Gen. 12:7-8).**

BACK TO THE ALTAR

"And Abram went up out of Egypt, he, and his wife, and all that he had, and Lot with him, into *(from)* the south *(if Abraham went 'down' into Egypt in Gen. 12:10, Grace brings him 'up' out of Egypt, as recorded in this Verse; they left the south to go north, back to Canaan).*

"And Abram was very rich in cattle, in silver, and in gold *(these were the Blessings of God, but it did not make up for his lapse of Faith).*

"And he went on his journeys from the south even to Beth-el, unto the place where his tent had been at the beginning, between Beth-el and Hai;

"Unto the place of the Altar, which he had made there at the first: and there Abram called on the Name of the LORD. *(He went back to the mountaintop where his tent had been at the beginning, and there, doubtless with tears and shame, he called by Sacrifice on the Name of the Lord. His backslidings were forgiven, his soul was restored, and he resumes his true life as a pilgrim and a worshipper with his tent and his Altar, neither of which he had in Egypt. Until the Believer comes back to the Cross, of which the Altar is a Type, true Restoration cannot be found)*" **(Gen. 13:1-4).**

HE BUILT THERE AN ALTAR UNTO THE LORD

"And the LORD said unto Abram, after that Lot was separated from him *(directly Lot departs, God draws near to Abraham),* **Lift up now your eyes, and look from the place where you are northward, and southward, and eastward, and westward** *(the Lord tells Abraham that the Promises are given to him, and not to Lot)***:**

"For all the land which you see, to you will I give it, and to your seed forever. *(The modern Palestinians should look at the statement, 'and to your seed forever.')*

"And I will make your seed as the dust of the earth *(Sarah is barren, and yet God promises a number beyond comprehension)***: so that if a man can number the dust of the earth, then shall your seed also be numbered.** *(This includes not only the Jews who serve the Lord, but also every Gentile Believer who has ever lived.)*

"Arise, walk through the land in the length of it and in the breadth of it; for I will give it unto you *(this is a walk of Faith)***.**

"Then Abram removed his tent, and came and dwelt in the plain of Mamre, which is in Hebron, and built there an Altar unto the LORD. *(There was no Altar in Sodom, which Lot chose. All who travel in that direction are in quest of something quite different from that. It is never the worship of God, but the love of the world that leads them thither. Abraham builds an Altar unto the Lord, which means that his Faith is reestablished in Christ, and what Christ will do to redeem humanity by dying on the Cross. Hebron, incidentally, was about 22 miles south of Jerusalem, on the way to Beer-sheba)***" (Gen. 13:14-18).**

THE GREAT REVELATION GIVEN TO ABRAHAM

"And they came to the place which God had told him of *(this would be the place of the threshingfloor which David bought, and where Solomon's Temple would be built)***; and Abraham built an Altar there** *(it is believed that the Holy of Holies, which contained the Ark of the Covenant in the Temple, was built over this exact spot)***, and laid the wood**

in order *(signifying the Cross)*, **and bound Isaac his son** *(typical of Jesus being nailed to the Cross)*, **and laid him on the Altar upon the wood** *(typical of Jesus stretched on the Cross)*.

"**And Abraham stretched forth his hand, and took the knife to slay his son** *(perhaps the Lord asked more of Abraham than He has ever asked of any man; when Abraham took the knife, his surrender was complete)*.

THE LORD WILL PROVIDE

"**And the Angel of the LORD** *(this was the Lord Himself)* **called unto him out of heaven, and said, Abraham, Abraham** *(He Who said, 'Abraham, Abraham,' was the same One Who said, 'Martha, Martha,' 'Simon, Simon,' and 'Saul, Saul'; the repetition denotes urgency)*: **and he said, Here am I.** *(It was the trial that God intended, not the act.)*

"**And He said, Lay not your hand upon the lad, neither do you any thing unto him** *(Abraham didn't have to kill the boy to prove himself to God, but he had to fully intend to do so, and that he did!)*: **for now I know that you fear God, seeing you have not withheld your son, your only son from Me** *(should have been translated, 'for I the knowing One knew that you feared God, and that you would not withhold your son, your only son, from Me')*.

"**And Abraham lifted up his eyes, and looked, and behold behind him a ram caught in a thicket by his horns** *(this is the doctrine of Substitution plainly laid out; the ram was offered up in Sacrifice instead of his son; likewise, Jesus was offered up as our Substitute)*: **and Abraham went and took the ram, and offered him up for a Burnt Offering in the stead of his son** *(even though the Doctrine of Substitution is clearly set forth here, its corresponding Doctrine of Identification is not so clearly stated, that awaiting Moses [Num. 21:9]; but still, we are seeing here the very heart of the Salvation Plan)*.

"And Abraham called the name of that place Jehovah-jireh *(meaning 'the Lord will provide')*: **as it is said to this day, In the mount of the LORD it shall be seen.** *(Should read, 'in this mount Jehovah shall be seen'; this was fulfilled in II Sam. 24:25; I Chron. 21:26; II Chron. 7:1-3)*" **(Gen. 22:9-14).**

THE WAY OF REDEMPTION

As stated, this was one of the greatest Revelations ever given to any man. Abraham would be shown the way of Redemption, which would be by God giving His Only Son as a Sacrifice, typified in what the Lord asked of Abraham.

However, while the Lord showed Abraham the *"Way of Salvation,"* which would be by death of an innocent victim, in this case a ram, typical of the coming Christ, yet, He would not show him the manner of that death, in other words, how it would be carried out, which would be the Cross, that would be given to Moses.

THE DELIVERANCE OF THE CHILDREN OF ISRAEL

Even though the following has already been given in another answer in this Volume, still, due to the significance of the subject matter, the Bible being the Story of *"Jesus Christ and Him Crucified,"* I felt that the following must be repeated. I think by now we should be beginning to see what the Bible is all about. Everything in the Old Testament, which is of God, pointed toward the coming Redeemer and the price He would pay, all typified by the Sacrificial system; however, as we go forward, we will see how that more and more this is enlarged, in other words, making it more and more clear. All Salvation is in the Cross as all Sanctification is in the Cross. In fact, every single thing we receive from the Lord, and I mean everything, comes to us from the Source, which is the Lord Jesus Christ, and by the Means of the Cross of Christ.

A LAMB FOR AN HOUSE

"Speak ye unto all the congregation of Israel, saying *(another great lesson learned here is the fact that neither Moses nor Aaron introduced any legislation of their own, either at this time or later. The whole system, Spiritual, political, and ecclesiastical, was received by Divine Revelation, commanded by God, and merely established by the agency of the two brothers. This proclaims the fact that Salvation is all of God and none of man. This problem presents itself when man attempts to insert his means and ways into that which God has devised, which, in fact, the modern church is now doing),* **In the tenth day of this month they shall take to them every man a lamb, according to the house of their fathers, a lamb for an house:**
* *(In the Fourth Chapter of Genesis, it is a lamb for each person.*
* *Now it is a lamb for each house.*
* *Upon the giving of the Law, it would be a lamb for the entirety of the nation.*
* *But when Jesus came, He would be the Lamb for the entirety of the world [Jn. 1:29].*

"*The offering up of the Lamb in Sacrifice was a Type of Christ, and what He would do at the Cross, all on our behalf. The Lamb represented innocence and gentleness. The Prophets represented the tender compassion of God for His People under the figure of the Shepherd and the Lamb [Isa. 40:11], and, ultimately, the intention of God for His People used the lamb as an important symbol; therefore, the Lamb was a worthy symbol of our Saviour, Who, in innocence, patiently endured suffering as our Substitute [I Pet. 1:19]).*

A LAMB WITHOUT BLEMISH

"And if the household be too little for the lamb, let him and his neighbor next unto his house take it

according to the number of the souls; every man according to his eating shall make your count for the lamb. *(Every person had to partake of the Passover. This was mandatory. Even though the lamb represented the entire house, it had to be partaken by each and every individual in that house. It is the same as it regards Salvation, which is always very personal.)*

"Your lamb shall be without blemish *(Christ was without blemish, Who the Lamb represented, 'holy, harmless, undefiled' — a 'lamb without spot' [I Pet. 1:19])*, **a male of the first year** *(meant to portray the virile manhood of Christ; in other words, He didn't die in the throes of old age, but rather in the prime of manhood)*: **you shall take it out from the sheep, or from the goats** *(the 'goats' then represented were different from our goats presently; then they were very similar to the sheep, actually, with their long flowing mane, even more beautiful than the sheep)*:

KILL THE LAMB

"And you shall keep it up until the fourteenth day of the same month *(they were to select the animal on the tenth day, and then kill it on the fourteenth day [Vs. 3]; it was to be minutely inspected during these four days, that no trace of illness would be observed; representing Christ, it had to be perfect)*: **and the whole assembly of the congregation of Israel shall kill it in the evening.** *(The actual Hebrew says, 'between the two evenings,' which was about 3 p.m. This was the exact time that Jesus died on the Cross of Calvary [Mat. 27:46])*.

THE BLOOD APPLIED

"And they shall take of the blood *(which represented the shed Blood of the Lord Jesus Christ)*, **and strike**

it on the two side posts and on the upper door post of the houses, wherein they shall eat it *(eat the Passover; in I Cor. 5:7-8, we have the Divine Authority for our regarding the contents of Exodus Chapter 12, as typical of what our Blessed Saviour did on the Cross; at the deliverance of the Children of Israel from Egypt, the blood, which represented the shed Blood of Christ, was to be put on the side posts and the upper posts of the house; later, it would be applied to the Mercy Seat on the Great Day of Atonement; now, by Faith, it is applied to our hearts [Jn. 3:16; Eph. 2:13-18]).*

THEY SHALL EAT THE ROASTED LAMB

"And they shall eat the flesh in that night *(in essence, Jesus was referring to this in Jn. 6:53-55; of course, He wasn't speaking of His flesh literally being eaten, but was speaking rather of our Faith in Him and what He would do for us at the Cross; our Faith must be in the entirety of His Finished Word),* **roast with fire** *(this spoke of the Judgment of God that would come upon Him as the Sin-Bearer, which was death, instead of us),* **and unleavened bread** *(this typified the Perfection of Christ; He was Holy, harmless, and undefiled [Heb. 7:26], of which the lack of leaven was a Type);* **and with bitter herbs they shall eat it** *(the 'bitter herbs' were to remind the Children of Israel of the slavery which they had experienced in Egypt [Ex. 1:14]; as well, the Cross ever reminds us presently of that from which we were redeemed, abject slavery to Satan).*

EAT ALL OF IT, LET NONE OF IT REMAIN

"Eat not of it raw, nor sodden at all with water *(this speaks of accepting Christ, but without the Cross, which God cannot condone),* **but roast with fire** *(speaks of the Cross and the price paid there);* **his head with his legs, and with the purtenance thereof.** *(The purtenance pertained* *to the intestines, which were removed and washed, and then placed back in the animal and, as obvious here, to be eaten when the lamb was consumed. This speaks of partaking of all of the Cross. Sin goes to the very vitals; therefore, for sin to be properly addressed, and in every capacity, everything that Christ did at the Cross must be accepted, and without fail.)*

"And you shall let nothing of it remain until the morning *(all of it must be consumed, referring to the fact that we must accept all of Christ, or else we will not have any of Christ; untold millions attempt to accept Christ as a good man, a great example, even a miracle worker, but they care not for the Cross; if Christ is to be had at all, He can only be had by and through the Cross; otherwise, we have 'another Jesus' [II Cor. 11:4])***; and that which remains of it until the morning you shall burn with fire.** *(This tells us that Christ cannot be received in stages. He can only be received in totality. Burning the remainder 'with fire' once again points to the Cross. We must always remember, Christ is the Source, while the Cross is the Means.)*

THE LORD'S PASSOVER

"And thus shall you eat it; with your loins girded, your shoes on your feet, and your staff in your hand *(proclaims the fact that they were leaving Egypt; after the Law was given, and Israel was safely ensconced in the Promised Land, they were to eat the Passover resting, and for all the obvious reasons)***; and you shall eat it in haste** *(the same admonition, however, should hold true for the modern Believer, in that we should be eagerly awaiting the moment when the Trump of God shall sound and, thereby, we will be raptured away [I Thess. 4:13-18])***: it is the LORD's Passover.** *(Concerning this, Pink says, 'The Death of Christ glorified God if never a single sinner had been Saved by the virtue of it. The more we study the teaching of Scripture on* *this subject, and the more we lay hold by simple Faith of what the Cross meant to God, the more stable will be our peace, and the deeper our joy and praise.' The Passover was ever a type of the Cross. In I Cor. 5:7, we read, 'Christ our Passover.' He is now 'our' Passover, because He was first the 'LORD's Passover.')*

THE JUDGMENT

"For I will pass through the land of Egypt this night, and will smite all the firstborn in the land of Egypt, both man and beast; and against all the gods of Egypt I will execute judgment: I am the LORD. *(The words 'pass through' could be translated 'go through,' since the word used is entirely unconnected with the 'Passover.' According to Ex. 12:23, the Lord did not personally go through the land of Egypt that particular night, but rather that He used an Angel. The 'beasts' were included because animal worship was an important part of the religion of the Egyptians. So, the Lord directed His Judgment against every facet of Egyptian life and living.)*

WHEN I SEE THE BLOOD

"And the blood shall be to you for a token upon the houses where you are *(the blood applied to the door posts meant that their Faith and trust were in the Pascal Lamb; the blood then applied was only a 'token,' meaning that it was then but a symbol of One Who was to come, Who would redeem mankind by the shedding of His Life's Blood)***: and when I see the blood, I will pass over you** *(this is, without a doubt, one of the single most important Scriptures in the entirety of the Word of God; the lamb had taken the fatal blow; and because it had taken the blow, those in the house would be spared; it was not a question of personal worthiness, self had nothing whatever to do in the matter; it was* *a matter of Faith; all under the cover of the blood were safe, just as all presently under the cover of the Blood are safe; this means that they were not merely in a savable state, but rather that they were 'saved'; as well, they were not partly Saved and partly exposed to Judgment, they were wholly Saved, and because there is no such thing as partial Justification; the Lord didn't say, 'When I see you,' or, 'When I see your good works,' etc., but, 'When I see the blood'; this speaks of Christ and what He would do at the Cross in order that we might be Saved, which pertained to Him giving Himself in Sacrifice, which necessitated the shedding of His Precious Blood [I Pet. 1:18-19]),* **and the plague shall not be upon you to destroy you, when I smite the land of Egypt.** *(Salvation from the 'plague' of Judgment is afforded only by the shed Blood of the Lamb, and Faith in that shed Blood)"* **(Ex. 12:3-13).**

THE LAW OF GOD

The Law of God, at times referred to as the *"Law of Moses,"* could be said to be in three parts. They are:

1. The Ceremonial: this concerned itself with the sacrifices that were offered twice a day plus the many sacrifices that were offered daily by the people of Israel. It also concerned the Great Day of Atonement which came once a year.

2. The Ritual: this concerned the Feast days along with all the rituals performed by the Priests on a constant basis, such as trimming the lamps twice a day, offering up Incense on the Altar, etc. It also concerned itself with all laws that pertained to how man treated his fellowman.

3. The Moral: this basically pertained to the Ten Commandments.

Every facet of the Law, and I mean every part, pointed to Christ in His Atoning, Mediatorial, or Intercessory work, all on man's behalf.

THE BRAZEN ALTAR

While everything about the Law, as stated, was of immense significance, still, one might say that the *"Brazen Altar"* was the most important of all. This was where atonement was made for sin.

One might say that the Ark of the Covenant was more important. In essence, that is true; however, the High Priest on the Great Day of Atonement could not go into the Holy of Holies without the blood of the sacrifice, which was to be placed on the Mercy Seat. Of course, this came from the Brazen Altar. One might say, and be absolutely Scripturally correct, that the Ark of the Covenant was typical of the very Throne of God; however, the only way one can get to the Throne is by the Means of the slain lamb, which we will address elsewhere in this article.

Concerning the Brazen Altar, the Scripture says:

"**And you shall make an Altar** *(typified the Cross)* **of Shittim Wood** *(the Humanity of Christ)*, **five cubits long** *(seven and one-half feet long)*, **and five cubits broad; the Altar shall be four square** *(it is the same Gospel for all of mankind, whether north, south, east, or west)*: **and the height thereof shall be three cubits** *(four and one-half feet)*.

"**And you shall make the horns** *(speaks of total dominion over sin, which would be purchased at the Cross)* **of it upon the four corners thereof** *(signifying that Salvation is the same for all)*: **his horns shall be of the same: and you shall overlay it with brass.** *(This Altar of indestructible wood was to be 'overlaid with copper.' Until the metallurgy of the not-too-distant past, copper had a greater resistance to fire, even than gold or silver. It would consequently protect the wood, that it would not catch fire and be consumed. Pink says, 'The copper plates on the Altar protected it from the fervent heat and prevented it from being burned up; so Christ passed through the fires of God's wrath without being* consumed. *He is mighty to save, because He was mighty to endure')*" **(Ex. 27:1-2).**

MOSES AND THE MANNER OF DEATH

While the Lord gave to Abraham the fact that there must be the death of an innocent victim as it regards the coming Sacrifice, still, He did not tell Abraham as to how that death would be. As stated, that would be given to Moses.

Concerning the manner of death, which would pay the price for man's Redemption, the Scripture says:

"**And they journeyed from Mount Hor by the way of the Red Sea, to compass the land of Edom: and the soul of the people was much discouraged because of the way** *(the 'way' is not always easy, but this difficult way was their own doing; if their fathers had believed the Lord, they would have been in the Promised Land approximately thirty eight years before)*.

"**And the people spoke against God, and against Moses, Wherefore have you brought us up out of Egypt to die in the wilderness? For there is no bread, neither is there any water; and our soul loathes this light bread** *(hates the Manna. They had the same heart of rebellion as their fathers. Wherever the Believer finds himself, and no matter how difficult may seem the way at present, he must not complain. To do so presents a gross insult to the Lord, and for many and varied reasons. We should thank the Lord, and do so daily, irrespective of the circumstances. If the 'way' is hard, we should try to learn the lesson which the Lord is trying to teach us, and ask Him to deliver us. He will!)*.

THE FIERY SERPENTS

"**And the LORD sent fiery serpents among the people,**

and they bit the people; and much people of Israel died. *(It says that the 'LORD' sent these fiery serpents. Let all understand, everything which happens to a Believer, be it negative or positive, is either 'caused' by the Lord, or 'allowed' by the Lord. Believers belong to the Lord. As such, Satan can do nothing against us, unless the Lord allows it.)*

"Therefore the people came to Moses, and said, We have sinned, for we have spoken against the LORD, and against you; pray unto the LORD, that He take away the serpents from us. And Moses prayed for the people. *(This is the first and only recorded occasion on which the people directly ask for the intercession of Moses.)*

LOOK AND LIVE

"And the LORD said unto Moses, Make thee a fiery serpent, and set it upon a pole *(the 'serpent,' i.e., 'sin and Satan,' was the reason for the Cross, and the pole was a Type of the Cross)***: and it shall come to pass, that everyone who is bitten, when he looks upon it, shall live** *(everyone who looks to Christ and the Cross has the sentence of death abated and, therefore, shall 'live')***.**

"And Moses made a serpent of brass *(copper)***, and put it upon a pole and it came to pass, that if a serpent had bitten any man, when he beheld the serpent of brass, he lived.** *(Approximately four hundred years earlier, the Lord had shown, as stated, Abraham the manner of Salvation; it would be through the death of an innocent victim, namely the Son of God [Jn. 8:36]; it was to Moses, however, as recorded here, that the Lord proclaimed the way that the Son of God would die; it would be by the Cross, symbolized by the serpent on the pole)***" (Num. 21:4-9).**

THE PLAGUE WAS STAYED

When David became the king of Israel, he numbered Israel

without paying the half-shekel of silver demanded by the law. This stated that Israel's prosperity was anchored solely in the shed blood of the Lamb. In fact, in the manner of Atonement, all worshippers stood on one common ground — the slain lamb. David ignored, to his peril, this extremely important command of the Lord. As a result, a plague was sent by God upon Israel that resulted in the deaths of seventy thousand men (II Sam. 24:15).

To stop the plague, David was told by the Lord to build an Altar and offer sacrifices, and to do so at a certain place. It was the threshing floor of Araunah the Jebusite where, in fact, the coming Temple would be built. Concerning this the Scripture says:

> "And David built there an Altar unto the LORD, and offered Burnt Offerings and Peace Offerings. So the LORD was entreated for the land, and the plague was stayed from Israel. *(There is a 'plague' called 'sin' that is destroying this world, and causing multiple hundreds of millions to be eternally lost. There is only one cure for that plague, and that is the precious, atoning, Vicarious Offering of the Blood of the Lord Jesus Christ, which was done at the Cross, and our acceptance of Him. All the churches in the world will never stay the 'plague.' All the good works, good intentions, money, religion, prestige, or education will not stop this plague of sin. Only the precious Blood of Jesus Christ can, here symbolized by the 'Altar')"* **(II Sam. 24:25).**

THE DEDICATION OF THE TEMPLE

When the Temple was finished and Solomon dedicated it, it was done so on the merit, one might say, of the shed Blood of the Lamb, all typifying Christ. In fact, a staggering number of sacrifices were offered. The Scripture says:

> "And the king, and all Israel with him, offered sacrifice before the LORD *(proclaiming the fact that Israel's safety,*

protection, blessing, and prosperity depended solely upon the shed Blood of the Lamb).

"And Solomon offered a sacrifice of Peace Offerings, which he offered unto the LORD, two and twenty thousand oxen, and an hundred and twenty thousand sheep. So the king and all the Children of Israel dedicated the House of the LORD. *(The tremendous number of sacrifices offered typified the great Sacrifice of Christ. But yet, even though all these sheep and oxen were offered, they still were insufficient to take away sin. They only covered sin until Christ would come [Heb. 10:4], Who would take sin away [Jn. 1:29].)*

THE GREAT ALTAR

"The same day did the king hallow the middle of the Court that was before the House of the LORD: for there he offered Burnt Offerings, and Meat Offerings, and the fat of the Peace Offerings: because the Brazen Altar that was before the LORD was too little to receive the Burnt Offerings, and Meat Offerings, and the fat of the Peace Offerings. *(In fact, the great Altar was thirty feet wide and thirty feet long, actually the same size as the Holy of Holies, signifying that His Answer to sin, which is the Cross, is as great as His Throne, signified by the Holy of Holies. But yet, even the great Altar was too small to receive all the Offerings, so the entirety of the Court was used, at least for the slaughter. No doubt, this lasted for several days.)*

THE MEANING OF THE SACRIFICES

"And at that time Solomon held a feast, and all Israel with him, a great congregation, from the entering in of Hamath unto the river of Egypt, before the LORD our God, seven days and seven days, even fourteen days. *(All the people were required to eat their portion of the 'Peace Offerings,' which signified that 'Peace with God'*

had been restored, now that the proper Burnt Offer-ings had been sacrificed. The Burnt Offerings signified that the Lord would give His all, His Perfection, to the people. The Sin and Trespass Offerings signified that the people would give their sin and trespasses to the Lord)"
(**I Ki. 8:62-65**).

It took all of these different Offerings to symbolize the one Sacrifice of our Lord.

THE PROPHECY OF ISAIAH

The great Prophecy of Isaiah concerning the Crucifixion of Christ presents itself as so all-encompassing that it literally defies description.

Even though this great Fifty-third Chapter is quoted voluminously, especially considering all the notes from **THE EXPOSITOR'S STUDY BIBLE**, still, I think it would be most profitable to quote its entirety.

THE REVELATION OF THE LORD

"Who has believed our report? and to whom is the arm of the LORD revealed? *('Our report,' refers to this very Prophecy, as well as the other Messianic Prophecies delivered by Isaiah. To Israel was 'the arm of the LORD revealed.' And to Israel is ascribed the 'unbelief,' which destroyed them.*

"The Revelation of 'the arm of the LORD' requires the eye of Faith to see it. Unbelief can always assign the most plainly providential arrangements to happy accident. It takes Faith to believe the report that is revealed.)

THE INCARNATION

"For He shall grow up before Him as a tender plant,

and as a root out of dry ground: He has no form nor comeliness; and when we shall see Him, there is no beauty that we should desire Him. *(To God's Eye, Israel, and the entirety of the Earth for that matter, were a 'dry ground,' but that Eye rested with delight upon one tender plant which had a living root. It was Jesus!*

"The Hebrew verbs in these Verses [through Verse 7] are to be regarded as 'perfects of prophetic certitude.' This means that in the mind of God all has been finished before the foundation of the world and done so in the Divine Counsels [I Pet. 1:18-20].

"The words, 'Before Him,' mean 'before Jehovah' — under the fostering care of Jehovah. God the Father had His Eye fixed upon the Son with a watchfulness and tenderness and love.

"This 'sapling' from the house of David shall become the 'root' out of which His Church will grow. The Messiah will be a fresh sprout from the stump of a tree that had been felled, i.e., from the destroyed Davidic Monarchy.

"The words 'He has no form nor comeliness,' refer to the fact that He had none during His sufferings, but now He has it more than anyone else except the Father and the Holy Spirit [Eph. 1:20-23; Phil. 2:9-11; Col. 1:15-18; I Pet. 3:22].

"The words, 'There is no beauty that we should desire Him,' refer to His sufferings, which include His peasant upbringing and, as a consequence, His poverty, as well as His lack of association with the aristocracy!)

REJECTED

"He is despised and rejected of men; a man of sorrows, and acquainted with grief: and we hid as it were our faces from Him; He was despised, and we esteemed Him not. *(Him being 'rejected of men' means 'One from Whom men held themselves aloof.' Why? He was pure*

Holiness and they were pure corruption.

"'A man of sorrows,' refers to Jesus taking all the sorrows of humanity upon Himself.

"'Acquainted with grief,' actually refers to diseases and sicknesses, for that's what the word 'grief' in the Hebrew means.

"'And we hid as it were our faces from Him,' describes the treatment of the Servant by His fellowmen. Again, why? He was not the type of Messiah they wanted!

"'He was despised, and we esteemed Him not,' refers to the fact that the religious leadership of Israel esteemed Him not at all. He came to deliver men from sin, but that wasn't the type of deliverance they desired!)

SMITTEN OF GOD

"Surely He has borne our griefs, and carried our sorrows: yet we did esteem Him stricken, smitten of God, and afflicted. *(Twelve times within the space of nine Verses the Prophet asserts, with the most emphatic reiteration, that all the Servant's sufferings were vicarious; i.e., borne for man to save him from the consequences of his sins, to enable him to escape punishment. In other words, Jesus did this all for us.*

"'Yet we did esteem Him stricken, smitten of God, and afflicted,' proclaims the fact that because He died on a Cross, Israel assumed that He died under the curse of God, because Moses had said, 'For he who is hanged is accursed of God' [Deut. 21:23].

"What they did not understand was that He was not accursed, neither in Himself was cursed, but, in fact, was 'made a curse for us.'

"Israel assumed He was 'smitten of God,' and, in a sense, He was. He suffered in our stead, actually as our Substitute, which means that the blow that should have come to us instead went to Him. But yet, it was not for His sins,

because He had none, but instead was for our sins. He was 'afflicted' for us. As stated, He was our Substitute.)

WOUNDED FOR OUR TRANSGRESSIONS

"But He was wounded for our transgressions, He was bruised for our iniquities: the chastisement of our peace was upon Him; and with His stripes we are healed. *('He was wounded for our transgressions,' pertains to the manner in which He died, which was the price He paid for the Redemption of humanity.*

" 'He was bruised for our iniquities,' means that what He suffered was not at all for Himself, but all for us. It was for our iniquities. Look at the Cross, and then say, 'My sin did this.'

" 'The chastisement of our peace was upon Him,' means that if peace between God and man was to be restored, all which Adam lost, then Jesus would have to bring it about. Here is the simple doctrine of the Gospel — the Death of Christ. All other founders of religions base their claims upon their life and their teaching — their death was a calamity, and without significance. But the Death of Christ was His Glory, and forms the imperishable foundation of the one and only Salvation. His purpose in coming was to die.

" 'And with His stripes we are healed,' definitely pertains to physical healing, but is far greater in meaning than that. Its greater meaning refers to being healed of the terrible malady of sin.)

THE INIQUITY OF US ALL

"All we like sheep have gone astray; we have turned every one to his own way; and the LORD has laid on Him the iniquity of us all. *(Sheep without a shepherd get lost easily. Man, as sheep, has wandered from the right path;*

he has become so hopelessly lost that it is impossible for him, within his own means, to come back to the right path. Therefore, the Lord had to come from Heaven down to this wilderness called Earth and, thereby, seek and save man, who is lost.

"'We have turned everyone to his own way,' refers to the fact that the whole world, collectively and individually, has sinned and come short of the Glory of God. This 'erroneous way' has led to death, suffering, sorrow, heartache, loneliness, despair, and pain. This is the reason that everything that man touches dies! Whereas everything that God touches lives! So, man desperately needs God's touch, i.e., 'the Atonement of Calvary.'

"'And the LORD has laid on Him the iniquity of us all,' refers to the total price He paid for our total Salvation. The penalty for every sin for all of humanity and for all time was laid on Christ. God the Father, as the primary disposer of all things, lays upon the Son the burden which the Son voluntarily accepts. He comes into the world to do the Father's Will, and the Father's Will is to secure the Salvation of man, at least for those who will believe.)

AS A LAMB TO THE SLAUGHTER

"He was oppressed, and He was afflicted, yet He opened not His Mouth: He is brought as a lamb to the slaughter, and as a sheep before her shearers is dumb, so He opens not His Mouth. *(The first phrase refers to all that was done to Him in His humiliation, suffering, and agony. He could so easily have vindicated Himself from every charge; therefore, He self-abased Himself.*

"It seemed like an admission of guilt and, in fact, was, but not His guilt but the guilt of those who were accusing Him, as well as the entirety of the world.

"Of all the Levitical Offerings [five total], the 'lamb' was the animal most used; hence, John the Baptist would

say, *'Behold the Lamb of God, which takes away the sin of the world' [Jn. 1:29].)*

FOR THE TRANSGRESSION OF MY PEOPLE

"He was taken from prison and from judgment: and who shall declare His generation? For He was cut off out of the land of the living: for the transgression of My people was He stricken. *('He was taken from prison and from judgment,' refers to a violence which cloaked itself under the formalities of a legal process.*

" 'And who shall declare His generation,' refers to the fact of Him being 'cut off' [Dan. 9:26], which means that He would have no posterity.

" 'For the transgression of My people was He stricken,' can be summed up in what He suffered, and all on our behalf. This must never be forgotten: every single thing He suffered was not at all for Himself, or for Heaven in any capacity, but all for sinners.)

HE HAD DONE NO VIOLENCE

"And He made His grave with the wicked, and with the rich in His death; because He had done no violence, neither was any deceit in His mouth *('And He made His grave with the wicked,' means that He was appointed such by the religious hierarchy of Israel, but Joseph of Arimathea, a rich man, asked that Jesus be buried in his personal tomb instead, and so He was. 'Because He had done no violence, neither was any deceit in His mouth,' proclaims the sinlessness of Christ, and forms the main argument in the Epistle to the Hebrews for the superiority of the New Covenant over the old [Heb. 7:26-28; 9:14].*

"As no other man was ever without sin, it follows that the Servant of this present Chapter is, and can be no other than, Christ.)

AN OFFERING FOR SIN

"Yet it pleased the LORD to bruise Him; He has put Him to grief: when You shall make His soul an offering for sin, He shall see His seed, He shall prolong His days, and the pleasure of the LORD shall prosper in His Hand. *('Yet it pleased the LORD to bruise Him,' refers to the sufferings of Christ, which proceeded from the 'determinate counsel and foreknowledge of God' [Acts 2:23], and which, being permitted by Him, were in some way His doing. It 'pleased Him' moreover that they should be undergone, for the Father saw with satisfaction the Son's self-sacrifice, and He witnessed with joy man's Redemption and Deliverance effected thereby.*

"'He has put Him to grief,' actually says 'He has put Him to sicknesses' or 'He has made Him sick.' This spoke of the time He was on the Cross bearing our sins and 'sicknesses' [Mat. 8:16-17; I Pet. 2:24]. And yet, while all sin and sickness were atoned at the Cross, the total effects of such will not be completely dissipated until the coming Resurrection [Rom. 8:23].

"'When You shall make His soul an offering for sin,' is powerful indeed! The word 'Offering' in the Hebrew is 'Asham,' and means 'a Trespass Offering,' an 'Offering for sin.'

"Offerings for sin, or 'Guilt Offerings,' were distinct from 'Sin Offerings.' The object of the former was 'satisfaction'; of the latter, 'expiation.' The Servant of Jehovah, was, however, to be both. He was both the 'Sin Offering' and the 'Guilt Offering.')

THE JESUS DIED SPIRITUALLY THEORY

"This completely destroys the idea that Jesus died spiritually on the Cross, meaning that He became a sinner on the Cross, and died and went to Hell as all sinners,

and was born again in Hell after three days and nights of suffering, etc. None of that is in the Word of God. While Jesus definitely was a 'Sin Offering,' He was not a sinner, and did not become a sinner on the Cross. To have done so would have destroyed His Perfection of Sacrifice, which was demanded by God. In other words, the Sacrifice had to be perfect, and He was Perfect in every respect.

" 'He shall see His seed,' refers to all His 'true follow-ers,' which include all who have ever been Born-Again.

" 'He shall prolong His days,' refers to His Resurrection.

" 'And the pleasure of the LORD shall prosper in His Hand,' refers to the great victory that He would win at Calvary, which will ultimately restore everything that Adam lost.)

THE TRAVAIL OF HIS SOUL

"He shall see the travail of His soul, and shall be satisfied: by His knowledge shall My righteous Servant justify many; for He shall bear their iniquities. *(The 'travail of His soul' pertains to His Sacrifice for sin, which has resulted in the Restoration of man, at least for those who will believe.*

" 'And shall be satisfied,' refers to the fact that even though the price was high, actually beyond comprehension, still, it was worth the Redemption it accomplished.

"What Jesus did at the Cross made it possible for man to be fully and totally 'justified' in the Eyes of God, which comes about by man exhibiting Faith in Christ and what Christ did at the Cross.)

A PORTION WITH THE GREAT

"Therefore will I divide him a portion with the great, and He shall divide the spoil with the strong: because He has poured out His soul unto death: and He was

numbered with the transgressors; and He bore the sin of many, an made intercession for the transgressors. *(To be appointed with the great and to divide the spoil with the strong is figurative language expressive of full victory. It means here that Christ, by His Death, delivers from Satan mankind who was held captive.*

"'Because He has poured out His soul unto death,' means that Christ not only died for man, but, as it were, 'poured out His soul' with His Own Hand to the last drop. The expression emphasizes the duration and the voluntariness of the Messiah's sufferings. In other words, He laid down His Own Life and no man took it from Him [Jn. 10:18].

HE BORE THE SIN OF MANY

"'And He was numbered with the transgressors' refers to the actions of the Jews toward Him. He was crucified between two thieves. He was condemned as a 'blasphemer' [Mat. 26:65], crucified with malefactors [Lk. 23:32], called 'that deceiver' [Mat. 27:63], and regarded generally by the Jews as accursed [Deut. 21:23].

"'And He bore the sin of many, and made Intercession for the transgressors,' is, in the Hebrew, an act, though begun in the past, not yet completed. The 'Intercession for transgressors' was begun on the Cross with the compassionate words, 'Father, forgive them; for they know not what they do' [Lk. 23:34]. This Intercession for Believers has continued ever since and will ever continue [Rom. 8:34; Heb. 7:25]; such Intercession is made possible by what Christ did at the Cross)" **(Isa. 53:1-12).**

THE LORD JESUS CHRIST

All the Patriarchs of old pointed to Christ. As well, the Prophets, even as we have quoted some of them, pointed directly to Christ and what He would do to redeem humanity. As we

have stated, the Sacrificial system was given by God at the very
dawn of time in order that fallen man might have forgiveness
of sins and have communion with Him. Regrettably, few took
advantage of this most wonderful gift.

Yet, all of that, and we continue to speak of the Sacrificial
system, was meant to point to the reality that would come and
would fulfill all of these Promises and Predictions.

THE ACTUAL DEATH OF JESUS

While all four Gospels give an account of the price paid at
Calvary's Cross, to conserve space, we will quote Matthew.

"Now from the sixth hour *(12 Noon)* there was darkness over all the land until the ninth hour *(3 p.m. — for
these three hours, God would literally hide His Face from
His Son; during this time, Jesus did bear the sin penalty of
mankind [II Cor. 5:21].*

" *'This darkness' was not the result of an eclipse, for
then the moon was full; it was brought on by God in that He
could not look upon His Son as He did bear the sin penalty
of the world).*

"And about the ninth hour Jesus cried with a loud
voice *(showing He didn't die from weakness, but rather laid
down His Own Life [Jn. 10:17-18])*, **saying, Eli, Eli, Lama
Sabachthani? That is to say, My God, My God, why
have You forsaken Me?** *(The question as to why God had
forsaken Him was not asked in a sense of not knowing, but
in a sense of acknowledging the act. God didn't deliver Him,
even as He always had, because, to have done such, would
have forfeited Redemption for mankind. Incidentally, Jesus
spoke in Aramaic, which was commonly used by the Lord.)*

THE RESPONSE OF THE MOCKERS

"Some of them who stood there, when they heard

that, said, This *man* calls for Elijah *(this would have referred to Jews, because Romans would have known nothing about Elijah)*.

"And straightway *(immediately)* one of them ran, and took a sponge, and filled *it* with vinegar, and put *it* on a reed, and gave Him to drink *(the evidence is, it touched His lips, and He died; it had nothing to do with His Life or Death)*.

"The rest said, Let be, let us see whether Elijah will come to save Him *(said in mockery!)*.

"Jesus, when He had cried again with a loud voice, yielded up the ghost *(He freely laid down His Life, meaning that He didn't die from His wounds; as well, He didn't die until the Holy Spirit told Him to do so [Heb. 9:14])*.

THE VEIL OF THE TEMPLE

"And, behold, the Veil of the Temple *(that which hid the Holy of Holies; Josephus said it was sixty feet high from the ceiling to the floor, four inches thick, and was so strong, that four yolk of oxen could not pull it apart)* was rent in twain from the top to the bottom *(meaning that God alone could have done such a thing; it also signified that the price was paid completely on the Cross; signified by the rent Veil; regrettably, some say, the Cross didn't finish the task with other things required; this Verse says differently)*; and the earth did quake, and the rocks rent *(represented an earthquake, but had nothing to do with the renting of the Veil, which took place immediately before this phenomenon)*;

PARADISE WAS EMPTIED

"And the graves were opened; and many bodies of the Saints which slept arose *(does not teach 'soul sleep' as some claim, but rather that the bodies of the Sainted dead do sleep; not the soul and the spirit, which then went to*

Paradise, but since the Cross, at death, now go to be with Christ [Phil. 1:23]),

"**And came out of the graves after His Resurrection, and went into the Holy City** *(Jerusalem)*, **and appeared unto many** *(while all were delivered out of Paradise, and taken to Heaven, some, even many, stopped over in Jerusalem for a short period of time, 'and appeared unto many'; how many there were, we aren't told, and to whom they appeared, we aren't told; Matthew alone gives this account).*

THE FIRST GENTILE AFTER THE DEATH OF CHRIST TO RENDER A TESTIMONY OF FAITH

"**Now when the Centurion, and they who were with him, watching Jesus, saw the earthquake, and those things that were done, they feared greatly, saying, Truly this was the Son of God** *(he was the first Gentile to render this testimony of Faith; tradition affirms that the Centurion's name was Longinus, and that he became a devoted follower of Christ, preached the Faith, and died a martyr's death).*

"**And many women were there beholding afar off, which followed Jesus from Galilee, ministering unto him** *(concerns those who came from Galilee, and were with Him unto the end)*:

"**Among which was Mary Magdalene** *(Jesus had delivered her [Mk. 16:9; Lk. 8:2])*, **and Mary the mother of James and Joseph** *(probably the wife of Cleophas [Jn. 19:25])*, **and the mother of Zebedee's children.** *(Salome [Mk. 15:40] the mother of James and John)*" **(Mat. 27:45-56).**

THE RESURRECTION OF CHRIST

The Resurrection of Christ, the Ascension of Christ, and the

Exaltation of Christ were, as should be obvious, of tremendous significance; however, those great happenings were not because of Redemption, but rather the results of Redemption afforded at the Cross of Christ.

THE RESURRECTION OF CHRIST

Despite the fact that Jesus had oftentimes told His Disciples that the Religious leaders of Israel would kill Him and that He would rise from the dead on the third day, still, none believed Him. In fact, there doesn't seem to be a single individual who believed that He would rise from the dead after they witnessed His Death at Calvary, at least, the part they saw. Nevertheless, He did!

The Scripture says:

"In the end of the Sabbath *(the regular weekly Sabbath, which was every Saturday)*, as it began to dawn toward the first *day* of the week *(this was just before daylight on Sunday morning; Jesus rose from the dead some time after sunset on Saturday evening; the Jews began the new day at sunset, instead of midnight, as we do presently)*, came Mary Magdalene and the other Mary to see the sepulcher *(they wanted to put spices on the Body of Christ)*.

"And, behold, there was a great earthquake *(presents the second earthquake, with the first taking place when Christ died [Mat. 27:51])*: for the Angel of the Lord descended from Heaven *(was probably observed by the Roman soldiers, who alone witnessed it and gave the account)*, and came and rolled back the stone from the door *(Christ had already risen from the dead and had left the Tomb when the stone was rolled away; His glorified Body was not restricted by obstacles)*, and sat upon it *(this was done as a show of triumph; in other words, death was vanquished!)*:

THE ANGEL

"**His countenance was like lightning, and his raiment white as snow** *(there is no evidence that any of the women or Disciples saw this glorious coming of the Angel; however, the next Verse tells us that the Roman guards did see it, and were terrified!)*:

"**And for fear of Him** *(the Angel)* **the keepers** *(guards)* **did shake, and became as dead** *men* *(inasmuch as this happened at night, the situation was even more frightful)*.

"**And the Angel answered and said unto the women** *(this was just before dawn and after the soldiers had run away)*, **Do not fear: for I know that you seek Jesus, who was crucified** *(the Angel now uses this word, 'Crucified,' in a most glorious manner; it is now 'the Power of God and the Wisdom of God' [I Cor. 1:23-24])*.

INSTRUCTIONS GIVEN BY THE ANGEL

"**He is not here** *(is the beginning of the most glorious statement that could ever fall upon the ears of mere mortals)*: **for He is risen** *(a dead and risen Saviour is the life and substance of the Gospel [I Cor. 15:1-4])*, **as He said** *(the Angel brought to the attention of the women, the fact that Christ had stated several times that He would be crucified and would rise from the dead)*. **Come, see the place where the Lord lay** *(they were looking for a corpse, but instead, would find a risen Lord; they were looking for a Tomb containing a corpse, but instead, would find it empty)*.

"**And go quickly, and tell His Disciples that He is risen from the dead** *(the Disciples should have been the ones telling others, but because of unbelief, the women will tell them; this is the greatest Message that humanity has ever received)*; **and, behold, He goes before you into Galilee; there shall you see Him** *(He would reveal Himself to whom and to where He so desired)*: **lo, I have told you** *(guarantees the certitude of this action)*" **(Mat. 28:1-7).**

THE REVELATION OF THE CROSS
WAS GIVEN TO PAUL

After the Crucifixion and Resurrection of Christ, the Apostles, by and large, preached the Resurrection. They were, in a sense, shouting it from the housetops that Jesus had risen from the dead, and rightly so!

As it regards the Cross of Christ, they had no knowledge as to what that meant for that Revelation had not yet been given. In fact, it would be given to the Apostle Paul. He said:

"**But I certify you, Brethren** *(make known)*, **that the Gospel which was preached of me** *(the Message of the Cross)* **is not after man.** *(Any Message other than the Cross is definitely devised by man.)*

"**For I neither received it of man** *(Paul had not learned this great Truth from human Teachers)*, **neither was I taught** *it* *(he denies instruction from other men)*, **but by the Revelation of Jesus Christ.** *(Revelation is the mighty Act of God whereby the Holy Spirit discloses to the human mind that which could not be understood without Divine Intervention)*" **(Gal. 1:11-12).**

In fact, the Revelation of the Cross of Christ was, in effect, the meaning of the New Covenant. If so desired, one could turn it around and say, *"The meaning of the New Covenant is the meaning of the Cross of Christ."*

As stated, this great Truth, this great Revelation, was given to the Apostle Paul, which he gave to us in his fourteen Epistles, that is, if he wrote the Book of Hebrews, which I believe he did.

In giving us the meaning of the Crucifixion and what it means to us, which is the greatest Truth ever known or heard by man, He said:

CRUCIFIED WITH HIM

"Know you not, that so many of us as were baptized into Jesus Christ *(plainly says that this Baptism is into Christ and not water [I Cor. 1:17; 12:13; Gal. 3:27; Eph. 4:5; Col. 2:11-13])* **were baptized into His Death?** *(When Christ died on the Cross, in the Mind of God, we died with Him; in other words, He became our Substitute, and our identification with Him in His Death gives us all the benefits for which He died; the idea is that He did it all for us!)*

WE WERE BURIED WITH HIM

"Therefore we are buried with Him by Baptism into death *(not only did we die with Him, but we were buried with Him as well, which means that all the sin and transgression of the past were buried; when they put Him in the Tomb, they put all of our sins into that Tomb as well)*:

WE WERE RAISED WITH HIM AS WELL

"That like as Christ was raised up from the dead by the Glory of the Father, even so we also should walk in newness of life *(we died with Him, we were buried with Him, and His Resurrection was our Resurrection to a 'Newness of Life').*

THE LIKENESS OF HIS DEATH AND THE LIKENESS OF HIS RESURRECTION

"For if we have been planted together *(with Christ)* **in the likeness of His Death** *(Paul proclaims the Cross as the instrument through which all Blessings come; consequently, the Cross must ever be the Object of our Faith, which gives the Holy Spirit latitude to work within our lives)*, **we shall be also** *in the likeness* **of** *His* **Resurrection.** *(We can have* the 'likeness of His Resurrection,' i.e., 'live this Resurrection Life,' only as long as we understand the 'likeness of His Death,' which refers to the Cross as the means by which all of this is done)" **(Rom. 6:3-5).**

THE LAW OF THE SPIRIT
OF LIFE IN CHRIST JESUS

We find from Paul's writings that the Holy Spirit works entirely within the parameters of the Finished Work of Christ. In fact, He will work in no other manner. Paul said:

"For the Law *(that which we are about to give is a Law of God, devised by the Godhead in eternity past [I Pet. 1:18-20]; this Law, in fact, is 'God's Prescribed Order of Victory')* **of the Spirit** *(Holy Spirit, i.e., 'the way the Spirit works')* **of Life** *(all life comes from Christ, but through the Holy Spirit [Jn. 16:13-14])* **in Christ Jesus** *(any time Paul uses this term or one of its derivatives, he is, without fail, referring to what Christ did at the Cross, which makes this 'life' possible)* **has made me free** *(given me total Victory)* **from the Law of Sin and Death.** *(These are the two most powerful Laws in the Universe; the 'Law of the Spirit of Life in Christ Jesus' alone is stronger than the 'Law of Sin and Death'; this means that if the Believer attempts to live for God by any manner other than Faith in Christ and the Cross, he is doomed to failure)"* **(Rom. 8:2).**

THE MEANING OF THE GOSPEL

The great Apostle also said:

"For Christ sent me not to baptize *(presents to us a Cardinal Truth)***, but to preach the Gospel** *(the manner in which one may be Saved from sin)***: not with wisdom of words** *(intellectualism is not the Gospel)***, lest the Cross**

of Christ should be made of none effect. *(This tells us in no uncertain terms that the Cross of Christ must always be the emphasis of the Message)*" **(I Cor. 1:17).**

THE POWER OF GOD

Paul also tells us what the Power of God actually is, which is needed desperately by every Believer. He said:

"**For the preaching** *(Message)* **of the Cross is to them who perish foolishness** *(Spiritual things cannot be discerned by unredeemed people, but that doesn't matter; the Cross must be preached just the same, even as we shall see)*; **but unto us who are Saved it is the Power of God.** *(The Cross is the Power of God simply because it was there that the total sin debt was paid, giving the Holy Spirit, in Whom the Power resides, latitude to work mightily within our lives)*" **(I Cor. 1:18).**

In these few short words, we are told here as to how the Power of God works. It is by the preaching of the Cross, which tells us how the Holy Spirit works. The Holy Spirit doesn't demand much of us, but He does demand that our Faith be exclusively in the Cross of Christ and maintained exclusively in the Cross of Christ. Then, He will work mightily on our behalf, doing what He Alone can do. In fact, it is impossible for the Believer to live a victorious life without understanding the Message of the Cross and abiding therein.

THE ONLY WAY IS THE CROSS OF CHRIST

The great Apostle went on to say to the Church at Corinth:

"**And I, Brethren, when I came to you, came not with excellency of speech or of wisdom** *(means that he depended not on oratorical abilities, nor did he delve into* *philosophy, which was all the rage of that particular day)*, **declaring unto you the Testimony of God** *(which is Christ and Him Crucified)*.

"**For I determined not to know any thing among you** *(with purpose and design, Paul did not resort to the knowledge or philosophy of the world regarding the preaching of the Gospel)*, **save Jesus Christ, and Him Crucified.** *(That and that alone is the Message which will save the sinner, set the captive free, and give the Believer perpetual victory)*" **(I Cor. 2:1-2).**

OVERCOMING THE WORLD, THE FLESH, AND THE DEVIL

The Apostle said:

"**But God forbid that I should glory** *(boast)*, **save in the Cross of our Lord Jesus Christ** *(what the opponents of Paul sought to escape at the price of insincerity is the Apostle's only basis of exultation)*, **by Whom the world is crucified unto me, and I unto the world.** *(The only way we can overcome the world, and I mean the only way, is by placing our Faith exclusively in the Cross of Christ and keeping it there)*" **(Gal. 6:14).**

VICTORY OVER SATAN

The Apostle then said:

"**Blotting out the handwriting of Ordinances that was against us** *(pertains to the Law of Moses, which was God's Standard of Righteousness that man could not reach)*, **which was contrary to us** *(Law is against us, simply because we are unable to keep its precepts, no matter how hard we try)*, **and took it out of the way** *(refers to the penalty of the Law being removed)*, **nailing it to His Cross** *(the Law with its decrees was abolished in Christ's Death, as if Crucified with Him)*;

"*And* **having spoiled principalities and powers** *(Satan and all of his henchmen were defeated at the Cross by Christ Atoning for all sin; sin was the legal right Satan had to hold man in captivity; with all sin atoned, he has no more legal right to hold anyone in bondage)*, **He** *(Christ)* **made a show of them openly** *(what Jesus did at the Cross was in the face of the whole universe)*, **triumphing over them in it.** *(This triumph is complete and it was all done for us, meaning we can walk in power and perpetual victory due to the Cross)*" **(Col. 2:14-15).**

I think by now it is obvious that Paul preached the Cross. That was his Message and his Message alone!

THE VISION OF JOHN THE BELOVED OF THE THRONE OF GOD

In John's great Vision of the Throne of God, he gives us even greater insight into the Cross of Christ. This is what he said:

"**And one of the Elders said unto me, Weep not** *(states that man's dilemma has been solved)*: **behold, the Lion of the Tribe of Judah, the Root of David, has prevailed to open the Book, and to loose the Seven Seals thereof** *(presents Jesus Christ).*

"**And I beheld, and, lo, in the midst of the Throne and of the four Beasts, and in the midst of the Elders, stood a Lamb as it had been slain** *(the Crucifixion of Christ is represented here by the word 'Lamb,' which refers to the fact that it was the Cross which redeemed mankind; the slain Lamb Alone has Redeemed all things)*, **having seven horns** *(horns denote dominion, and 'seven' denotes total dominion; all of this was done for you and me,* *meaning that we can have total dominion over the powers of darkness, and in every capacity; so there is no excuse for a lack of victory)* **and seven eyes** *(denotes total, perfect, pure, and complete illumination of all things spiritual, which is again made possible for you and me by the Cross; if the Believer makes the Cross the Object of his Faith, he will never be drawn away by false doctrine)***, which are the Seven Spirits of God sent forth into all the Earth.** *(Signifying that the Holy Spirit, in all His Perfection and universality, functions entirely within the parameters of the Finished Work of Christ; in other words, it is required that we ever make the Cross the Object of our Faith, which gives the Holy Spirit latitude, and guarantees the 'dominion,' and the 'illumination' [Isa. 11:2; Rom. 8:2])"* **(Rev. 5:5-6).**

THE NEW HEAVENS AND THE NEW EARTH

In the last two Chapters of Revelation we find the New Heaven and the New Earth, meaning that Satan is no more, with all of his demons and fallen Angels locked away in the Lake of Fire forever. In fact, there is no more sin in the Universe, meaning that the totality of the Cross of Christ has now taken effect.

Seven times in Chapters Twenty-one and Twenty-two, which denote this Perfect Age to come, John the Beloved uses the name *'Lamb,'* as it regards the Lord Jesus Christ (21:9, 14, 22-23, 27; 22:1, 3).

Why did the Holy Spirit choose the name *"Lamb,"* referring to the Son of God, in these two Chapters?

Of course, we know that the word *"Lamb,"* as used here, refers to our Lord, but, more particularly, refers to what He did at Calvary's Cross.

So, why bring up the Cross at this particular time when all sin is forever gone and will never be enacted again?

The reason is this:

IT IS THE CROSS OF CHRIST WHICH WILL
MAKE THE PERFECT AGE POSSIBLE

What Jesus did at the Cross not only addressed itself to the Fall of man, but, also the revolution engaged by Lucifer against God, which is the cause of all of this pain and suffering. This means that the Cross of Christ, in essence, what He did there, has far greater import than any of us realize. In fact, it is impossible for us to fully comprehend the value, the worth, and, yes, the glory of that event. The New Heaven and the New Earth are the result of the Cross.

In fact, this Covenant is so perfect, so without fault, so without error, that the Apostle Paul referred to it as *"the Blood of the Everlasting Covenant"* (Heb. 13:20), which means that it will never have to be amended, will never wear out, will never need replacing, because it is all in Christ.

I think that when one understands the Bible as one should understand the Bible, it becomes obvious that the Story of this Book is the Story of *"Jesus Christ and Him Crucified."*

"Thrice blessed Spirit! Giver of Salvation,
"Purchased by Jesus on the Cross of shame;
"Dwell in our hearts; transform them with Your Beauty,
"Fairest adorning of our Saviour's dear Name."

"Your sevenfold Grace bestow upon us freely:
"Love, deep and full, to God and all mankind;
"Joy in the Lord, mid every earthly sorrow;
"Peace, calm and sweet, that guards heart and mind."

"Make us long-suffering, mid earth's provocations,
"Gentleness give us, when enduring wrong;
"Goodness impart, that we e'en foes may succour;
"Faithfulness grant, to change our toil to song."

"Meekness bestow, with humble self-abasement,

"And self-control, through Your controlling Mights:
"And as we list to every call of duty,
"May we do all as in Your searching Sight."

"Then with the gift of Holiness within us;
"We not less human, but made more Divine;
"Our lives replete with Heaven's supernal beauty,
"Ever declare that beauty, Lord, is Thine."

CHAPTER TWENTY-ONE

Why Is The Great Truth Of The Cross Of Christ Greatly Ignored Or Even Rejected?

QUESTION:

WHY IS THE GREAT TRUTH OF THE CROSS OF CHRIST GREATLY IGNORED OR EVEN REJECTED?

ANSWER:

The major reason is unbelief!

IGNORANCE?

When the Lord in 1997 first began to open up this great Truth to me, and that was after some six years of two prayer meetings a day, to say I was elated would be a gross understatement. With the understanding of the Cross, many pieces began to fall into place. The understanding of failure, as it regards the Believer, comes into view. The understanding as to how the Holy Spirit works, which is a phenomenal truth, was then made obvious. In other words, my whole world changed, and in every respect.

To be sure, what the Lord had given me was not something new, not at all! It was what had originally been given to the Apostle Paul, and he gave it to us in his fourteen Epistles.

THE TEACHING GIVEN BY PAUL IS NOT ALTOGETHER EASY TO UNDERSTAND

I would say, and I think I am correct, that what the Lord gave to Paul is very, very difficult to understand. Peter, himself, under the inspiration of the Holy Spirit also said the same thing.

"Wherefore, beloved, seeing that you look for such things *(if one believes the Bible, one will believe its account of Endtime events)*, be diligent that you may be found of Him in Peace, without spot, and blameless *(which can be done only by the Believer ever making the Cross the Object of his Faith).*

"**And account *that* the longsuffering of our Lord is Salvation** *(His longsuffering, which refers to this Day of Grace that has now lasted longer than any other Dispensation, is in order to bring the unredeemed to Himself)*; **even as our beloved Brother Paul also according to the wisdom given unto him has written unto you** *(doesn't say which Epistle, but probably refers to Hebrews)*;

"**As also in all *his* Epistles, speaking in them of these things** *(proclaims the fact that Paul's Epistles are inspired)*; **in which are some things hard to be understood** *(could refer to Prophecy, or to the great teaching Paul gave on the Cross)*, **which they that are unlearned and unstable wrest, as *they do* also the other Scriptures, unto their own destruction.** *(This presents the fact that some Christians purposely twist the Scriptures, attempting to make them mean something the Holy Spirit never intended.)*

THE ERROR OF THE WICKED

"**You therefore, beloved, seeing you know these *things* before** *(the Holy Spirit, through Peter, tells those to whom the Apostle was writing that they were not without understanding regarding what was being taught)*, **beware lest you also, being led away with the error of the wicked** *(refers to being led away from the Cross)*, **fall from your own steadfastness** *(refers here to the proper application of one's Faith; the Cross of Christ must always be the Object of the Saint's Faith; if we shift our Faith to anything else, we 'fall' [Gal. 5:4])*.

"**But grow in Grace** *(presents the only way the Saint can grow)*, **and *in* the knowledge of our Lord and Saviour Jesus Christ.** *(This 'knowledge' refers not only to Who Christ is [the Lord of Glory] but, as well,* *what He did in order that we might be Redeemed, which points to the Cross.)* **To Him** *be* **Glory both now and forever. Amen.** *(This refers to such belonging to Him, because He is the One Who paid the price for man's Redemption)*" **(II Pet. 3:14-18).**

WHY IS WHAT PAUL TAUGHT ABOUT THE CROSS DIFFICULT TO UNDERSTAND?

It is difficult simply because that which the Lord gave to Paul proclaims the Holy Spirit bringing us from *"walking after the flesh"* to *"walking after the Spirit"* (Rom. 8:1, 3-5, 8-9).

"Walking after the flesh" comes naturally to us as human beings. So, to transfer our thinking, our actions, in fact, all that we do, to *"walking after the Spirit"* is not something that is done quickly or easily. Part of the reason it's so difficult is because of a lack of understanding as it regards these great truths.

In fact, unless the Believer is privileged to have a teacher who understands the Message of the Cross, it is highly unlikely that he would ever begin to understand what Paul taught.

THE MEDIA

When the Lord in 1997 began to open up to me the Message of the Cross, this which we are teaching you, I immediately began to teach it over Radio and Television, plus in written form in our publications. As it regards teaching over the media, I taught the subject for several weeks and then went to something else, as one normally would. Every time, I would come back to the Message of the Cross.

After this happened several times, I was leaving my office to go to the Radio Studio for our morning program, *"A Study In The Word"*, when the moment I walked out the door to get in the car, the Spirit of the Lord came on me. The Lord spoke forcibly to my heart saying, *"I want you to teach this subject of the Cross without stopping until I tell you otherwise."* And, then He said to me, *"Now, are you going to do what I want you to do?"*

What the Lord spoke to my heart, as stated, was so forceful that it scared me. I made the consecration immediately that I would begin to teach this great Word of the Cross and I would not stop until the Lord said otherwise. That's been twelve years ago at the time of this dictation and the Lord has given me no instructions to stop yet, except for a very short period of time to deal with the Holy Spirit and Prophecy, etc.

The more that one learns about this great subject of the Cross, the more that one begins to realize that it covers every aspect of Biblical instruction. In other words, if one properly teaches the Cross, one will, as well, teach every other subject in the Bible because they are all interlaced, so to speak.

ELATION!

When the Lord first began to open this up to me, knowing that the church as a whole had no understanding whatsoever of this great subject, which is the cause of so many problems, I foolishly thought that instantly the response would be very positive.

While I was certainly correct that there was much ignorance as it regards this great subject, still, the response was totally opposite as to what I thought it would be. There was outright opposition in some circles, but, mostly we were just ignored.

While it is true that the church was and is ignorant of this great subject, still, I found to my dismay that it is a *"wilful ignorance."* In other words, the church as a whole doesn't know this great Truth, which, as stated, is anything but new, but, has no desire to know. That's a different type of ignorance, which translates into unbelief.

However, at the time of this writing, May of 2009, more and more preachers are beginning to understand what we're saying and are desiring to hear more. In fact, many of these preachers, and more are being added constantly, are as versed in this great subject as I am or as any of my Associates, for which we thank the Lord. But, as a whole, the problem of unbelief still reigns.

UNBELIEF

Unbelief is a problem that has prevailed from day one. For instance, the religious leaders of Israel did not believe that Jesus was their Messiah, even though He fulfilled the Scriptures in totality. Their unbelief was without reason, which characterizes most unbelief.

As another example, untold millions presently, despite every type of evidence to the contrary, don't believe in the Baptism with the Holy Spirit with the evidence of speaking with other Tongues. Millions fall into the same category as it regards the Rapture. They simply don't believe that it will happen. And, as it regards the Message of the Cross, even though it is unmistakably the Word of God, which with a little investigation could be easily ascertained, unbelief doesn't bother to investigate.

WHAT THE SPIRIT IS SAYING TO THE CHURCHES

In the seven Messages proclaimed by our Lord to the seven Churches of Asia, which, in effect, characterized the entire Church Age, Jesus basically closed each Message with the words, *"He who has an ear, let him hear what the Spirit says unto the churches"* (Rev. 2:7, 11, 17, 29; 3:6, 13, 22). In fact, many Scholars believe that the Laodicean church pictures the modern church. At any rate, it closes with the words, *"He who has an ear, let him hear what the Spirit says unto the churches."*

I firmly believe that the *"Message of the Cross"* is *"what the Spirit is presently saying to the modern church."* If that is the case, then this Message takes on a brand-new complexion. While anything from the Lord is of supreme significance, still, when emphasis is placed on anything by the Holy Spirit, everything changes.

It is terribly debilitating to reject anything that is given by the Lord, irrespective as to what it is; however, if what is being rejected is His primary Thrust, the situation then becomes critical. Let me give a Biblical example.

ANOTHER GOSPEL

When Paul or his associates founded the churches in Galatia, a tremendous work for God was carried out, as should be obvious. After stabilizing these churches, the Apostle was called to other fields of endeavor.

After he had gone elsewhere, interlopers came in with the so-called gospel of Law. These were Jews either from Jerusalem or Judea. They professed to believe in Christ, even to the fact that He was the Messiah of Israel, but, in fact, they were enemies of the Cross. They were preaching Law, meaning that all the men and the boys had to be circumcised, that is, if they were to be a complete Believer. In fact, that's at least one of the reasons that Paul told the Believers in the church in Colosse that, *"you are complete in Him, Who is the Head of all principality and power"* (Col. 2:10).

The Apostle told the Galatians, *"If you be circumcised, Christ shall profit you nothing."* He then said, *"Christ is become of no effect unto you, whosoever of you are justified by the Law; you are fallen from Grace"* (Gal. 5:2, 4).

He wrote these things to them after he had already written, *"But though we, or an Angel from Heaven, preach any other gospel unto you than that which we have preached unto you, let him be accursed"* (Gal. 1:8).

The Word, which the Lord had given to Paul was the meaning of the New Covenant and was the Message of *"Grace, Faith, and Righteousness."* It was all centered up in the Cross, hence, the great Apostle saying, *"Christ sent me not to baptize, but to preach the Gospel: not with wisdom of words, lest the Cross of Christ should be made of none effect"* (I Cor. 1:17).

Paul did not write these things because he had a wounded ego. He wrote them because the Holy Spirit told him to say these exact words and, as well, through these statements, and especially

Galatians 1:8, we are told how serious the matter was and is.

The problem in the Early Church was *"another gospel,"* which tried to take the place of the Cross and, as well, the problem presently is *"another gospel."* In one sense of the word, the situation is worse presently than it was even in Paul's day.

That means that if this Message of the Cross is rejected, the same pronouncement is made that was made by Paul, *"let him be accursed."*

Let it be understood, the Message of the Cross is not something new or is it optional. It's what was given to the Apostle Paul and, in reality, is the meaning of the New Covenant. It is the Gospel (1 Cor. 1:17-18, 23; 2:2).

PRIDE

The problem of pride is far larger in things of this nature than most people realize. To give an example, one of the leaders in a particular Pentecostal denomination made the statement that if Revival came, it would come in their denomination. In other words, he was saying, whatever happened in other denominations was of little consequence, if any at all. Pure and simple, that is pride. Many preachers, as well, are loath to admit that there is something respecting the Gospel that they don't know.

A PERSONAL EXPERIENCE

Some time back, one of my associates and I were speaking with another preacher. He pastored a quite large church and was a very able individual. We were discussing the Message of the Cross. I was startled at his answer.

He said, in essence, *"This Message is, no doubt, necessary for some, but all of us don't need it."*

I don't think I've ever heard a more ridiculous answer than that.

In other words, he was stating that some Christians were very weak; therefore, they needed the Message of the Cross, but, people such as himself were more mature than having need of the simple Message of the Cross.

The tragedy is the dear brother was ridiculing the very thing that could have Saved him. A short time after that conversation, he was found to be having a tremendous problem in his life, which destroyed his ministry and wrecked the church. Nevertheless, there are many, many preachers who feel the same way. They are too proud to admit their need for what the Lord has prepared for them.

THE MESSAGE OF THE CROSS

The Message of the Cross as designed by the Lord, and I might quickly add, *"foreordained before the foundation of the world,"* is an absolute necessity for every single Believer. In fact, as it regards the unsaved, every single person who has made things right with God, and down through the many, many centuries, even from the dawn of time, has been Saved as a result of what Jesus did at the Cross. Every single Believer has enjoyed the Blessings of God, and all because of the Cross. Everything the dear brother had from the Lord, which we have just mentioned, had been made available to him because of the Cross of Christ. As we've said over and over, the Lord Jesus is the Source of all things we receive from God, while the Cross is the Means by which these things are given. It is our Faith in that Finished Work that enables us to receive what has been given, and it is our Faith alone. So, when anyone ignores or rejects the Message of the Cross, they have rejected the only means through which the things of God come to us.

ENEMIES OF THE CROSS

Paul said:

"Brethren, be followers together of me *(be 'fellow-imitators')*, and mark them which walk so as you have us for an example *(observe intently).*

"**(For many walk** *(speaks of those attempting to live for God outside of the Victory and rudiments of the Cross of Christ)*, **of whom I have told you often, and now tell you even weeping** *(this is a most serious matter)*, *that they are* **the enemies of the Cross of Christ** *(those who do not look exclusively to the Cross of Christ must be labeled 'enemies')*:

"**Whose end** *is* **destruction** *(if the Cross is ignored, and continues to be ignored, the loss of the soul is the only ultimate conclusion)*, **whose God** *is their* **belly** *(refers to those who attempt to pervert the Gospel for their own personal gain)*, **and** *whose* **glory** *is* **in their shame** *(the material things they seek, God labels as 'shame')*, **who mind earthly things.)** *(This means they have no interest in heavenly things, which signifies they are using the Lord for their own personal gain)*" **(Phil. 3:17-19).**

"Make me a captive, Lord, And then I shall be free;
"Force me to render up my sword, And I shall conqueror be.
"I sink in life's alarms, When by myself I stand;
"Imprison me within Your Arms, And strong shall be my
*   hand."*

"My heart is weak and poor, Until You it master find:
"It has no spring of action sure, It varies with the wind,
"It cannot freely move, Till You have wrought its chain,
"Enslave it with Your matchless Love, And deathless it
*   shall reign."*

"My power is faint and low, Till I have learned to serve:
"It wants the needed fire to glow, It wants the breeze to
*   nerve;*
"It cannot drive the world, Until You itself be driven;
"Its flag can only be unfurled, When You shall breathe
*   from Heaven."*

"My will is not my own, Till You have made it Thine;
"If it would reach the Monarch's Throne, It must its
    crown resign:
"It only stands unbent, Amid the clashing strife,
"When on Your bosom it has leant, And found in You its
    life."

CHAPTER TWENTY-TWO

How Does Christ Intercede For The Saints?

QUESTION:

HOW DOES CHRIST INTERCEDE FOR THE SAINTS?

ANSWER:

The Presence of Christ at the Throne of God, which means that God accepted His Sacrifice, proclaims the Intercession of Christ on our behalf and guarantees its veracity.

ENTIRE SANCTIFICATION?

There is a particular doctrine referred to as *"entire sancti-fication,"* which, in a sense, teaches that a person can come to a particular place in the Lord to where they will not again sin. The Bible does not teach such.

This doctrine, in effect, teaches that one is Saved; and then, secondly, they are sanctified; and then, thirdly, they are baptized with the Holy Spirit.

The Bible teaches that Sanctification is an instant work and, at the same time, a progressive work. Let me explain:

The moment any believing sinner comes to Christ, at that moment they are totally, completely, absolutely sanctified. In effect, and to be brief, the word *"Sanctification"* means *"to be made clean."* Justification means *"to be declared clean."* Of course, one has to be made clean before one can be declared clean. The Scripture says:

"Do you not know that the unrighteous shall not inherit the Kingdom of God? *(This shoots down the unscriptural doctrine of Unconditional Eternal Security.)* Be not deceived *(presents the same words of our Lord, 'let no man deceive you' [Mk. 13:5])*: neither fornicators, nor idolaters, nor adulterers, nor effeminate, nor abusers of themselves with mankind *(the proof of true Christianity is the changed life),*

"Nor thieves, nor covetous, nor drunkards, nor revilers, nor extortioners, shall inherit the Kingdom of God *(refers to those who call themselves 'Believers,' but yet continue to practice the sins mentioned, whom the Holy Spirit says are not saved, irrespective of their claims).*

"And such were some of you *(before conversion)*: but you are washed *(refers to the Blood of Jesus cleansing from all sin)*, but you are Sanctified *(one's position in Christ)*, but you are Justified *(declared not guilty)* in the Name of the Lord Jesus *(refers to Christ and what He did at the Cross, in order that we might be Saved)*, and by the Spirit of our God. *(Proclaims the Third Person of the Triune Godhead as the Mechanic in this great Work of Grace)*" (I Cor. 6:9-11).

In this Passage please note Verse 11.

• *"But you are Washed"*: When a person comes to Christ, in the Mind of God, as they exhibit Faith in Christ, such a person is washed clean by the precious Blood of Jesus Christ.

• *"But you are Sanctified"*: This means to be made clean, and because one has been washed, spiritually speaking, which specifies one's position in Christ. In effect, it is a position of perfection, simply because it is in Christ.

• *"But you are Justified"*: Due to being washed and, thereby, Sanctified, one can be declared *"not guilty."* However, Justification is greater than a verdict of *"not guilty." It means a*lso to be *"innocent."* It means, as well, that one is looked at by God as having never sinned in all of his or her life. But, it goes even a step further and means that one is *"perfect."* One can be declared such and, in fact, is declared such upon Faith, but only in Christ. In other words, upon Faith the Lord gives the believing sinner the perfection of Christ. In fact, God can accept no less.

OUR POSITION OF SANCTIFICATION

The position of Sanctification is an instant work. It takes

place at conversion and is the same for all Believers. This position never changes, irrespective of the situation regarding the Believer. It is a position that is unmovable, unchangeable and, as long as Faith is maintained in our Lord, is eternal. That is the position given to the Believer the moment such a person accepts Christ (Rom. 5:1-2). However, all of us know and realize that while this may be our *"position"* in Christ, it is not exactly our *"condition."*

THE CONDITION OF THE BELIEVER

While the Believer's position in Christ never changes, the truth is, our condition does change and, in fact, is changing constantly. To say it a different way, our *"condition"* is not up to our *"position"* in Christ. In fact, that is the Work of the Holy Spirit, meaning that He works with us, endeavoring to bring our *"condition"* up to our *"position."* It is a lifelong task on our part.

PROGRESSIVE SANCTIFICATION

While we are Sanctified, at the same time, we are being Sanctified. That is progressive Sanctification. Paul said:

"**And the very God of Peace Sanctify you wholly** *(this is 'progressive Sanctification,' which can only be brought about by the Holy Spirit, Who does such as our Faith is firmly anchored in the Cross, within which parameters the Spirit always works; the Sanctification process involves the whole man)*; **and** *I pray God* **your whole spirit and soul and body** *(proclaims the make-up of the whole man)* **be preserved blameless unto the coming of our Lord Jesus Christ.** *(This refers to the Rapture. As well, this one Verse proclaims the fact that any involvement, whether righteous or unrighteous, affects the whole man, and not just the physical body or the soul* *as some claim)"* (I Thess. 5:23).

ENTIRE SANCTIFICATION?

There is a teaching to which some subscribe, which is according to the following:

• They teach that a person is Saved by Grace through Faith, which is absolutely correct (Eph. 2:8).

• They then teach that Sanctification is also a definite work of Grace, which must be entered into after the person is Saved. In other words, after a person is Saved, they then should go to the Altar seeking Sanctification. They teach that this is a definite work of Grace and, when it happens, the person will not sin again.

• They then teach that such a person, then Sanctified, is now a fit candidate for the Baptism with the Holy Spirit.

This doctrine is wrong on two counts:

1. By teaching Sanctification as a definite work of Grace, they are at the same time teaching that Justification by Faith is incomplete. In other words, they are somewhat teaching a partial justification.

As we've said many times, and continue to say, all false doctrine begins by an improper understanding of the Atonement, i.e., *"the Cross."*

2. And, as stated, the Bible does not teach sinless perfection. Anyone who thinks such simply does not know what sin actually is or else, they have a very elevated picture of themselves. Let us say it again:

The moment the Believer comes to Christ, at that moment, they are fully, totally, and completely Sanctified (I Cor. 6:11). That is our position in Christ and a position, we might quickly add, that never changes; however, the truth is, while every Believer has such a position in Christ, that is not our *"condition."* In fact, our condition is far beneath the position of perfection. This is a great part of the Work of the Holy Spirit Who now resides within our hearts and lives and does so in order to bring our *"condition"* up to our *"position."*

CAN THE BELIEVER BE BROUGHT TO A PLACE IN CHRIST THAT HIS CONDITION, AS HIS POSITION, IS PERFECT?

No!

In the Eyes of God our position in Christ is perfect, and simply because it is in Christ; however, due to the fact that every Believer still has a sin nature, our condition cannot be brought to a place of perfection. Yet, the Bible most definitely does teach that *"sin is not to have dominion over us"* (Rom. 6:14).

Concerning perfection, Paul said:

"**That I may know Him** *(referring to what Christ did at the Cross)***, and the power of His Resurrection** *(refers to being raised with Him in 'Newness of Life' [Rom. 6:3-5])***, and the fellowship of His sufferings** *(regarding our Trust and Faith placed in what He did for us at the Cross)***, being made conformable unto His death** *(to conform to what He did for us at the Cross, understanding that this is the only means of Salvation and Sanctification)***;**

"**If by any means I might attain unto the Resurrection of the dead.** *(This does not refer to the coming Resurrection, but rather the believing sinner being baptized into the Death of Christ [refers to the Crucifixion], and raised in 'Newness of Life,' which gives victory over all sin [Rom. 6:3-5, 11, 14].)*

NOT PERFECT

"**Not as though I had already attained, either were already perfect** *(the Apostle is saying he doesn't claim sinless perfection)***: but I follow after** *(to pursue)***, if that I may apprehend** *(Paul is pursuing absolute Christlikeness)* **that for which also I am apprehended of Christ Jesus.** *(He* *was saved by Christ for the purpose of becoming Christlike, and so are we!)*

"Brethren, I count not myself to have apprehended *(in effect, repeats what he said in the previous Verse)***: but** *this* **one thing** *I do***, forgetting those things which are behind** *(refers to things the Apostle had depended upon to find favor with God, and the failure that type of effort brought about [Phil. 3:5-6])***, reaching forth unto those things which are before** *(all our attention must be on that which is ahead, and not on what is past; 'those things' consists of all the victories of the Cross)***,**

"I press toward the mark *(this represents a moral and spiritual target)* **for the prize of the high calling of God** *(Christlikeness)* **in Christ Jesus** *(proclaims the manner and means in which all of this is done, which is the Cross [I Cor. 1:17-18; 2:2])***.**

TO BE SPIRITUALLY MATURE

"Let us therefore, as many as be perfect *(should have been translated, mature)***, be thus minded** *(have our minds on what Christ has done at the Cross, and was done for us)***: and if in anything you be otherwise minded, God shall reveal even this unto you.** *(This means that some were actually otherwise minded. But through the words of Paul, the Holy Spirit was going to show them the right way, which is to pull them back to the Cross.)*

"Nevertheless, whereto we have already attained *(progress)***, let us walk by the same rule, let us mind the same thing.** *(Let us walk the same path, that of the Cross [Lk. 9:23-24])***" (Phil. 3:10-16).**

THE EPISTLE TO THE GALATIANS

This entire Epistle, basically, was written by Paul to the Believers in the churches in Galatia, who had been Saved by

Grace through Faith, but were now trying to be sanctified by the means of self. In other words, they had been Saved by Faith and now they are trying to sanctify themselves by works.

What had happened?

It was Paul who founded these churches in Galatia. To be sure, they had had the proper teaching, the right kind of teaching. In fact, the teaching they received was from the man who had been given the meaning of the New Covenant by the Lord Jesus Christ. So, what they had been taught was the very best that could be taught. So, how in the world could they have this type of foundation and then revert to *"works,"* trying to sanctify themselves?

The flesh is very appealing to Believers. As we've explained many times, the *"flesh,"* as used by the Holy Spirit through Paul, referred and refers to the personal ability, talent, education, strength, intellect, motivation, etc., of the individual. In other words, it's indicative to human beings and what we can do as mortals.

While these things within themselves aren't necessarily wrong, the truth is, they are woefully inadequate to achieve the task that is before us. In other words, the Believer simply cannot walk in victory while depending on the flesh. But, the following must quickly be noted:

If the Believer doesn't understand the Message of the Cross, in other words, not only is our Salvation in the Cross of Christ, but, our Sanctification as well, such a Believer will resort to the flesh because there is nowhere else to go. Our faith is either in the flesh, i.e., *"self,"* or else, it is in the Cross of Christ. There is no in-between. As the believing sinner cannot be Saved unless he exhibits Faith in Christ, likewise, the Believer cannot be sanctified unless one's Faith is exclusively in Christ and the Cross. But, the sadness is, while the modern church has understanding respecting the Cross of Christ concerning Salvation, it has virtually no understanding at all as it regards Sanctification referring to the Cross. While one can be Saved in this posture, one cannot even remotely live a victorious life.

To answer the question posed sometime back, *"How could these Galatians fall for false doctrine when they had had the greatest teaching on the face of the earth?"* As stated, the flesh is very appealing.

FALSE APOSTLES

After Paul had founded these Churches and then had gone on to other fields of endeavor, false apostles came into the Churches, telling the people that to be complete in Christ, the men had to be circumcised, etc. That's the reason that Paul said, *"That if you be circumcised, Christ shall profit you nothing"* (Gal. 5:2).

Every Believer should read those words very, very carefully. If one so desires, he can place any type of *"work"* in place of *"circumcised,"* and the results will be the same, *"Christ shall profit you nothing."* This means that if any Believer is trusting in the Lord's Supper, Water Baptism, fasting, or any such thing to bring them victory, *"Christ shall profit you nothing."*

While the things mentioned aren't wrong within themselves and, in fact, are viable Christian doctrines, still, if one places one's faith in such, the truth is, we are substituting something for the Cross of Christ, which God will never honor. God honors Christ and what He did at the Cross alone. If our Faith is in anything else, again I state, *"Christ shall profit you nothing."*

THE INTERCESSORY WORK OF CHRIST

I would hope from what information we have given that it would be easily understandable as to why we need the Intercession of Christ and need it on a constant basis.

Paul said:

"Wherefore He *(the Lord Jesus Christ)* **is able also to save them to the uttermost** *(proclaims the fact that Christ Alone has made the only true Atonement for sin; He did* *this at the Cross)* **who come unto God by Him** *(proclaims the only manner in which man can come to God)*, **seeing He ever lives to make intercession for them.** *(His very Presence by the Right Hand of the Father guarantees such, with nothing else having to be done.)*

"For such an High Priest became us *(presents the fact that no one less exalted could have met the necessities of the human race)*, **Who is Holy, harmless, undefiled, separate from sinners** *(describes the spotless, pure, Perfect Character of the Son of God as our Great High Priest; as well, this tells us Christ did not become a sinner on the Cross, as some claim, but was rather the Sin-Offering)*, **and made higher than the Heavens** *(refers to the fact that He is seated at the Right Hand of the Father, which is the most exalted position in Heaven or Earth)*;

THE LORD ALONE CAN FUNCTION IN THE CAPACITY OF INTERCESSOR

"Who needs not daily *(refers to the daily sacrifices offered by the Priests under the old Jewish economy)*, **as those High Priests, to offer up sacrifice, first for his own sins, and then for the people's** *(refers to the work of the Jewish High Priest on the Great Day of Atonement, which specified their unworthiness; Christ did not have to function accordingly)*: **for this He did once, when He offered up Himself.** *(This refers to His Death on the Cross, which Atoned for all sin — past, present, and future, making no further sacrifices necessary.)*

"For the Law *(Law of Moses)* **makes men High Priests which have infirmity** *(refers to the fact that the system was imperfect because it depended on frail men)*; **but the word of the oath** *(the Promise of God that He was going to institute a superior Priesthood, far superior to the old Levitical Order [Ps. 110:4])*, **which was since the Law** *(refers to the fact that the Oath was given some five hundred years* *before the Law was given to Moses)*, **makes** the Son *(the Lord Jesus)*, **Who is consecrated** *(means that He, and He Alone, can function in this capacity)* **forevermore.** *(This Covenant is perfect because the Son is Perfect, because what He did at the Cross is Perfect, which means it will never have to be replaced.)*

OUR GREAT HIGH PRIEST

"Now of the things which we have spoken *this is* **the sum** *(refers to what Paul will now give as it regards the meaning of all this)*: **We have such an High Priest, Who is set on the Right Hand of the Throne of the Majesty in the Heavens.** *(The very fact that Christ is now seated in the Heavens at the Right Hand of God proves His Work is a Finished Work)*" **(Heb. 7:25-28; 8:1).**

HOW DOES THE LORD MAKE INTERCESSION FOR US?

His very Presence at the Throne of God tells us that God has accepted His Sacrifice with, in effect, the Intercession already made. If, in fact, the Lord had to do something else in order to bring about intercession, this would mean that Calvary was not a Finished Work. It is a Finished Work and His very Presence at the Throne of God guarantees our Intercession.

The idea is, our Lord does not have to do anything as it regards intercession on our behalf, such as turning to the Father and asking Him to forgive us, etc.

In fact, the actual prayer and petition of His Intercession is given to us in the Psalms. It was given by the Holy Spirit and prayed through David, but, actually, represented and is, in fact, our Lord's Intercession on our part, and for time and eternity. We must understand that Jesus is the True Man, the True Israel, and the True Church. Unless we understand that, we will misunderstand exactly Who Christ really is.

CHRIST THE TRUE MAN, THE TRUE ISRAEL AND THE TRUE CHURCH

Williams says, *"God having been dishonored by human unbelief and disobedience, it was necessary that a Man should be born who would perfectly love, trust and serve Him; and Who would be the True Man, True Israel, and True Church.*

"God's moral glory demanded that sin should be judged; that sinners should repent, confess and forsake sin and worship and obey Him; and being God, His nature required perfection in these emotions of the heart and will.

"Such perfection was impossible to fallen man, and it was equally out of his power to provide a sacrifice that could remove his guilt and restore his relationship with God.

"The Psalms reveal Christ as satisfying in these relationships all the Divine requirements. He, though Himself sinless, declares Himself in these Psalms to be the True Advocate; and He expresses to God the abhorrence of sin accompanied by the repentance and sorrow which man ought to feel and express but will not and cannot. Similarly, the Faith, love, obedience and worship which man fails to give, Christ perfectly renders.

"Thus, as the High Priest of His people, He, the True Advocate, charges Himself with the guilt of our sins; declares them to be His Own; confesses them, repents of them, declaring at the same time His Own sinlessness; and atones for them. Thus, the Psalms, in which the Speaker declares His sinfulness and His sinlessness, become quite clear of comprehension when it is recognized Who the Speaker actually is."[1]

THE WORK OF THE MESSIAH

On the Cross, our Lord became: *"The Burnt Offering, the Meal Offering, the Peace Offering, the Sin Offering, and the Trespass Offering."*

The Gospels record the fact that Jesus prayed; the Psalms furnish the very words of the prayer.

THE PRAYER

The Fifty-first Psalm is a prayer, as is obvious, prayed by David; however, in reality, it was more than that. It is actually the intercessory prayer of our Lord on our behalf. It was prayed one time and need never be prayed again.

When we ask the Lord for forgiveness of sin and we are sincere of heart (I Jn. 1:9), we can rest assured that the prayer of intercession has already been prayed for us and accepted by God. That's the reason that John beautifully wrote:

"**If we confess our sins** *(pertains to acts of sin, whatever they might be; the sinner is to believe [Jn. 3:16]; the Saint is to confess)*, **He** *(the Lord)* **is faithful and just to forgive us** *our* **sins** *(God will always be true to His Own Nature and Promises, keeping Faith with Himself and with man)*, **and to cleanse us from all unrighteousness.** *('All,' not some. All sin was remitted, paid for, and put away on the basis of the satisfaction offered for the demands of God's Holy Law, which sinners broke, when the Lord Jesus died on the Cross.)*

"**If we say that we have not sinned** *(here, John is denouncing the claims of sinless perfection; he is going back to Verse 8, speaking of Christians who claimed they had no sin nature)*, **we make Him a liar** *(the person who makes such a claim makes God a liar, because the Word says the opposite)*, **and His Word is not in us.** *(If we properly know the Word, we will properly know that perfection is not in us at present, and will not be until the Trump sounds)*" (I Jn. 1:9-10).

MERCY

Now we commence with the very words prayed by our Lord as it regards intercession on our part. As stated, it's a prayer that God has already heard and answered. It need not be prayed

again. So, when the Believer asks forgiveness for sin, whatever that sin might be, this petition is in the Face of God, and it is a prayer, as stated, that has already been answered; consequently, we can be sure and certain of His Mercy.

"Have Mercy upon me, O God, according to Your lovingkindness: according unto the multitude of Your tender mercies blot out my transgressions. *(This is a Psalm of David, written when Nathan the Prophet came unto him after the sin with Bath-sheba and the murder of her husband Uriah [II Sam., Chpt. 12]. This Psalm was given by the Holy Spirit to David when, his heart broken and contrite because of his sin against God, he pleaded for pardon through the Atoning Blood of the Lamb of God, foreshadowed in Exodus, Chapter 12. Thus, he was not only fittingly provided with a vehicle of expression in Repentance and Faith, but he was also used as a channel of prophetic communication.*

"David, in his sin, Repentance, and Restoration, is a forepicture of Israel. For as he forsook the Law and was guilty of adultery and murder, so Israel despised the Covenant, turned aside to idolatry [spiritual adultery], and murdered the Messiah.

"Thus, the scope and structure of this Psalm goes far beyond David. It predicts the future confession and forgiveness of Israel in the day of the Messiah's Second Coming, when, looking upon Him Whom they pierced, they shall mourn and weep [Zech., Chpts. 12-13].

"As well, this is even more perfectly a vivid portrayal of the Intercessory Work of Christ on behalf of His People. Even though David prayed this prayer, the Son of David would make David's sin [as well as ours] His Own, and pray through him that which must be said.

"This means that this is the truest prayer of Repentance ever prayed, because it symbolizes the Intercessory Work of the Son of David.)

WASH ME

"**Wash me thoroughly from my iniquity, and cleanse me from my sin** *(man's problem is sin, and man must admit that; the only remedy for sin is 'Jesus Christ and Him Crucified,' to which David, in essence, appealed [Heb. 10:12]; the Blood of Jesus Christ alone cleanses from all sin [I Jn. 1:7])*.

THE ACKNOWLEDGMENT OF TRANSGRESSIONS

"**For I acknowledge my transgressions: and my sin is ever before me** *(the acknowledgement of Verses 3 and 4 is the condition of Divine forgiveness; all sin, in essence, is committed against God; therefore, God demands that the transgressions be acknowledged, placing the blame where it rightfully belongs — on the perpetrator; He cannot and, in fact, will not, forgive sin that is not acknowledged and for which no responsibility is taken)*.

ALL SIN IS AGAINST GOD

"**Against You, You only, have I sinned, and done this evil in Your sight: that You might be justified when You speak, *and* be clear when You judge.** *(While David's sins were against Bath-sheba, her husband Uriah, and all of Israel, still, the ultimate direction of sin, perfected by Satan, is always against God.*

"All sin is a departure from God's Ways to man's ways.

"David is saying that God is always 'justified' in any action that He takes, and His 'judgment' is always perfect.)

ORIGINAL SIN

"**Behold, I was shaped in iniquity; and in sin did my mother conceive me.** *(Unequivocally, this Verse proclaims the fact of original sin. This Passage states that all are* *born in sin, and as a result of Adam's Fall in the Garden of Eden.*

"When Adam, as the federal head of the human race, failed, this means that all of humanity failed. It means that all who would be born, would, in effect, be born lost.

"As a result of this, the Second Man, the Last Adam, the Lord Jesus Christ, had to come into this world, in effect, God becoming Man, to undo what the original Adam did. He would have to keep the Law of God perfectly, which He did, all as our Substitute, and then pay the penalty for the terrible sin debt owed by all of mankind, for all had broken the Law, which He did by giving Himself on the Cross of Calvary [Jn. 3:16].

"To escape the judgment of original sin, man must be 'born again,' which is carried out by the believing sinner expressing Faith in Christ and what Christ did at the Cross [Jn. 3:3; Eph. 2:8-9].)

TRUTH

"Behold, You desire truth in the inward parts: and in the hidden part You shall make me to know wisdom *(man can only deal with the externals, and even that not very well; God Alone can deal with the 'inward parts' of man, which is the source of sin, which speaks of the heart; in other words, the heart has to be changed, which the Lord Alone can do [Mat. 5:8])***.**

WHITER THAN SNOW

"Purge me with hyssop, and I shall be clean: wash me, and I shall be whiter than snow. *(The petition, 'purge me with hyssop,' expresses a figure of speech. 'Purge me with the blood which on that night in Egypt was sprinkled on the doorposts with a bunch of hyssop' [Ex. 12:13, 22] portrays David's dependence on 'the Blood of the Lamb.'*

"David had no recourse in the Law, even as no one has recourse in the Law. The Law can only condemn. All recourse is found exclusively in Christ and what He did for us at the Cross, of which the slain lamb and the blood on the doorposts in Egypt were symbols [Ex. 12:13].)

JOY AND GLADNESS

"Make me to hear joy and gladness; that the bones which You have broken may rejoice. *(Forgiveness for the past never exhausts the fullness of pardon. There is provision for the future.*

"The expression, 'bones which You have broken,' presents a figure of speech meaning that one cannot proceed until things have been made right with God. It is as though a man's leg is broken, and he cannot walk. Unforgiven sin immobilizes the soul the same as a broken bone immobilizes the body.)

BLOT OUT ALL OF MY INIQUITIES

"Hide Your face from my sins, and blot out all my iniquities. *(Unforgiven sin stares in the Face of God. This can only be stopped when the sins are put away, which can only be done by proper Confession and Repentance, with the Blood of Jesus being applied by Faith. When this is done, the 'iniquities' are 'blotted out' as though they had never existed. This is 'Justification by Faith' [Rom. 5:1]).*

A RIGHT SPIRIT

"Create in me a clean heart, O God: and renew a right spirit within me. *(David's heart was unclean. Sin makes the heart unclean. The word 'create' is interesting. It means the old heart is infected by sin, is diseased, and cannot be salvaged. God must, spiritually speaking, 'create*

a clean heart' [Ezek. 18:31].
"*Also, it is impossible for any individual to have a 'right spirit' if there is unconfessed sin.)*

THE HOLY SPIRIT

"**Cast me not away from Your Presence; and take not Your Holy Spirit from me.** *(If sin is unconfessed and rebellion persists, God will ultimately 'cast away' the individual 'from His Presence.' He will also 'take the Holy Spirit' from the person. This refutes the doctrine of unconditional eternal security.)*

RESTORATION

"**Restore unto me the joy of Your Salvation; and uphold me with Your free spirit.** *(Part of the business of the Holy Spirit is 'restoration,' but only if the individual meets God's conditions, as David did, and as we must do. With unconfessed sin, all 'joy' is lost. With sin confessed, cleansed, and put away, the 'joy of Salvation' returns. A clean heart, a willing spirit, and a steadfast will are then given by the Holy Spirit.)*

TRUE REPENTANCE

"**Then will I teach transgressors Your ways; and sinners shall be converted unto You.** *(Before Repentance, David was in no condition to proclaim God's Truth to 'transgressors,' because he was a transgressor himself.*
"*Upon true Repentance, David was now ready to teach and to preach, and the Holy Spirit attested to that.)*

DELIVERANCE

"**Deliver me from blood guiltiness, Oh God, Thou God**

of my Salvation: and my tongue shall sing aloud of Your Righteousness.** *(This refers to the terrible sin of having Uriah, the husband of Bath-sheba, killed [II Sam. 11:14-21].*

"Only the consciously pardoned sinner can 'sing aloud' of God's Righteousness. Unpardoned men can speak of His Mercy, but their thoughts about it are unholy thoughts.)

PRAISE UNTO THE LORD

"O LORD, open Thou my lips; and my mouth shall show forth Your praise. *(Proper praise to the Lord cannot go forth as long as there is unconfessed sin. This is the reason for such little praise in most churches, and far too often the praise which actually is offered is hollow. True praise can only come from a true heart!)*

SACRIFICE?

"For You desire not Sacrifice; else would I give it: You delight not in Burnt Offering. *(No penance, sacraments, or costly gifts of churches or men regarding expiation of past sins, are desired or accepted by God. Only Faith and trust in Christ and what He has done for us at the Cross can be accepted by the Lord.*

"Unfortunately, the world tries to create a new god, while the church tries to create another sacrifice. There is only one Sacrifice for sin [Heb. 10:12].)

A BROKEN AND CONTRITE HEART

"The sacrifices of God are a broken spirit: a broken and a contrite heart, O God, You will not despise. *(True Repentance will always include a 'broken spirit' and a 'broken and contrite heart.' Such alone will accept Christ and what Christ has done at the Cross. God will accept nothing less.)*

BUILD THOU THE WALLS OF JERUSALEM

"**Do good in Your good pleasure unto Zion: build Thou the walls of Jerusalem.** *(Verses 18 and 19 are not, as some think, a meaningless addition to the Psalm by some later writer. They both belong to the structure and prophetic scope of the Psalm.*

"*David's sin, confession, and Restoration illustrate this future chapter in Israel's history. With their idolatry [spiritual adultery] and murder forgiven, they will go forth as messengers of the Gospel to win other nations to a whole-hearted Faith and service in and for Christ.*

"*Upon Israel's Repentance, the Lord will once again 'build Thou the walls of Jerusalem.')*

THE LORD IS PLEASED

"**Then shall You be pleased with the sacrifices of Righteousness, with Burnt Offering and Whole Burnt Offering: then shall they offer bullocks upon Your Altar.** *(The Sacrificial program under the old system was lawful, because it pointed to the coming Redeemer. Since Christ and the Cross, they are no longer necessary, and for all the obvious reasons. Why the symbol when the substance is available?*

"*During the Millennial Reign, the Sacrificial system will be restored, but only as a memorial of what Christ has done at the Cross [Ezek., Chpts. 40-48])*" **(Ps. 51:1-19).**

CHRIST INTERCEDES ON OUR BEHALF FOR WHAT?

For sin!

In fact, Christ Alone can intercede on behalf of this problem. He is the One Who paid the price at Calvary's Cross. He is the One Who satisfied the demands of a thrice-Holy God. He is the One Who satisfied the demands of the broken Law. He is the One Who atoned for all sin, and He Alone can intercede on behalf of this dread problem.

For those who would be so foolish as to think they don't need this intercession, should think again! In fact, without such Intercession by Christ, we wouldn't last a full day.

Every Born-Again person in this world is Saved at the present time, and remains Saved, because of what Jesus did at the Cross and, thereby, His Intercession on our behalf. We must never forget that!

THE HOLY SPIRIT IS AN INTERCESSOR AS WELL!

Paul also said:

"**Likewise the Spirit** *(Holy Spirit)* **also helps our infirmities** *(the help given to us by the Holy Spirit is made possible in its entirety by and through what Jesus did at the Cross)***: for we know not what we should pray for as we ought** *(signals the significance of prayer, but also that without the Holy Spirit, all is to no avail)***: but the Spirit itself** *(Himself)* **makes intercession for us** *(He petitions or intercedes on our behalf)* **with groanings which cannot be uttered** *(not groanings on the part of the Holy Spirit, but rather on our part, which pertains to that which comes from the heart and cannot properly be put into words)***.**

"**And He Who searches the hearts** *(God the Father)* **knows what** *is* **the Mind of the Spirit** *(what the Spirit wants done, and not what we want done)***, because He** *(Holy Spirit)* **makes intercession for the Saints according to** *the Will of* **God.** *(The overriding goal of the Spirit is to carry out the Will of God in our lives, and not our personal wills; in other words, the Spirit is not a glorified bellhop)***"** (Rom. 8:26-27).

Whereas Christ intercedes on our behalf, the Holy Spirit intercedes for us according to the following:

• He helps us: This speaks of the Holy Spirit coming to our aid. He doesn't take the entire load, but He does help us in this endeavor, whatever it might be. This means that the Holy Spirit comes to our aid in our spiritual problems and difficulties, not by taking over the responsibility for them and, as well, not by giving us an automatic deliverance without any effort on our part, but by showing us how to work out our problems and overcome the difficulties with His Help.

• *"Infirmities,"* as used here, is not speaking of that which is physical, but, rather, that which is Spiritual. He gives us Guidance and Direction into all Truth. He takes those things of Christ, which pertains to what Christ did for us at the Cross, and reveals such to us (Jn. 16:14-15).

• Prayer: He helps us to pray, guiding us into the right way. Paul specifically stated that we do not know what the specific, detailed objects of prayer in any given emergency or situation might be. In effect, Paul actually said, *"We do not know 'the what' we should pray for,"* indicating the particular what. Many times we don't even know what to say in prayer, with only a *"groan"* coming from our heart; however, the Holy Spirit takes that groan as an acceptable petition, lays it before the Father in terminology we did not know nor could we find, but, of course, the Holy Spirit, Who is God, knows exactly what we should say and says it for us.

• We, as Believers, need the Intercession of Christ and the Holy Spirit, as should be obvious. In fact, we wouldn't make it at all without it. Thank God it is available to all Believers, whomever they might be and wherever they might be.

"Christ, from Whom all Blessings flow,
"Perfecting the Saints below,
"Hear us, who Your nature share,
"Who Your mystic body are."

"Join us, in one spirit join,
"Let us still receive of Thine;

"Still for more on You we call,
"You who fillest all in all."

"Move, and actuate, and guide:
"Diverse gifts to each divide;
"Place according to Your Will,
"Let us all our work fulfill."

"Sweetly may we all agree,
"Touch with loving sympathy:
"Kindly for each other care;
"Every member feel its share."

"Love, like death, has all destroyed,
"Rendered all distinction void;
"Names, and sects, and parties fall:
"You, Oh Christ, are all in all."

CHAPTER TWENTY-THREE

How Do I Apply The Cross To My Life Daily?

QUESTION:

HOW DO I APPLY THE CROSS TO MY LIFE DAILY?

ANSWER:

In fact, the application of the Cross, according to the Scriptures, most definitely is on a daily basis, so to speak. It is all done by Faith in Christ. This means that our Faith is placed exclusively in Christ and what He did for us at the Cross, which then gives the Holy Spirit liberty to work within our lives. However, and I think one can say without fear of Scriptural contradiction, it is most definitely a *"daily choice."*

TAKE UP YOUR CROSS DAILY

Faith is never a once for all settled thing, one might say. Inasmuch as our Faith is attacked on a constant basis by the powers of the enemy, likewise, we, on a constant basis, even daily, must renew our Faith, which means that we do not move it elsewhere, but maintain it in the Cross. Please remember the following:

Every attack by Satan against the Child of God, whether it's in the realm of spiritual things, financial, physical, domestical, etc., is for but one purpose and that is to destroy our Faith, or else to seriously weaken it.

WHAT IS FAITH?

The Scripture says:

"Now Faith is the substance *(the title deed)* of things hoped for *(a declaration of the action of Faith)*, the evidence of things not seen. *(Faith is not based upon the senses, which yield uncertainty, but rather on the Word of God)*" (Heb. 11:1)

The Holy Spirit said:

"But without Faith *(in Christ and the Cross; anytime Faith is mentioned, always and without exception, its root meaning is that its Object is Christ and the Cross; otherwise, it is faith God will not accept) it is* impossible to please *Him (faith in anything other than Christ and the Cross greatly displeases the Lord)*: for he who comes to God must believe that He is *(places Faith as the foundation and principle of the manner in which God deals with the human race)*, and *that* He *(God)* is a rewarder of them who diligently seek Him. *(Seek Him on the premise of Christ and Him Crucified)*" (Heb. 11:6).

WHY FAITH?

We might say that Faith is the coin of the realm, which alone spends in God's Economy.

No doubt, God chose Faith with which to deal with the human race for many and varied reasons; however, possibly the greatest reason of all is the equality of Faith. Anyone, rich, poor, great, small, irrespective of race, color, or creed, can evidence Faith. In other words, it is equal for all!

THE OBJECT OF FAITH

The Object of our Faith must, and without fail, be the Cross of Christ or else it's not faith that God will recognize. In fact, every human being in the world, even the atheist, has faith. To be sure, it's not faith in God or His Word, nevertheless, it is faith, but, not faith that God will recognize.

That's the reason that Capitalism produces the greatest economy on Earth. It is because Capitalism is based on faith. Countries that adopt socialism, or communism, etc., greatly shortchange their people, because it rules out faith.

Again, the only Faith that God will recognize is Faith in Christ and what Christ has done for us at the Cross. That's the reason He said to the Children of Israel just before they were delivered from Egyptian bondage:

> "When I see the Blood *(which speaks of the Cross of Christ)* I will pass over you" (Ex. 12:13).

FAITH AND THE CROSS

Faith and the Cross are so intertwined, so melded together, so one in essence, one might say, that when one begins to fully understand the Cross, then Faith is understood.

There have been more books written on Faith in the last 50 years, I suppose, than all the balance of the Church Age put together. Regrettably, most of the teaching contained in these books was and is unscriptural.

How do I know that?

I know it because the Cross of Christ is, by and large, divorced from Faith. I realize that people talk much about *"Faith in the Word."* That is a proper statement; however, that which says too much concludes by saying much of nothing.

First of all, we must understand that the story of the Bible is the story of man and his Fall and, above all, our Redemption, all made possible by the Cross of Christ. One might say that the short phrase, *"Christ and Him Crucified,"* is the Story of the Bible. The Crucifixion of Christ is stamped on the first page of human history, and I speak of the Sacrificial system instituted by the Lord so sinful man could have forgiveness of sins and communion with Him. It is characterized first of all in the Fourth Chapter of Genesis. The Crucifixion of Christ is then stamped on every sacrifice, of which there were untold millions.

So, for it to be Faith that God will recognize, it must have the Cross of Christ as its Object.

TAKE UP THE CROSS DAILY

Jesus said:

"And He said to *them* all, if any *man* will come after Me *(the criteria for Discipleship)*, let him deny himself *(not asceticism as many think, but rather that one denies one's own willpower, self-will, strength, and ability, depending totally on Christ)*, and take up his cross *(the benefits of the Cross, looking exclusively to what Jesus did there to meet our every need)* daily *(this is so important, our looking to the Cross; that we must renew our Faith in what Christ has done for us, even on a daily basis, for Satan will ever try to move us away from the Cross as the Object of our Faith, which always spells disaster)*, and follow Me *(Christ can be followed only by the Believer looking to the Cross, understanding what it accomplished, and by that means alone [Rom. 6:3-5, 11, 14; 8:1-2, 11; I Cor. 1:17-18, 21, 23; 2:2; Gal. 6:14; Eph. 2:13-18; Col. 2:14-15).*

"For whosoever will save his life shall lose it *(try to live one's life outside of Christ and the Cross)*: but whosoever will lose his life for My sake, the same shall save it. *(When we place our Faith entirely in Christ and the Cross, looking exclusively to Him, we have just found 'more abundant life' [Jn. 10:10])*" (Lk. 9:23-24).

ONE OF THE MOST IMPORTANT SCRIPTURES

The Church, by and large, and from the very beginning, seemingly has misunderstood this Passage (Lk. 9:23-24) given by Christ. Completely misinterpreting it, it has not realized its tremendous benefits. In fact, this is one of the greatest Passages found in the entirety of the Word of God. It is the secret of all Blessings.

First of all, *"denying oneself"* doesn't refer to asceticism, as stated, which refers to denying oneself of all pleasurable activity, etc.

In other words, to be a little foolish, sleep without a pillow, don't put sugar in your tea, etc. That is to say, make life as coarse, as harsh, as Spartan as it can be made, which is supposed to denote some type of holiness.

It doesn't!

That's not what Jesus was talking about at all. In the first place, there's nothing we can do within ourselves that can make us holy, that is a work of the Holy Spirit within our hearts and lives, carried out by and through our Faith in Christ and what He has done for us at the Cross.

Likewise, *"taking up the Cross,"* in the mind of most Believers, corresponds to suffering. In other words, the more one suffers the more that one has taken up the Cross.

Understanding that, unless one has a death wish, he certainly isn't in the market for suffering, this Passage is discussed, but at a distance, and avoided at all costs. No wonder!

The word *"daily"* is ignored altogether. No, Jesus wasn't speaking of suffering, but, in reality, the very opposite. Stop and think about it a moment.

Either Christ finished His great Work at Calvary or He didn't. I happen to believe that He did, which means that there is nothing I can add to what He has already done; however, when we talk about *"suffering,"* or some such like effort on our part, whether we realize it or not, this means that what Christ did at the Cross was insufficient and that we have to add our effort (suffering) to His. I hope that one can see how this is an insult to the Lord. In a sense, we are to renew our Faith daily, which simply means to keep believing daily.

THE TRUTH

The truth is, Luke 9:23-24 are two of the greatest Passages found in the entirety of the Word of God as it regards Blessings. When Jesus told us to take up our Cross daily, this referred to the benefits of all that He did at Calvary. This means that these Passages are loaded with Blessings.

Likewise, the Twenty-fourth Verse holds the same Blessings. When we lose our life in Christ, this is the greatest thing that could ever be done, meaning that we've just found our life. If we refuse to lose it in Christ, well, then it is truly lost. Outside of Christ there is no life, no Blessing, no Salvation, nothing! In Christ there is everything.

CANNOT BE MY DISCIPLE

When Jesus addressed this subject again, He said:

"**And whosoever does not bear his Cross** *(this doesn't speak of suffering, as most think, but rather ever making the Cross of Christ the Object of our Faith; we are Saved and we are victorious, not by suffering, although that sometimes will happen, or any other similar things, but rather by our Faith, but always with the Cross of Christ as the Object of that Faith)*, **and come after Me** *(one can follow Christ only by Faith in what He has done for us at the Cross; He recognizes nothing else)*, **cannot be My Disciple** *(this statement is emphatic! If it's not Faith in the Cross of Christ, then it's Faith that God will not recognize, which means that such people are refused)*" **(Lk. 14:27).**

WHAT DO I DO?

A dear lady wrote me some time back, rather confused as to what she should do on a daily basis in applying the Cross to her heart and life. She asked, *"Should I repeat 10 times. . . ?"*

"Should I memorize a certain prayer?" she went on to say!

To be sure, her letter wasn't written in sarcasm. She was completely serious. And, once you think about it a little bit, most Believers fall into the same category.

What do I mean by that?

The modern church is so accustomed to functioning in the flesh, in other words, things we do, that it's lost sight of what Faith actually means.

No! As far as trying to do something as it concerns taking up the Cross daily, we are to do nothing. In fact, it was already done at Calvary some two thousand years ago.

As we said at the first of the article, it is merely a matter of Faith. On a daily basis, we should reinforce our Faith in Christ and what He has done for us at the Cross.

THE MODERN CHURCH AND WORKS

I think possibly one could say without fear of contradiction that the modern church is a veritable beehive of religious activity. They are doing everything from handing out bottles of water on the corner to passing motorists to cooking meals for those who have suffered some misfortune, etc., to a hundred and one other things that we could name. While all of this may or may not be good, the problem with it is, in the minds of these people, they are trying to transfer their works into Righteousness. I'm sorry but that will never play.

Righteousness is something that is freely given to us as we evidence Faith in Christ and what He did for us at the Cross. It is the Cross of Christ that made the imputation of Righteousness possible. Simple Faith in Christ and what He did for us gives us an instant, pure, perfect Righteousness of God. Let us say it again, *"it is all by Faith,"* but it must be Faith in Christ and the Cross or else it's not recognized by the Lord.

That being correct, do you realize that precious little Faith by the modern church is actually recognized by the Lord?! Considering that the Cross of Christ is not even understood respecting Sanctification, much less taught and preached, this means whatever it is the modern church refers to as faith is, by and large, totally ignored by the Lord.

Someone said the other day, *"Brother Swaggart, you propose the Cross of Christ as the answer for everything."*

To be sure, that person was finally beginning to hear what we have been saying. That's exactly what I'm saying. Everything, and I mean everything, that we receive from the Lord is all, and without exception, made possible by the Cross of Christ.

Let's go back to our original subject. The way we apply

the Cross of Christ to our life daily is to simply have Faith on a daily basis that what Christ did at the Cross answers every question and solves every problem. Such Faith evidenced will then give the Holy Spirit the liberty to work in our lives and to do what He Alone can do (Rom. 8:1-2, 11).

"A mind at perfect peace with God;
"Oh, what a word is this!
"A sinner reconciled through blood;
"This, this indeed is peace."

"By nature and by practice far,
"How very far from God;
"Yet now by Grace brought near to Him,
"Through Faith in Jesus' Blood."

"So nigh, so very nigh to God,
"I cannot nearer be;
"For in the Person of His Son,
"I am as near as He."

"So dear, so very dear to God,
"More dear I cannot be;
"The love wherewith He Loves the Son,
"Such is His Love to me."

"Why should I ever anxious be,
"Since such a God is mine?
"He watches o'er me night and day,
"And tells me 'Mine is Thine.'"

CHAPTER TWENTY-FOUR

Why Is The Cross Of Christ So Important As It Regards The Holy Spirit?

QUESTION:

WHY IS THE CROSS OF CHRIST SO IMPORTANT AS IT REGARDS THE HOLY SPIRIT?

ANSWER:

The Cross of Christ is a legal work. It provides the legal means for the Holy Spirit to carry out His Work.

THE HOLY SPIRIT AND HIS WORK

The Holy Spirit is God. There is one God manifested in Three Persons, God the Father, God the Son, and God the Holy Spirit. These are one in essence but not one in number (Mat. 28:19).

Everything that's been done on this Earth by the Godhead has been done by and through the Ministry, Agency, Office, and Person of the Holy Spirit. There has been one exception and that is the First Advent of Christ; however, the Holy Spirit, to be sure, superintended that from beginning to end. The Scripture says:

"Now the Birth of Jesus Christ was on this wise: When as His Mother Mary was espoused *(engaged)* to Joseph, before they came together *(before they were married)*, she was found with Child of the Holy Spirit. *(By decree of the Holy Spirit)*" (Mat. 1:18).

When Jesus began His Public Ministry, the Scripture says:

"And Jesus, when He was baptized *(this was the beginning of His earthly Ministry)*, went up straightway *(immediately)* out of the water *(refers to Baptism by immersion and not by sprinkling)*: and, lo, the heavens were opened unto Him *(the only One, the Lord Jesus Christ, to Whom the heavens would be opened)*, and he saw the Spirit of

God *(Holy Spirit)* **descending like a dove, and lighting upon Him** *(John saw a visible form that reminded him of a dove)***:**

"**And lo a Voice from Heaven, saying** *(the Voice of God the Father)***, This is My Beloved Son, in Whom I am well pleased.** *(The Trinity appears here: the Father speaks, the Spirit descends, and the Son prays [Lk. 3:21])*" **(Mat. 3:16-17).**

THE TEMPTATION OF JESUS

"**Then** *(immediately after the descent of the Holy Spirit upon Him)* **was Jesus led up** *(urgently led)* **of the Spirit** *(Holy Spirit)* **into the wilderness** *(probably close to Jericho)* **to be tempted of the Devil** *(as the Last Adam, He would be tempted in all points like as we are [Heb. 4:15; I Cor. 15:21-22, 45, 47])*" **(Mat. 4:1).**

THE SPIRIT OF THE LORD UPON CHRIST

"**And He came to Nazareth, where He had been brought up** *(makes vivid the fact that Jesus was Very Man, even as He was Very God)***: and, as His custom was** *(in our language presently, He was faithful to Church)***, He went into the Synagogue on the Sabbath day, and stood up for to read** *(it was common to ask visitors to expound on the Word)***.**

"**And there was delivered unto Him the Book** *(Scroll)* **of the Prophet Isaiah. And when He had opened the Book, He found the place where it was written** *(Isa. 61:1)***,**

"**The Spirit of the Lord** *is* **upon Me** *(we learn here of the absolute necessity of the Person and Work of the Holy Spirit within our lives)***, because He has anointed Me** *(Jesus is the ultimate Anointed One; consequently, the Anointing of the Holy Spirit actually belongs to Christ, and the Anointing we have actually comes by His Authority [Jn. 16:14])* **to**

preach the Gospel to the poor *(the poor in spirit)*; **He has sent Me to heal the brokenhearted** *(sin breaks the heart, or else is responsible for it being broken; only Jesus can heal this malady)*, **to preach Deliverance to the captives** *(if it is to be noticed, He didn't say to 'deliver the captives,' but rather 'preach Deliverance,' which refers to the Cross [Jn. 8:32])*, **and recovering of sight to the blind** *(the Gospel opens the eyes of those who are spiritually blind)*, **to set at liberty them who are bruised** *(the vicissitudes of life at times place a person in a mental or spiritual prison; the Lord Alone, and through what He did at the Cross, can open this prison door)*,

"To preach the acceptable Year of the Lord. *(It is believed that the day on which Jesus delivered this Message was the first day of the year of Jubilee)*" **(Lk. 4:16-19).**

THE DEATH OF CHRIST ON THE CROSS WAS SUPERINTENDED BY THE HOLY SPIRIT

The Scripture says:

"How much more shall the Blood of Christ *(while the sacrifice of animals could cleanse from ceremonial defilement, only the Blood of Christ could cleanse from actual sin; so that throws out every proposed solution other than the Cross)*, **Who through the Eternal Spirit offered Himself without spot to God** *(in this phrase, we learn Christ did not die until the Holy Spirit told Him to die; in fact, no man took His Life from Him; He laid it down freely [Jn.10:17-18]; as well, the fact that Jesus 'offered Himself without spot to God' shoots down the unscriptural doctrine that 'Jesus died Spiritually' on the Cross; had He died Spiritually, meaning He became a sinner on the Cross, He could not have offered Himself without spot to God, as should be obvious; God could only accept a perfect Sacrifice; when He died on the Cross, He took upon Himself the sin penalty of the human* *race, which was physical death; inasmuch as His Offering of Himself was Perfect, God accepted it as payment in full for all sin — past, present, and future, at least for those who will believe [Jn. 3:16])*, **purge your conscience from dead works to serve the Living God?** *('Dead works' are anything other than simple Faith in the Cross of Christ, i.e., 'the Blood of Christ')*" **(Heb. 9:14).**

THE RESURRECTION OF OUR LORD FROM THE DEAD BY THE HOLY SPIRIT

The Scripture says:

"But if the Spirit *(Holy Spirit)* **of Him** *(from God)* **Who raised up Jesus from the dead dwell in you** *(and He definitely does)*, **He Who raised up Christ from the dead shall also quicken your mortal bodies** *(give us power in our mortal bodies that we might live a victorious life)* **by His Spirit Who dwells in you.** *(We have the same power in us, through the Spirit, that raised Christ from the dead, and is available to us only on the premise of the Cross and our Faith in that Sacrifice)*" **(Rom. 8:11).**

BEFORE THE CROSS OF CHRIST THE HOLY SPIRIT WAS LIMITED AS TO WHAT HE COULD DO

Paul said:

"For *it is* **not possible that the blood of bulls and of goats should take away sins.** *(The word 'impossible' is a strong one. It means there is no way forward through the blood of animals. As well, it applies to all other efforts made by man to address the problem of sin, other than the Cross)*" **(Heb. 10:4).**

At the very dawn of time, in fact, immediately after the Fall

of Adam and Eve, the Lord instituted the Sacrificial system, which pertained to an innocent victim, a lamb, if you will, which would serve as a substitute until our Lord would come. Even though this served as a stopgap measure, so to speak, still, it was woefully insufficient to take away sins. In a sense, the blood of animals did serve to atone for sin in that sin was covered, but not taken away. As a result, the sin debt remained as a part of every individual, even the greatest Patriarchs and Prophets. Because of sin still being present, the Holy Spirit could not come into Believers to dwell. He did come into some Believers in order to help them carry out a task that was assigned to them, but, when the task would be completed, the Holy Spirit would leave. There is no hint in the Scriptures that, even with the few inhabited by the Holy Spirit, the Spirit helped them as it regards Sanctification. As stated, He was limited to the task for which the certain person had been called. David is a perfect example.

THE SPIRIT OF THE LORD CAME UPON DAVID

"Then Samuel took the horn of oil, and anointed him in the midst of his brethren *(this was Samuel's last and crowning work; he would train the man who more nearly than any other approached unto the ideal of the theocratic king, and was to Israel the Type of their coming Messiah; it was Samuel's wisdom in teaching his young men music which gave David the skill to be the sweet singer of the Sanctuary; and we may feel sure also that when David arranged the service of the House of God, and gave Priests and Levites their appointed duties [I Chron. 23:26], the model which he set before him was that in which he had so often taken part with Samuel at Ramah, with, of course, the Lord guiding it all)*: and the Spirit of the LORD came upon David from that day forward *(which would be the means by which all things good were accomplished in David's life; David's name would be the very first human name in the New Testament and the very last human name in the New*

Testament; in fact, the Messiah would be referred to as 'the Son of David,' because He would come through the lineage of David's family [II Sam., Chpt. 7])" **(I Sam. 16:13).**

We find the very opposite with Saul.

THE DEPARTURE OF THE SPIRIT OF THE LORD

When Saul was chosen by the Lord to be king, which was not the Will of God, but because the people insisted, Samuel told him, *"And the Spirit of the LORD will come upon you, and you shall prophesy with them, and shall be turned into another man"* **(I Sam. 10:6).**

But, because of sin and rebellion, ultimately the Scripture says:

"But the Spirit of the LORD departed from Saul, and an evil spirit from the LORD troubled him. *(The Spirit of the Lord did not arbitrarily depart from Saul, but did so because Saul no longer wanted God. Because the Holy Spirit was not wanted, an evil spirit was allowed to go to Saul and trouble him, but only because of Saul's rebellion)"* **(I Sam. 16:14).**

THE WORDS OF CHRIST

Our Lord addressed this as well, even as He spoke to His chosen Disciples a short time before the Crucifixion. He said to them:

"And I will pray the Father, and He shall give you another Comforter *('Parakletos,' which means 'One called to the side of another to help'),* **that He may abide with you forever** *(before the Cross, as previously stated, the Holy Spirit could only help a few individuals, and then only for a period of time; since the Cross, He lives in the hearts and* *lives of Believers, and does so forever)*;

"*Even* **the Spirit of Truth** *(the Greek says, 'The Spirit of the Truth,' which refers to the Word of God; actually, He does far more than merely superintend the attribute of Truth, as Christ 'is Truth' [I Jn. 5:6])*; **Whom the world cannot receive** *(the Holy Spirit cannot come into the heart of the unbeliever until that person makes Christ his or her Saviour; then He comes in)*, **because it sees Him not, neither knows Him** *(refers to the fact that only Born-Again Believers can understand the Holy Spirit and know Him)*: **but you know Him** *(would have been better translated, 'But you shall get to know Him')*; **for He dwells with you** *(before the Cross)*, **and shall be in you.** *(Which would take place on the Day of Pentecost and forward, because the sin debt has been forever paid by Christ on the Cross, changing the disposition of everything)*" **(Jn. 14:16-17).**

CAPTIVES!

As stated, before the Cross when Believers died, due to the fact that animal blood was insufficient to take their sins away, meaning the sin debt remained, instead of going to Heaven, they went to Paradise, i.e., *"Abraham's Bosom."* Actually, they were held captive by Satan. While he could not hurt them in any manner, and in actuality they were comforted, still, they were in a place they did not desire to be. No doubt, the Evil One hoped to get them over into the burning side, with this part being separated from Abraham's Bosom by a great gulf (Lk. 16:19-31).

To be frank, their Salvation depended totally on Christ going to the Cross and there atoning for all sin.

Immediately after the Cross was a fact, Jesus went down into this place and liberated every soul there, taking them to Heaven with Him. Now, when Believers die and, in fact, ever since the Cross, the soul and spirit immediately go to be with Christ (Phil. 1:23). As should be obvious, the Cross of Christ changed everything.

THE CROSS PAID THE SIN DEBT

With the sin debt lifted, due to the price being paid at Calvary's Cross, everything changed. Now, the moment a Person comes to Christ, instantly, the Holy Spirit comes into his heart and life, there to abide forever (Jn. 14:16).

The Cross of Christ was a legal work. Man owed a debt to God he could not pay. When Jesus gave His Life on Calvary's Cross, this paid the debt in totality, making it possible for Believers, upon the Merit of Christ, to enter boldly into the very Throne of Grace. As well, this can be done anytime by any Believer, and as many times as necessary (Heb. 4:16).

THE NEW COVENANT

Paul tells us how that debt was paid. He said:

"For where a Testament *is (Covenant)*, there must also of necessity be the death of the testator. *(This refers to the death of Christ, Who was charged to make a New Covenant on the part of man.)*

"For a Testament *is* of force after men are dead *(this tells us in no uncertain terms that the death of Christ on the Cross was a legal matter)*: otherwise it is of no strength at all while the testator lives. *(This simply means it is not valid until the individual to whom the Will belongs dies, as is the case of any Testament or Will.)*

"Whereupon neither the First *Testament* (Old Covenant) was dedicated without blood *(but it was only the blood of animals)*.

ANIMAL BLOOD

"For when Moses had spoken every Precept to all the people according to the Law *(this was referred to as the 'Law of Moses')*, he took the blood of calves and of

goats *(proclaims the seal of the Old Covenant, which was 'shed blood'; of course, it was a type of the Shed Blood of Christ)*, **with water** *(as the blood witnessed to the nature of His Atoning Death [Jn. 19:34], the water witnessed to His full and proper humanity)*, **and scarlet wool** *(wool is normally white, which symbolizes the Righteousness of Christ; however, it was dyed red, which portrayed the fact that it took the Blood of Christ to make this Righteousness available to man)*, **and hyssop** *(a bushy plant, which typified His Death on the Cross as a man; in Egypt the blood was applied to the doorpost with hyssop [Ex. 12:22])*, **and sprinkled both the Book, and all the people** *(referred to the Book of Leviticus, with the Tribe of Levi Ordained for Tabernacle Service, pertaining to the people; the sprinkling of the blood was the ratification of the Covenant, and symbolized the Blood of Christ which would ultimately be shed and applied by Faith to the hearts and lives of believing sinners [the blood was mixed with water])*,

THE BLOOD OF THE TESTAMENT

"Saying, This *is* **the Blood of the Testament** *(presents that which made the Old Covenant valid)* **which God has enjoined upon you** *(This presents the fact that everything in the First Covenant, exactly as in the New Covenant, is all of God and not at all of man.)*

"Moreover he sprinkled with Blood both the Tabernacle, and all the Vessels of the Ministry. *(This particular Verse portrays the awfulness of sin, and that it has contaminated everything on this Earth.)*

"And almost all things are by the Law purged with blood *(some few things were purged with water, but almost all with blood)*; **and without shedding of blood is no remission.** *(The shed Blood of Christ on the Cross is the only solution for the sins, the ills, and the problems of this world. The problem of the world, and of the Church as well, is that* *it has ever sought to substitute something else. But let all know, it is alone the Cross! The Cross! The Cross!)*

"*It was* therefore necessary that the patterns of things in the heavens should be purified with these *(everything that pertained to the Tabernacle and all of its Sacred Vessels was a copy of that which was in Heaven; inasmuch as the Vessels and the Tabernacle were touched by men, they had to be purified by Blood, i.e., 'animal blood')*; **but the heavenly things themselves with better sacrifices than these.** *(If man were to enter Heaven, the abode of God, there would have to be a better sacrifice than that of animal blood.)*

A BETTER SACRIFICE

"For Christ is not entered into the Holy Places made with hands *(Christ did not enter the earthly Tabernacle or Temple, regarding the offering up of His Precious Blood on the Mercy Seat)***, which are the figures of the true** *(presents the fact that these 'figures' were only temporary)*; **but into Heaven itself, now to appear in the Presence of God for us** *(presents the purpose and reason for the Cross; all of it was done 'for us')*:

"Not yet that He should offer Himself often *(refers to the fact that the one Sacrifice of Christ, which was the Offering of Himself on the Cross, was eternally sufficient for the cleansing from all sin — past, present, and future; it will never need to be repeated)*, **as the High Priest enters into the Holy Place every year with blood of others** *(refers to the High Priest of Israel of Old, who went into the Holy of Holies once a year on the Great Day of Atonement, carrying animal blood)*;

"For then must He *(the Lord Jesus)* **often have suffered since the foundation of the world** *(presents the fact that He wasn't functioning as the High Priests of Israel who, as stated, had to offer sacrifice yearly)*: **but now once in the end of the world has He appeared to put away sin by**

the Sacrifice of Himself. *(This presents the One Sacrifice of Christ as sufficient for all time. The phrase, 'In the end of the world,' should have been translated, 'in the consummation of the ages.' As well, by the Sacrifice of Himself, He didn't merely cover sin, but rather 'took it away' [Jn. 1:29].)*

CHRIST TOOK THE PENALTY OF OUR SINS

"And as it is appointed unto men once to die *(due to the Fall, all men are under the sentence of death, and, in fact, all have died Spiritually, which means to be separated from God)***, but after this the Judgment** *(the answer to the Spiritual death of man is Christ and what He did at the Cross; if Christ the Saviour is rejected, all will face Christ the Judge; for as death was inevitable, the Judgment is inevitable as well)***:**
"So Christ was once offered to bear the sins of many *(the Cross was God's Answer to sin and, in fact, the only answer)***; and unto them who look for Him shall He appear the second time without sin unto Salvation.** *(This refers to the Second Coming. 'Without sin' refers to the fact that the Second Coming will not be to atone for sin, for that was already carried out at the Cross at His First Advent. The Second Coming will bring all the results of Salvation to this world, which refers to all that He did at the Cross. We now only have the 'Firstfruits' [Rom. 8:23])***"**
(Heb. 9:16-28).

"When I saw the cleansing Fountain,
"Open wide for all my sin,
"I obeyed the Spirit's wooing,
"When He said, Will you be clean?"

"Though the Way seems straight and narrow,
"All I claimed was swept away;
"My ambitions, plans, and wishes,

"At my feet in ashes lay."

"Then God's Fire upon the Altar,
"Of my heart was set aflame;
"I shall never cease to praise Him,
"Glory, Glory to His Name."

"Blessed be the Name of Jesus,
"I'm so glad He took me in;
"He's forgiven my transgressions,
"He has cleansed my heart from sin."

"Glory, Glory to the Father,
"Glory, Glory to the Son,
"Glory, Glory to the Spirit,
"Glory to the Three in One."

"I will praise Him, I will praise Him,
"Praise the Lamb for sinners slain;
"Give Him glory, all ye people,
"For His Blood can wash away each stain."

CHAPTER TWENTY-FIVE

How Do You Know That Romans 6:3-4 Speaks Of The Crucifixion, Instead Of Water Baptism?

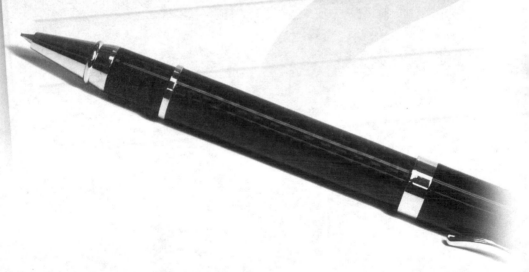

QUESTION:

HOW DO YOU KNOW THAT ROMANS 6:3-4 SPEAKS OF THE CRUCIFIXION, INSTEAD OF WATER BAPTISM?

ANSWER:

I know that because the associating Texts are speaking of the Crucifixion and not Water Baptism. As well, I know it because Paul is using the Words *"Baptism,"* and *"Baptize,"* in the figurative instead of the technical sense. On page sixteen of the *GREEK DICTIONARY OF THE NEW TESTAMENT* from *THE NEW STRONG'S EXHAUSTIVE CONCORDANCE OF THE BIBLE*,[1] we are given this information.

Incidentally, there are several Editions of the Strong's Concordance. Some go into more detail than others, as does the one I am using.

INTERPRETING ROMANS 6:3-4 AS WATER
BAPTISM IS ERRONEOUS

Most preachers, regrettably, interpret these two Scriptures as Water Baptism, which causes them to miss the proper meaning of the Sixth Chapter of Romans, one of the single most important Chapters in the Bible. Most Christians read this Chapter and, as it begins, think that Paul is speaking of Water Baptism. Considering that they have been baptized in water they, by and large, dismiss the balance of the Chapter, thereby, missing the greatest teaching given in the Bible as it regards how a Believer is to live for God. In fact, I think one can say without fear of contradiction that the Sixth Chapter of Romans carries the most important teaching for the Believer given anywhere in the Word of God. However, as stated, it is lost on most Christians because of an erroneous interpretation.

I suppose we have most all of the Study Bibles in our office that are being offered to the Christian public presently. I'm aware of only one Study Bible, other than THE EXPOSITOR'S STUDY BIBLE, which correctly interprets this Passage. As stated, that is sad, considering how important the teaching is as given here by Paul.

A BRIEF EXEGESIS OF THE SIXTH CHAPTER OF ROMANS

If one properly understands the Bible, it is understood that at least ninety-five percent of it is given over to telling Believers how to live for God. Of the fourteen Epistles written by Paul, to whom the meaning of the New Covenant was given (Gal. 1:12), virtually ninety percent of these Epistles are, as well, given over to telling Believers how to serve the Lord. Understanding that, one might say that the entirety of the Bible pushes toward the great Sixth Chapter of Romans, while that which follows harks back to what the Apostle taught us in this particular Chapter. That's how important it is. To think that Satan has corrupted the meaning in the minds of most Believers to where they do not properly understand what the great Apostle taught us is nothing less than tragic.

SIN

We must understand that Paul is speaking in this Chapter to Believers. He is not speaking to the unsaved because they would not understand at all that of which he said.

The first two Verses tell us that sin is the problem. Any Christian who claims he doesn't have a problem with sin needs to tell the Apostle Paul that he did not know what he was talking about. Yes, sin is the problem!

THE CROSS OF CHRIST

Pure and simple, Paul tells us in Verses 3 through 5 that the answer to the sin problem and, in fact, the only answer is the

Cross of Jesus Christ.

When Jesus died on the Cross, He died as our Substitute. Actually, He was referred to by Paul as the last Adam and the Second Man (I Cor. 15:45-47). So, in His earthly Ministry, and above all, His death on the Cross of Calvary, Jesus Christ being the Last Adam, was the True Man. So, when He hung on the Cross, in the Mind of God we were literally *"in Him"* when He died. As well, we were *"in Him"* when He was placed in the tomb and *"in Him"* when He was raised from the dead.

Now, how did this happen, seeing that we were not there and that we who are presently Saved live some two thousand years after the happening of the Cross?

FAITH

Whenever the believing sinner evidences Faith in Christ when he is Saved, in the Mind of God, such Faith places one in Christ. This is the reason that the Crucifixion is so important. It is far more than Jesus dying, even as He did. He was literally dying for the entirety of mankind, at least for all who will believe (Jn. 3:16).

THE DEATH OF THE OLD MAN

Paul said, *"Knowing this, that our old man is Crucified with Him, that the body of sin might be destroyed that henceforth we should not serve sin"* (Rom. 6:6).

Verses 6 through 10 tell us of the old man dying with Christ, which refers to what we were before conversion. This means that in the Mind of God, as it regards the conversion process, we did not merely become something, but rather, died as to what we were, and were raised in *"newness of life."* As stated, this all came by Faith. What we once were is dead. What we are now is:

"A new creature *(a new creation)*: old things are passed away *(what we were before Salvation)*; behold, all things

are become new. *(The old is no longer useable, with every-thing given to us now by Christ as 'new')*" **(II Cor. 5:17).**

FAITH ONCE AGAIN

Understanding this, how that we were in Christ when He died, were buried, and raised from the dead, and that what we were before conversion died with Him, and we were raised in *"newness of life,"* now we must:

"**Likewise reckon** *(account)* **you also yourselves to be dead indeed unto** *(the)* **sin** *(while the sin nature is not dead, we are dead unto the sin nature by virtue of the Cross and our Faith in that Sacrifice, but only as long as our Faith continues in the Cross)*, **but alive unto God** *(living the Resurrection Life)* **through Jesus Christ our Lord** *(refers to what He did at the Cross, which is the means of this Resurrection Life)*" **(Rom. 6:11).**

SANCTIFICATION

Verses 12 and 13 tell us that inasmuch as we are now *"dead indeed unto the sin nature,"* and due to what Jesus did for us at the Cross and our Faith in that Finished Work, we do not have to allow the sin nature to rule us as it did before Salvation. We now have the means to *"yield ourselves unto God"* (Vs. 13). However, this is possible only as long as the Cross of Christ remains the Object of our Faith.

THE DOMINION OF SIN BROKEN

After Verses 2 and 3, probably one can say that the pivotal Scripture of this great Chapter, and maybe the entirety of the Bible, is *"For sin shall not have dominion over you"* (Vs. 14). This means that the sin nature will no longer have dominion over us as Believers, as stated, as we continue to exercise Faith in Christ and what He did for us at the Cross. Never forget, the Cross of Christ must ever be the Object of our Faith. This being the case, the Holy Spirit, Who works exclusively within the parameters of the Finished Work of Christ, will work mightily on our behalf, developing His Fruit within our hearts and lives.

NO LONGER UNDER LAW BUT UNDER GRACE

Verses 15 through 23 tell us that we are no longer under Law, but rather, under Grace.

Grace is simply the Goodness of God given to undeserving Saints. It is a product of the Cross of Christ. In other words, it is the Cross which has made everything possible, including the Grace of God, which gives the Holy Spirit latitude to work within our lives.

That being the case, we can now live a life of Holiness and Righteousness unto the Lord. It is all made possible by the Cross and carried out by the Holy Spirit. In fact, the Eighth Chapter of Romans proclaims to us the manner in which the Holy Spirit works. As stated, it is by and through the Cross of Christ, which gives the Holy Spirit the legal means to do all that He does. It is found in Romans 8:2.

Someone has rightly said that the Sixth Chapter of Romans proclaims the mechanics of the Holy Spirit, in other words, how He works. It is said that the Eighth Chapter of Romans proclaims the dynamics of the Holy Spirit, which tells us what He does in our hearts and lives once we understand how He does it.

In brief, that is the basic intent of the great Sixth Chapter of Romans.

(For a more detailed analysis of the great Sixth Chapter of Romans, please see our Study Guide, *"GOD'S PRESCRIBED ORDER OF VICTORY, The Cross of Christ Series"*.)

THE FIGURATIVE USE OF CERTAIN WORDS

Paul used any number of words in a figurative sense because

the word that he used explained what he was teaching better than any other. For instance, he said, *"For I was alive without the Law once: but when the Commandment came, sin revived, and I died"* (Rom. 7:9). Here, as well, he used the word *"died"* in a figurative sense. It does not mean that he died physically, as should be obvious, but rather, he failed the Lord, and the word *"died,"* explaining that failure, was the word the Holy Spirit desired that he use.

He did the same thing in Romans 8:10. He said, *"And if Christ be in you, the body is dead because of sin."*

Physically speaking, the body was not dead in that sense. Nevertheless, he used the word *"dead"* in a figurative sense to explain what he was endeavoring to teach. It meant that the physical body had been rendered helpless because of the Fall; consequently, the Believer trying to overcome by willpower presents a fruitless task.

Paul was not the only one to use words in a figurative sense. John the Baptist said:

"I indeed baptize you with water unto Repentance: but He Who comes after me is mightier than I, Whose Shoes I am not worthy to bear: He shall Baptize you with the Holy Spirit, and with fire" (Mat. 3:11).

Here, John the Baptist uses the word *"Baptize"* in connection with the Holy Spirit. I think it should be obvious that John the Baptist was not speaking of Water Baptism. Actually, he used the same word in both cases, the first word *"baptize"* referring to water, and the second word *"Baptize"* referring to the Holy Spirit. Once again, as it regards the Holy Spirit, John the Baptist was using the word figuratively.

WHY DID PAUL USE THE WORDS *"BAPTIZE"* AND *"BAPTIZED"* IN ROMANS 6:3-5?

We must understand that every word that every Bible writer wrote, all the way from Moses to John the Beloved who closed out the Canon of Scripture with the great Book of Revelation, was given by the Holy Spirit. In other words, the Holy Spirit searched through the vocabulary of each writer and selected each word that He wanted in every sentence and, thereby, moved upon the individual to use that word. They did not do this through some type of automatic writing, but rather, in full control of their faculties. Inspiration is the Holy Spirit working accordingly in the hearts and lives of these writers, whomever they might have been. This is why the Bible is error free, at least as it regards the original manuscripts.

That's why Jesus said, *"Man shall not live by bread alone, but by every Word that proceeds out of the Mouth of God"* (Mat. 4:4).

Paul used the words *"Baptize"* and *"Baptized"* simply because those are the words the Holy Spirit desired to be used, and because they explained more fully than any other words what happens to the Believer as it regards the Crucifixion of Christ and the Believer being *"in Christ."* Incidentally, Paul used the term *"in Christ,"* or one of its derivatives, over one hundred times in his fourteen Epistles. Always and without exception, it refers to the Death, Burial, and Resurrection of Christ and us being in Him when all of this took place. As we have stated, we gain all of this by the simple act of Faith in Him.

In the strict sense of the word, the word *"baptize"* means, as it refers to water, that the person is in the water and the water is in the person. Of course, in the practical sense, that cannot happen because, if it did, the person would drown; however, that's what it literally means.

Over television at times we have all seen ships that have sunk. It is a perfect description of Baptism. The ship is in the water and the water is in the ship.

Regarding Christ and the great act of the Cross, we are literally in Christ and He is in us. That did not end with the Cross but is maintained forever. Jesus said:

"At that day *(after the Resurrection, and the coming of the Holy Spirit on the Day of Pentecost)* **you shall know**

that I *am* in My Father *(speaks of Deity; Jesus is God!)*, and you in Me *(has to do with our Salvation by Faith)*, and I in you *(enables us to live a victorious life [Gal. 2:20])*" (Jn. 14:20).

So, the Holy Spirit through Paul used the words *"Baptize"* and *"Baptized"* simply because these words explained what the Holy Spirit wanted explained better than any other words. That's why He had Paul to use them.

I should think by now that anyone reading the answer we have given would hardly think anymore that Paul is speaking here of Water Baptism. Actually, as it regards Water Baptism, while a viable, Scriptural Ordinance, still, it is not essential to Salvation, as important as it might be. Paul said this about Water Baptism:

"For Christ sent me not to baptize *(presents to us a Cardinal Truth)*, but to preach the Gospel *(the manner in which one may be Saved from sin)*: not with wisdom of words *(intellectualism is not the Gospel)*, lest the Cross of Christ should be made of none effect. *(This tells us in no uncertain terms that the Cross of Christ must always be the emphasis of the Message)*" (I Cor. 1:17).

THE CROSS OF CHRIST SAVES;
WATER DOES NOT SAVE

Concerning this Peter said:

"The like figure *(refers to Water Baptism as a symbol. As well, Peter is using the word 'baptism' in a figurative sense)* whereunto *even* baptism does also now save us *(speaks of the Baptism into Christ, which takes place at conversion; it is done by Faith, and has nothing to do with Water Baptism, although that serves as a symbol [Rom. 6:3-5])*, (not the putting away of the filth of the flesh *(proclaims the fact that Water Baptism cannot cleanse the soul)*, **but the answer of a good conscience toward God,)** *(refers to the fact that one engages in Water Baptism because one has already been made clean by Faith in the Lord Jesus, which in turn gives one a good conscience toward God)* **by the Resurrection of Jesus Christ** *(which refers to the Cross, and the Believing sinner being raised with Christ in 'newness of life' [Rom. 6:4-5]):*

"Who *(Jesus Christ)* **is gone into Heaven** *(His Mission is complete)*, **and is on the Right Hand of God** *(proclaims the fact that His Sacrifice was accepted)*; **Angels and authorities and powers being made subject unto Him.** *(This refers to all, whether Holy or unholy. The 'Cross' is the means by which all of this was done [Col. 2:14-15].)*

VICTORY OVER SIN

"Forasmuch then as Christ has suffered for us in the flesh *(refers to the Cross, with 'flesh' referring to the fact that He died physically, and not spiritually as some claim)*, **arm yourselves likewise with the same mind** *(doesn't mean we are to attempt to imitate Christ in suffering, but rather to make the fact He suffered our source of Victory; He suffered in the flesh that we might have Victory over the flesh)*: **for he who has suffered in the flesh has ceased from sin** *(refers to the struggle between the flesh and the Spirit; 'suffering in the flesh' by the Believer refers to stopping any dependence on self-effort, and depending totally on the Holy Spirit, Who demands that our Faith be in the Sacrifice of Christ [Rom. 8:1-2]);*

"That he no longer should live the rest of *his* time in the flesh to the lusts of men *(since being Saved, the sin nature is no longer to rule over us)*, **but to the Will of God.** *(This refers to the Divine Nature ruling over us, which comes about as a result of our total dependence on Christ and the Cross. In fact, Christ and the Cross are never to be* *separated, which refers to the benefits of the Cross coming down to us even unto this hour)"* **(I Pet. 3:21-22; 4:1-2).**

THE APOSTLE PAUL AND THE NEW COVENANT

It is obvious to all who are serious students of the Bible that it was to Paul that the meaning of the New Covenant was given **(Gal. 1:1-12),** and from that, we know and understand, and without contradiction, that Paul preached the Cross. While, of course, the Resurrection, the Ascension, and the Exaltation of Christ constituted that which was, as well, of extreme significance, still, these great happenings were the *"result"* of the Atonement and not the cause. There is no place in his fourteen Epistles that Paul held up anything but the Cross of Christ as the element of Redemption. He did not preach Water Baptism as a means of Salvation, and neither did he preach anything else, as Scriptural as these other things may have been. So, to surmise that Paul was speaking of Water Baptism in Romans 6:3-5 shows an acute ignorance of the Word of God, and especially of Paul's Ministry **(Rom. 6:1-14; 8:1-2, 11; I Cor. 1:17-18, 23; 2:2; Gal., Chpt. 5; 6:14; Eph. 2:13-18; Col. 2:14-15; Heb. 13:20).**

THE MEANING OF WATER BAPTISM

The Scripture says:

"And Jesus, when He was baptized *(this was the beginning of His earthly Ministry),* **went up straightway** *(immediately)* **out of the water** *(refers to Baptism by immersion and not by sprinkling):* **and, lo, the Heavens were opened unto Him** *(the only One, the Lord Jesus Christ, to Whom the Heavens would be opened),* **and he saw the Spirit of God** *(Holy Spirit)* **descending like a dove, and lighting upon Him** *(John saw a visible form that reminded him of a dove):*

"And lo a Voice from Heaven, saying *(the Voice of God the Father)*, **This is My Beloved Son, in Whom I am well pleased** *(the Trinity appears here: the Father speaks, the Spirit descends, and the Son prays [Lk. 3:21])*" (Mat. 3:16-17).

Jesus standing in the water symbolized His actual death on the Cross. Being put under the water by John the Baptist symbolized the burial of Christ. Jesus being raised out of the water symbolized His Resurrection.

In some sense, it means the same thing with the Believer when we are baptized. Being in Christ, we died with Him, were buried with Him, and raised with Him in Newness of Life.

Water Baptism is only a symbol of the reality, but yet, a very important symbol, as should be obvious. It should be understood that there is no saving Grace whatsoever in Water Baptism. While every Believer, once coming to Christ, most definitely wants to be baptized, still, his or her Salvation does not await that particular ceremony.

Some attempt to claim the following Passage as falling into the category of Baptismal Regeneration. It doesn't!

The Scripture says:

"**Then Peter said unto them, Repent** *(admit that God is right, and we are wrong)*, **and be baptized every one of you in the Name of Jesus Christ** *(by the authority of that Name; there is no baptismal formula given in the Book of Acts; the only formula given was given by Christ in Mat. 28:19)* **for the Remission of sins** *(should have been translated, 'because of remission of sins'; one is Baptized in Water because one's sins have already been remitted due to Faith in Christ, and not that sins should be remitted)*, **and you shall receive the Gift of the Holy Spirit** *(Repentance guarantees Salvation, which makes the Believer ready to be Baptized with the Holy Spirit; one is not Baptized with the Spirit automatically at conversion;*

it is an experience that follows Salvation, and is always accompanied by speaking with other tongues [Acts 2:4; 10:44-46; 19:1-7])" **(Acts 2:38).**

"In the Cross of Christ I glory,
"Towering o'er the wrecks of time;
"All the light of sacred story,
"Gathers round its head sublime."

"When the woes of life o'ertake me,
"Hopes deceive, and fears annoy,
"Never shall the Cross forsake me:
"Lo! It glows with peace and joy."

"When the sun of bliss is beaming,
"Light and love upon my way,
"From the Cross the radiance streaming,
"Adds more luster to the day."

"Bane and blessing, pain and pleasure,
"By the Cross are sanctified;
"Peace is there that knows no measure,
"Joys that through all time abide."

CHAPTER TWENTY-SIX

What Did Paul Mean When He Said To The Church At Corinth, "I Determined To Know Nothing Among You Save Jesus Christ And Him Crucified"?

QUESTION:

WHAT DID PAUL MEAN WHEN HE SAID TO THE CHURCH AT CORINTH, "I DETERMINED TO KNOW NOTHING AMONG YOU SAVE JESUS CHRIST AND HIM CRUCIFIED"?

ANSWER:

He meant that this was the only Message that would save the soul and, as well, give Believers Victory over the world, the flesh, and the Devil.

Paul said to the Church at Corinth:

"And I, Brethren, when I came to you, came not with excellency of speech or of wisdom *(means that he depended not on oratorical abilities, nor did he delve into philosophy, which was all the rage of that particular day)*, declaring unto you the Testimony of God *(which is Christ and Him Crucified)*.

"For I determined not to know anything among you *(with purpose and design, Paul did not resort to the knowledge or philosophy of the world regarding the preaching of the Gospel)*, save Jesus Christ, and Him Crucified *(that and that alone is the Message which will save the sinner, set the captive free, and give the Believer perpetual Victory)*" (I Cor. 2:1-2).

PAUL IN ATHENS

Even though there is no concrete Scriptural proof, some Scholars believe that Paul's experience in Athens was the catalyst in a negative sense, one might say, which formed the thinking of the Apostle as to how he would approach Corinth.

Even though I personally make no claim whatsoever to scholarship, I do personally claim to be an avid Bible student.

I too, share the idea that Paul's experience in Athens caused him, quite possibly, to investigate his Message, and to do so minutely. To give a proper account, we must as well, I think, deal with the situation at Athens. The Scripture says:

"And then immediately the Brethren sent away Paul to go as it were to the Sea *(speaks of the Aegean, which was about 17 miles from Berea)*: but Silas and Timotheus abode there still *(remained in Berea)*.

"And they who conducted Paul brought him to Athens *(presents the chief city of Greece, famed for its learning)*: and receiving a commandment unto Silas and Timotheus for to come to him with all speed, they departed *(Paul sends the Message back with these men that Silas and Timothy are to come to Athens as soon as possible)*.

IDOLATRY

"Now while Paul waited for them at Athens, his spirit was stirred in him, when he saw the city wholly given to idolatry *(meaning it was full of idols)*.

"Therefore disputed he in the Synagogue with the Jews *(from the Scriptures, he would preach Jesus; the Scriptures then, at least as far as the Jews were concerned, were the Old Testament)*, and with the devout persons *(singles out the Jews who really seemed to be devoted to the Scriptures)*, and in the market daily with them that met with him *(this was a place in Athens where speakers generally gave forth)*.

"Then certain philosophers of the Epicureans *(those who claimed that gratification of the appetites and pleasures was the only end in life)*, and of the Stoics *(they taught that man was not to be moved by either joy or grief)*, encountered him *(challenged his statements about Christ)*. And some said, What will this babbler say? *(this presents the highest insult of which they could think.)* **Other some, He seems to be a setter forth of strange gods** *(in their minds, anything outside of Greek philosophy was of no consequence)*: **because he preached unto them Jesus, and the Resurrection** *(they didn't want a Resurrection, simply because they did not desire the idea of living this life over again; this shows they totally misunderstood what Paul said)*.

THE RESPONSE OF THE ATHENIANS

"And they took him, and brought him unto Areopagus *(refers to Mars' Hill which faces the Acropolis; this was the Supreme Court of Athens)*, **saying, May we know what this new doctrine, whereof you speak,** *is*? *(This presents Paul facing the Supreme Court Justices of Athens.)*

"For you bring certain strange things to our ears *(it's strange that those who brought Paul to this place labeled what he said as mere babblings, but yet, think it important enough to be taken to the highest Court in Athens)*: **we would know therefore what these things mean** *(presents a noble request to Paul, and an unparalleled opportunity)*.

"(For all the Athenians and strangers which were there spent their time in nothing else, but either to tell, or to hear some new thing.) *(With the great Philosophers now dead, Athens was attempting to live off the glory of former times.)*

TO THE UNKNOWN GOD

"Then Paul stood in the midst of Mars' Hill, and said, *You* **men of Athens, I perceive that in all things you are too superstitious** *(in this one sentence, he debunks all of their philosophies; they are guided by superstition, which is no way to live)*.

"For as I passed by, and beheld your devotions *(has*

reference to their objects of worship), **I found an Altar with this inscription, TO THE UNKNOWN GOD** *(by addressing the situation in this way, he could not be accused of preaching a foreign god to them)*. **Whom therefore you ignorantly worship, Him declare I unto you** *(refers to them acknowledging that maybe they did not have the last word on gods! Actually, they did not have any word at all)*.

THE LORD OF GLORY

"God Who made the world and all things therein *(presents God as the Creator)*, **seeing that He is Lord of Heaven and Earth** *(proclaims Him not only as Creator, but the constant Manager of all that He has created as well)*, **dwells not in Temples made with hands** *(He is bigger than that!)***;**
    "Neither is worshipped with men's hands *(the Second Commandment forbids the making of any graven image of God, or the worship of any type of statue, etc.)*, **as though He needed any thing** *(God needs nothing!)*, **seeing He gives to all life, and breath, and all things** *(presents His Creation needing what He provides, which is provided by no other source)***;**
    "And has made of one blood all nations of men for to dwell on all the face of the Earth *(proclaims all having their origin in Adam)*, **and has determined the times before appointed, and the bounds of their habitation** *(pertains to particular parts of the world, and those who occupy these areas; however, the statement, 'one blood all nations of men,' eliminates any type of racial superiority)***;**

IN THE LORD OF GLORY IS EVERYTHING

"That they should seek the Lord *(presents the chief end of all God's dealings with men [I Pet. 2:24; II Pet. 3:9;*

Jn. 3:15-20; Rev. 22:17]), **if haply they might feel after Him, and find Him** *(Paul is appealing to the action of logic and common sense in trying to address these Pagans)*, **though He be not far from every one of us** *(speaks of the Creator being very close to His Creation)*:

"**For in Him we live, and move, and have our being** *(proclaims God as the Source of all life [Heb. 1:3])*; **as certain also of your own poets have said, For we are also His offspring** *(presents a direct quote from Aratus of Tarsus, Paul's own country)*.

THE GODHEAD

"**Forasmuch then as we are the offspring of God** *(is offered by Paul in the sense of Creation; it does not mean the 'Fatherhood of God, and the Brotherhood of man,' as many contend)*, **we ought not to think that the Godhead is like unto gold, or silver, or stone, graven by art and man's device** *(Paul is saying that God is not a device of man, as all the Greek gods in fact were)*.

"**And the times of this ignorance God winked at** *(does not reflect that such ignorance was Salvation, for it was not! Before the Cross, there was very little Light in the world, so God withheld Judgment)*; **but now commands all men every where to repent** *(but since the Cross, the 'Way' is open to all; it's up to us Believers to make that 'Way' known to all men)*:

THE GREAT WHITE THRONE JUDGMENT

"**Because He has appointed a day** *(refers to the coming of the Great White Throne Judgment [Rev. 20:11-15])*, **in the which He will Judge the world in Righteousness by *that* Man Whom He has ordained** *(this Righteousness is exclusively in Christ Jesus and what He has done for us at the Cross, and can be gained only by Faith in Him*

[Eph. 2:8-9; Rom. 10:9-10, 13; Rev. 22:17]); *whereof* **He has given assurance unto all** *men*, **in that He has raised Him from the dead** *(refers to the Resurrection ratifying that which was done at Calvary, and is applicable to all men, at least all who will believe!).*

THE RESURRECTION

"And when they heard of the Resurrection of the Dead, some mocked *(the 'mocking' was caused by sheer unbelief)*: **and others said, We will hear you again of this** *matter (many were touched by Paul's Message, but regrettably procrastinated).*

"So Paul departed from among them *(they ascertained that he had broken none of their laws, so he was free to go, which he did!).*

"Howbeit certain men clave unto him, and believed *(these believed wholeheartedly, recognizing in Paul the true Words of Life)*: **among the which** *was* **Dionysius the Areopagite** *(he was a member of the Great Court of Athens; tradition says that he became the Pastor of the Church in Athens)*, **and a woman named Damaris** *(a person of prominence)*, **and others with them"** (Acts 17:14-34).

CORINTH

Now, Paul feels led of the Lord to go to the great city of Corinth in order to plant a Church. It was one of the largest cities in the Roman Empire and, as well, one of, if not the most wicked. It was noted basically for two things:

1. Vice: Over one hundred pagan temples graced its environs, populated by thousands of male and female prostitutes. The city was so wicked that for those who had thrown all convention to the wind, they were said to be *"Corinthianized,"* meaning, jaded beyond redemption.

2. Philosophy: Several great Philosophers had come out of

Corinth, which gave the city an air of intellectualism.

So, Paul was facing the two greatest evils of Satan, human philosophy and vice. Coming from Athens to Corinth, from the statements that he made at the beginning of his Epistle to the Corinthians, it seems that he may have been troubled in spirit.

THE CROSS OF CHRIST

As is obvious, Paul didn't preach the Cross at Athens. He rather, preached the Resurrection. While his message was dynamic to say the least, still, after the fact, it seems that he may have wondered if he really had the Mind of the Lord as it regarded his Message that particular day. Knowing that he was going into one of the very strongholds of Satan, he, no doubt, pondered in his mind as to what his approach should be.

If, in fact, something like this happened, and it very well could have, the Holy Spirit could have whispered to him, saying, *"Preach the Cross!"* Then the Spirit may have said, *"If the Cross will work at Corinth, it will work anywhere."*

That's the reason I believe the great Apostle said to the Corinthians, *"For I determined not to know any thing among you, save Jesus Christ, and Him Crucified"* (I Cor. 2:2).

PHILOSOPHY AND INTELLECTUALISM

Paul was one of the most educated men used by the Lord as it regards writing the Books of the Bible. As a result, had he been so minded, he could hold forth with anyone respecting the intellectual pursuit, but he realized that all the pontification in the world would not save one single soul and would not help one single Believer find Victory in Christ. Yet, that's where the modern church is. The message of the moment is *"morality"* and *"ethics."* Such sounds very good to the carnal ear and is eagerly accepted; however, the idea is that poor mortal man can change his situation by changing his habits, etc. As stated, all of this sounds good to the carnal mind, but, the truth is, it is worthless.

Man's condition is far worse than he even begins to realize. In fact, whatever a man needs, no matter his education, no matter his talent, no matter his efforts, within himself, the need cannot be met. Paul told us why. He said:

"**And if Christ** *be* **in you** *(He is in you through the Power and Person of the Spirit [Gal. 2:20])***, the body** *is* **dead because of sin** *(means that the physical body has been rendered helpless because of the Fall; consequently, the Believer trying to overcome by willpower presents a fruitless task)***; but the Spirit** *is* **life because of Righteousness.** *(Only the Holy Spirit can make us what we ought to be, which means we cannot do it ourselves; once again, He performs all that He does within the confines of the Finished Work of Christ)*" **(Rom. 8:10).**

Now, either religious man believes what Paul said or he doesn't believe it. Regrettably, he doesn't believe it, so self tries to improve self, which is impossible.

The great Apostle, as he was inspired by the Holy Spirit, is telling us that the Fall rendered man incapable of doing what needs to be done, of being what he needs to be. No matter how hard we try, no matter the effort put forth, we simply cannot do what needs to be done. But, the Holy Spirit can.

THE HOLY SPIRIT

As we know, the Holy Spirit is God. As such, He is Omnipotent, meaning all-powerful; Omniscient, meaning all-knowing; and, Omnipresent, meaning that He is everywhere. However, we must understand the way that He works.

The Holy Spirit will never force the issue. He will deal with us, work with us, and speak to us, but, if we insist on going in the opposite direction, He will let us go. To be sure, we will reap the results, but He will not force the issue.

The Holy Spirit works from two positions, which in reality,

are one and the same.

1. **He works strictly by and through the Word of God.** In fact, **He is the Author of the Word.** The Scripture says:

"**For the Prophecy** *(the word 'Prophecy' is used here in a general sense, covering the entirety of the Word of God, which means it's not limited merely to predictions regarding the future)* **came not in old time by the will of man** *(did not originate with man)*: **but Holy men of God spoke** *as they were* **moved by the Holy Spirit.** *(This proclaims the manner in which the Word of God was written and thereby given unto us)*" (**II Pet. 1:21**).

This means that if the Believer functions outside of the Word of God, such limits the Holy Spirit greatly as to what He desires to do.

2. **In the context of the Word of God, the Holy Spirit works exclusively within the parameters of the Finished Work of Christ, i.e.,** *"the Cross"* **(Rom. 8:2).** As we've said over and over, the Holy Spirit doesn't demand much of us, but He does demand that our Faith be exclusively in Christ and what Christ did for us at the Cross. That is a must (Rom. 6:1-14; 8:1-2, 10; I Cor. 1:17-18, 23; 2:2; Gal., Chpt. 5; 6:14; Eph. 2:13-18; Col. 2:14-15).

The Message of the Cross is the only viable Message given to us in the Word of God. Everything else is a work of man and, no matter how religious it may seem to be, will effect no positive results.

JESUS CHRIST AND HIM CRUCIFIED

So, when Paul said, *"For I determined not to know anything among you, save Jesus Christ, and Him Crucified,"* the word *"determined"* means that he had investigated the situation thoroughly with his conclusion being that the Cross of Christ was the only answer.

The word *"determined"* in the Greek is *"krino,"* and means to *"conclude, decree, to esteem, to judge."* This is a matter that he obviously had wrestled with for quite some time and had sought the Lord as to the proper direction. The word *"determined,"* as used here, means that the Apostle knew beyond the shadow of a doubt that the only message that was going to help anyone was the Message of *"Jesus Christ and Him Crucified."* Once you understand a little bit about it, then it becomes crystal clear as to why this is the case.

In effect, the great Apostle was saying then as well as now that no matter how good the other ways may seem to be, no matter how much they are applauded by the world and even the church, if the Message isn't *"Jesus Christ and Him Crucified,"* then it is useless. That's why the great Apostle also said:

"**I do not frustrate the Grace of God** *(if we make anything other than the Cross of Christ the Object of our Faith, we frustrate the Grace of God, which means we stop its action, and the Holy Spirit will no longer help us)*: **for if Righteousness** *come* **by the Law** *(any type of Law)*, **then Christ is dead in vain.** *(If I can successfully live for the Lord by any means other than Faith in Christ and the Cross, then the Death of Christ was a waste)*" (**Gal. 2:21**).

WHAT ABOUT ALL THE OTHER PROPOSED WAYS?

The truth is, the church lurches from one proposed solution to the other, all to no avail!

The following constitutes some of the ways proposed by the Church in order for one to live for God. Some of the things are very right in their own way and some of the things are very wrong. They are as follows:

1. Humanistic psychology: We have dealt with this in another question in this Volume and there is no point in covering the same ground again, except to say, one cannot embrace at the same time humanistic psychology and the Cross of Christ.

One or the other must go.

2. The Lord's Supper: Of course, this is a viable Biblical Doctrine and should be engaged by every Believer; however, to read more into the ceremony than we should is not Biblical. In other words, the ceremony itself contains no magic properties. I realize that some preachers claim that one can be healed by taking the Lord's Supper, or find prosperity, etc. While anything that is Scriptural brings a Blessing, that is, if it's followed correctly, still, there is nothing in the Word of God that substantiates some type of favored Blessing as a result of taking this Scriptural Ordinance.

Regrettably, some have tried to make the Lord's Supper into a Sacrament, meaning that the taking of such will bring about Salvation. It won't! It is for one basic purpose and that is to call to remembrance, and to do so constantly, the price that was paid at Calvary's Cross for our Redemption. That's why our Lord said, *"This do in remembrance of Me"* (I Cor. 11:24-26).

To be sure, there definitely is hurt in the taking of the Lord's Supper, if it is done *"unworthily"* (I Cor. 11:27).

What does that mean?

It means that if one's faith is in anything except Christ and what He did for us at the Cross, then we are *"not discerning the Lord's Body,"* which can bring on sickness or even premature death (I Cor. 11:29-30). That's why Paul told us to *"examine ourselves"* (I Cor. 11:28) and, as well, to *"judge ourselves"* (I Cor. 11:31).

3. Fasting: While fasting is another viable Biblical Doctrine, still, if one places one's faith in such, thinking that by the doing of such we can have victory over sin, such constitutes a wrong direction. There is only one Sacrifice for sin and that is what Christ did at the Cross. Paul wrote:

> **"But this Man** (*this Priest, Christ Jesus*), **after He had offered One Sacrifice for sins forever** (*speaks of the Cross*), **sat down on the Right Hand of God** (*refers to the great contrast with the Priests under the Levitical*

system, who never sat down because their work was never completed; the Work of Christ was a 'Finished Work,' and needed no repetition)" **(Heb. 10:12).**

Paul addressed this when he spoke of Water Baptism. While it is, as well, a viable Biblical Doctrine, still, the emphasis must never be Water Baptism or anything else, for that matter, other than *"the Cross of Christ."* The great Apostle said:

"For Christ sent me not to baptize, but to preach the Gospel: not with wisdom of words, lest the Cross of Christ should be made of none effect" (I Cor. 1:17).

4. Prayer: If, by making the following statements, some conclude that I am speaking against prayer, then I am making the case very poorly, or else, such an individual is trying to find fault. On a personal basis, my Grandmother taught me to pray when I was but a child. That means that I've had an avid prayer life all of my many years. In fact, I still hold to a regimen of two prayer meetings a day, morning and afternoon, which I feel the Lord told me to do in 1991. In fact, if any Christian doesn't have a prayer life, then he or she has very little relationship with the Lord; however, having said that, the truth is, people can turn prayer into works. In other words, they think if they pray so much, this will guarantee victory within their lives, etc. It won't! Once again, those attempting to do so, and I once did just that, are using prayer in a wrong way. Basically, prayer is supposed to be for relationship and petition.

5. Manifestations: The Lord at times will do great things for people, such as exhibiting His Power to such an extent that it will literally knock a person off his feet. I believe that! Yet, manifestations are not the answer for victorious, overcoming, Biblical living. Jesus said, *"You'll know the Truth, and the Truth will make you free"* (Jn. 8:32). If an individual doesn't know the Truth, which is Jesus Christ and Him Crucified, even though the Power of the Lord knocks one off of one's feet, that person, despite the Moving and Operation of the Holy Spirit in this respect, will get up exactly as he fell down. In other words,

there won't be any change in his life and simply because manifestations, as wonderful as they are in their own right, will not set the captive free.

6. Confession: When I use the word *"confession,"* I am speaking of that which is roundly taught in some circles, that for every problem we might have, we should find two or three Scriptures, memorize them, and confess them over and over again, which will bring the Lord into action on our behalf. Now, again, I memorize Scriptures constantly and quote them all the time, which every Believer ought to do; however, the mere act of doing something is not going to set anyone free.

THE PROBLEM IS SIN!

While the modern church will not admit to that, still, the problem with Believers is sin. If we think not, then we are not admitting the truth and we simply don't know the Word of God. The Sixth Chapter of Romans is the great Victory Chapter of the Bible. It's where Paul taught us how to have Victory over the sin nature. Some seventeen times in that one Chapter he mentions sin. Fifteen of those seventeen times, when he originally wrote the Text, he placed in front of the word *"sin"* what is now referred to as the definite article, making it read *"the sin."* This means that he wasn't speaking of acts of sin, but rather, the sin principle and, in fact, the sin nature. He only mentioned acts of sin one time in that Chapter and that is in the Fifteenth Verse.

While the word *"sin"* in the Fourteenth Verse does not have the definite article, still, Paul used it as a noun instead of a verb, meaning that he is still speaking of the sin nature or the evil nature, whichever way we would like to label such.

Now, while many deny that the Believer has a sin nature, my answer to that is very simple.

We must admit that Paul is writing to Believers and I hardly think that he would mention something seventeen times when it doesn't even exist.

In fact, in the first two Verses of Romans, Chapter 6, the

Apostle tells us that the problem is sin. He then tells us how to
have victory over sin, which is the placing of our Faith exclusively in Christ and the Cross, given to us in Verses 3 through 5.
Understanding that our Victory is in the Cross of Christ, and the
Cross of Christ alone, then the Apostle explains to us how that
we can now have victory over the sin nature. No, that doesn't
mean sinless perfection, but it does mean that we are to come
to the place that the sin nature will no longer have dominion
over us (Rom. 6:14).

After thorough investigation and knowing that the Cross of
Christ was the only answer to man's dilemma, whatever that
dilemma might be, the great Apostle stated, *"For I determined
not to know any thing among you, save Jesus Christ, and Him
Crucified"* (I Cor. 2:2).

"I've found a Friend in Jesus, He's everything to me;
"He's the Fairest of ten thousand to my soul!
"The 'Lily of the Valley,' in Him alone I see,
"All I need to cleanse and make me fully whole:
"In sorrow He's my comfort, In trouble He's my stay;
"He tells me every care on Him to roll;
"He's the 'Lily of the Valley,' the bright and Morning Star;
"He's the Fairest of ten thousand to my soul!"

"He all my grief has taken, and all my sorrows borne;
"In temptation He's my strong and mighty Tower,
"I've all for Him forsaken, I've all my idols torn,
"From my heart, now He keeps me by His Power,
"Though all the world forsake me, And Satan tempts
  me sore,
"Through Jesus I shall safely reach the goal;
"He's the 'Lily of the Valley,' the bright and Morning
  Star;
"He's the Fairest of ten thousand to my soul!"

"He'll never, never leave me, Nor yet forsake me here,

"While I live by Faith, and do His Blessed Will;
"A wall of fire about me, I've nothing now to fear:
"With His Manna He my hungry soul shall fill.
"When crowned at last in Glory, I'll see His Blessed
    Face,
"Where rivers of delight shall ever roll;
"He's the 'Lily of the Valley,' the bright and Morning
    Star;
"He's the Fairest of ten thousand to my soul!"

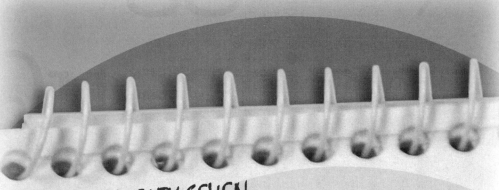

CHAPTER TWENTY-SEVEN

Why Is It That The Cross Doesn't Work For Me?

QUESTION:

WHY IS IT THAT THE CROSS DOESN'T WORK FOR ME?

ANSWER:

The Cross of Christ always works; it's you and I who at times don't work. We must understand that the Cross of Christ is not a magic wand that we wave over problems and the problems disappear. In fact, the Cross of Christ, one might say, is the door that leads to all of the great things of God. All of these things are learned slowly and most of the time with great difficulty.

MISUNDERSTANDING THE MESSAGE OF THE CROSS

Many people think of the Cross of Christ, at least when they first hear this Message, as a quick fix. To be sure, the Cross of Christ alone can, as the song says, *"fix it for you";* however, it is definitely not a quick fix. As we have stated, there are no magical qualities about the Message of the Cross. Let not the Believer think, upon embracing this great New Covenant, which the Lord has given unto us and for which He paid such a price, that the moment our Faith is there placed is the moment that all problems stop.

Not so!

To be sure, this Message is most definitely the key to *"more abundant life"* (Jn. 10:10). It is the one factor in this world, given to us by the Lord, which can set the captive free and it doesn't matter what the bondage might be. In fact, it would be impossible for us to overstate the benefits for which Jesus paid such a price. It is as Simon Peter said, *"a rejoicing with joy unspeakable and full of Glory"* (I Pet. 1:8), but, very few of these things come quickly or easily. Satan will contest every advancement we make, and do so with a venom that seems to defy description. He knows that such a person has found the key to victory and, if he can get that person, through discouragement, to simply quit, in other words to transfer his Faith from the Cross of Christ to something else, then the Evil One has won the battle. However, if we stay the course, Victory, and in a capacity we have never previously known, will be ours.

THE CROSS IS THE ENTRANCE ONE MIGHT SAY

Once one begins to understand the Cross of Christ, a proper understanding of the Word of God will begin to fall into place. In fact, I do not personally believe that anyone can properly understand the Bible unless one first of all understands the Cross. That doesn't mean one cannot understand some things about the Bible, for one certainly can; however, putting the pieces into place cannot come about until we understand the Atonement.

NO BELIEVER EVER MATURES BEYOND THE CROSS!

Williams says, *"The whole of the Christian life from beginning to end, day by day, moment by moment, is simply learning what it means to live by Grace through Faith alone in Christ alone."*[1]

The Child of God can Grow in Grace, come to the place of Spiritual Maturity, only by evidencing Faith in Christ and what Christ did at the Cross. The Cross of Christ must ever be the Object of our Faith, that and that alone! If, in fact, that is correct, and it most definitely is, considering that the modern church understands the Cross of Christ not at all, at least as it regards Sanctification, this means there isn't much maturity in the modern church. I think this should be obvious when we see those who claim to be Christians, even preachers, falling for that which is obviously unscriptural. It is a lack of maturity and because of the lack of the Cross.

WHAT IS THE ALTERNATIVE TO
THE CROSS OF JESUS CHRIST?

The only alternative is to fall back once again upon our own resources. Up beside Christ, what kind of resources do we have? What type of power and strength do we personally have?

Whatever it might be, it is understood, and graphically so, that we are no match within ourselves for the powers of darkness. So, the truth is, we have no alternative to the Cross of Christ, yet, the modern church keeps opting for that devised by man and, thereby, ignoring that provided by the Lord, i.e., *"the Cross."*

The Cross is God's Way and it is His only Way. The reason it is the only Way is because no other way is needed. Paul wrote:

"Then said He, Lo, I come to do Your Will, O God. *(The doing of the Will of God, as it regards Christ, pertained totally and completely to His Sacrifice of Himself on the Cross.)* He takes away the First *(the Old Covenant, which He did by the Sacrifice of Himself)*, that He may establish the Second *(the New Covenant which He did by going to the Cross, the only way it could be established).*

THE OFFERING OF THE BODY OF JESUS CHRIST

"By the which will *(the Sacrifice of Christ took away the First Covenant, satisfying its demands, and established the New Covenant)* we are Sanctified through the Offering of the Body of Jesus Christ once *for all.* *(This proclaims unequivocally that the only way the Believer can live a victorious life is by the Cross ever being the Object of his Faith.)*

"And every Priest stands daily Ministering and offering oftentimes the same Sacrifices, which can never take away sins *(proclaiming the insufficiency of this method)*:

"But this Man *(this Priest, Christ Jesus)*, after He had offered One Sacrifice for sins forever *(speaks of the Cross)*, sat down on the Right Hand of God *(refers to the great contrast with the Priests under the Levitical system, who never sat down because their work was never completed; the Work of Christ was a 'Finished Work,' and needed no repetition)*" **(Heb. 10:9-12).**

WHY IS IT SO FOOLISH TO REJECT THE CROSS?

To be frank, the way the question was formed in the heading presents a gross understatement. The word *"foolish"* is not nearly strong enough. To turn from the Cross of Christ is to turn from the only way of coming to God, the only way of having fellowship with God, and the only way of overcoming the world, the flesh, and the Devil. For one to exchange the free Grace of God, which comes to us solely by the means of the Cross, for the bondage of our own works is stupid indeed!

The Gospel of Grace says: God gives and gives and gives! The Law says: you must do and do and do! So, that being the case, why would most Believers desire Law over Grace?

That's a good question!

One of the reasons is, *"the doing of Religion is the most powerful narcotic there is,"* the doing of whatever makes us think that we are really righteous. Please understand the following:

There is absolutely nothing any Believer can do to make himself righteous, and I mean nothing! Righteousness is a free Gift from God and is freely given to anyone, irrespective as to what their past has been, if they will simply evidence Faith in Christ and what Christ has done for us at the Cross. Then a perfect, pure, untainted, unstained Righteousness will be imputed by God to such a believing soul (Rom. 5:1-2).

THE POWER THAT TRIES TO KEEP US UNDER

We quoted the following from THE EXPOSITOR'S STUDY BIBLE some Chapters back but it presents such a great Truth, that it needs, I think, to be repeated. It is said:

"The glad Tidings of Salvation is one thing; the struggle against the power that tries to keep the soul in bondage is quite another."

Many think that once the Cross of Christ is the Object of

their Faith all temptation will end and Satan will not be able to bother them again. Please understand that the Bible does not promise such a life. One day that will come, but, only when the Trump of God sounds (I Cor. 15). So, if you, as a Believer, think the Cross is not working because temptation is once again coming your way, you are misunderstanding the entirety of the great Plan of God.

In no place in the Word of God are we promised an uneventful life. To be frank, if such did come our way at this stage, it would not be for our benefit, but rather would play out to our hurt. Once again, allow me to quote from THE EXPOSITOR'S STUDY BIBLE:

"Satan will not easily allow his captives to go free; and God permits the bitter experience of Satan's power in order to exercise and strengthen Faith.

"That is ever the work of the Holy Spirit, the strengthening of our Faith. It is done in many ways; however, perhaps one could say, the greatest way of all is Satan's attacks against us. We don't like them! We certainly don't desire them in any fashion! But the truth is, such is necessary, that is if we are to 'Grow in Grace and the knowledge of the Lord.'"

IT IS WAR

We as Believers must understand that as long as we are in this world, and even though we understand the great Message of the Cross perfectly, none of this will exempt us from the opposition of the Evil One. In fact, Paul refers to this conflict as *"war"*; however, the Lord has shown us the way to have victory in this war, and we speak of Victory over the world, the flesh, and the Devil. Admittedly, it's not simple and it's not easy, but if we function according to the way laid down in the Word of God, we will win this war. In other words, sin will not have dominion over us (Rom. 6:14). There is nothing the Believer can do to escape the war, but most definitely we can have victory in this war. Paul said:

"**For though we walk in the flesh** *(refers to the fact that we do not yet have Glorified Bodies)*, **we do not war after the flesh** *(after our own ability, but rather by the Power of the Spirit)*:

"**(For the weapons of our warfare** *are* **not carnal** *(carnal weapons consist of those which are man-devised)*, **but mighty through God** *(the Cross of Christ [I Cor. 1:18])* **to the pulling down of strongholds;)**

"**Casting down imaginations** *(philosophic strongholds; every effort man makes outside of the Cross of Christ)*, **and every high thing that exalts itself against the Knowledge of God** *(all the pride of the human heart)*, **and bringing into captivity every thought to the obedience of Christ** *(can be done only by the Believer looking exclusively to the Cross, where all Victory is found; the Holy Spirit will then perform the task)*" **(II Cor. 10:3-5).**

As Paul says here, Satan will do everything within his power to erect *"strongholds"* of evil in our lives, and he will do so if we oppose him in the wrong way. However, if we place our Faith exclusively in Christ and what Christ has done for us at the Cross and refuse to allow it to be moved elsewhere, this *"war"* will be won. In the meantime, our Faith and strength in the Lord will grow mightily!

Yes, the Cross of Christ most definitely works and, in fact, is the only thing that will work. However, don't expect such to absolve us of all temptation, of all attacks by Satan, etc. That's not going to happen, but, as we have repeatedly stated, what the Lord gave to the Apostle Paul shows us the way to Victory, that is, if we will persevere, which means that we won't quit.

"*Take the Name of Jesus with you,*
"*Child of sorrow and of woe;*
"*It will joy and comfort give you,*
"*Take it then wherever you go.*"

"Take the Name of Jesus ever,
"As a shield from every snare.
"If temptations round you gather,
"Breathe that Holy Name in prayer."

"Oh, the precious Name of Jesus,
"How it thrills our souls with joy,
"When His loving Arms receive us,
"And His Songs our tongues employ!"

"At the Name of Jesus bowing,
"Falling prostrate at His Feet,
"King of kings in Heaven we'll crown Him,
"When our journey is complete."

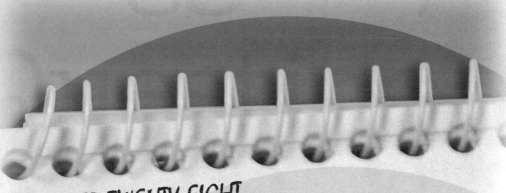

CHAPTER TWENTY-EIGHT

How Does Satan Respond To
The Message Of The Cross?

QUESTION:

HOW DOES SATAN RESPOND TO THE MESSAGE OF THE CROSS?

ANSWER:

He will do everything within his power to discourage the Believer, to try to get him to throw the Cross aside.

DOES THE MESSAGE OF THE CROSS WORK FOR EVERY BELIEVER?

I read an answer given by a particular Baptist preacher, as it regards the Cross, when someone stated to him, *"The Cross of Christ didn't work for me."* His answer was excellent. He said, *"Oh, yes, the Cross works and works beautifully well; it's me and you who don't work too well."*

How right he is!

When the Lord first gave me the Revelation of the Cross in 1997, I immediately began to preach it in our Church. Donnie, our grandson Gabriel, along with all of my associates, immediately began to preach this great Message as well. We also began to preach this great Word over the SonLife Network of Radio Stations (78 Stations), over the Internet, which goes all over the world, and over our Telecast, which at the time of this writing (2009) is going into one hundred and four countries of the world, and now the SonLife Broadcasting Network, a 24 hour, 7 day Television Network.

At any rate, at the outset and even continuing, after a fashion, to this hour, I had people say to me, *"I've tried the Cross and it doesn't work,"* or words to that effect. Many of these people were very sincere. They were not being sarcastic and neither were they demeaning the Message. Most of the time, things had happened that they did not understand and this was their response.

At the time, I hardly knew how to answer such complaints, meaning I either ignored them or else I chalked it up to unbelief, etc. The Lord, however, was to let me know that while some of these statements were definitely sarcastic and some were definitely from the realm of unbelief, the majority, as the Lord spelled it out to me, were people who were sincere but were falling by the wayside for a lack of knowledge.

THE REACTION OF SATAN TO THE MESSAGE OF THE CROSS

There is no way that one can adequately describe the hatred that Satan has for the Cross of Christ. It should be obvious seeing that it was at the Cross where he was defeated in totality (Rom. 6:3-14; 8:1-2, 11; I Cor. 1:17-18, 21, 23; 2:2; Col. 2:14-15). Knowing that the Cross of Christ is the one great factor in human history that can totally set the captive free presents the greatest knowledge of all. Actually, every single person who has ever been delivered from the ravages of sin and shame has been so because of what Jesus did at the Cross. No exceptions!

Satan, knowing that you, as a Believer, have heard the Message of the Cross, actually, the same Message given to us by the Apostle Paul, and knowing that you have now found the key to victory, will do everything within his power to discourage you, to disconcert you, and to try to cause you to doubt. He will do so by attacking you in every way possible, in fact, to a greater degree than ever before. This is what throws many Believers. They do not understand that, since they have now heard the Truth, Satan's efforts against them, his temptations, his pressure, and his oppression, are worse than ever. This throws many Believers. They don't understand what is happening but, hopefully, what you will now study in the answer to this particular question will give enlightenment and, thereby, show you the victory that awaits you, all in Christ Jesus.

A WORD FROM THE LORD

What I'm about to give you was not a dream or a vision,

and, yet, it was just as real as if it had been such.

It was a Saturday night. I had retired for bed and I honestly don't remember if I'd gone to sleep and awakened or if I had not yet gone to sleep. At any rate, my thoughts went to this question at hand as to exactly what happens to Believers when they first hear the Message of the Cross.

All of a sudden, it was like the Holy Spirit plastered on my mind the answer to this question, so clear, so concise, that I had no doubt it was from the Lord. Strangely and beautifully enough, He took me directly to the Fifth Chapter of Exodus. It was so real that I arose, turned on the light, and wrote down exactly what the Lord gave to me.

THE FIFTH CHAPTER OF EXODUS

The Fifth Chapter of Exodus relates to us Satan's opposition the moment that the demand was made by Moses and Aaron that the Children of Israel were to be set free, but, first, let's look at the plight of these people for a moment.

From the small group that came with Jacob into Egypt some two hundred and fifteen years before, Israel had grown to over two million in population. Despite their great numbers, they were slaves to the jackbooted heel of Pharaoh. The Scripture says concerning their plight:

"And the LORD said, I have surely seen the affliction of My People who are in Egypt, and have heard their cry by reason of their taskmasters; for I know their sorrows *(the Lord has 'seen,' He has 'heard,' and He 'knows')*;

"And I am come down to deliver them out of the hand of the Egyptians *(Egypt was a type of the world; 'the Lord delivers us from this present evil world'; He does so by the means of the Cross [Gal. 1:4])*, and to bring them up out of that land unto a good land and a large, unto a land flowing with milk and honey *(the Lord delivers us from something [sin] and, thereby, to something [Salvation], typified by Canaanland) . . ."* (Ex. 3:7-8).

THE LIE THAT SATAN ALMOST
MADE ME BELIEVE

If I remember correctly, it was 2003. I had come to the place in my thinking, regarding fellow Believers, that while there might be a few who were having problems, in reality, the majority were not, or so I had begun to reason in my mind.

It was a Sunday night. Donnie was preaching. He wasn't preaching on Moses and Aaron or the deliverance of the Children of Israel from Egyptian bondage; however, in the course of his Message he did mention the word that Moses gave to Pharaoh, *"Let My people go."*

When he said that, all of a sudden the Spirit of the Lord came all over me. I began to sob as the Lord began to speak to my heart. He said to me:

"Because they do not know My Word, the Church presently, is in the same condition as the Children of Israel were in Egypt."

His Word was unmistakable to me. My thinking that only a few Believers were so affected was far from the truth. The truth was that virtually the entirety of the Body of Christ, and we speak of those who are truly Saved, were, in fact, in bondage to Satan.

Why?

THE CROSS OF CHRIST AND SANCTIFICATION

While most Believers, and we speak of those who are truly Born-Again, have at least a modicum of understanding as it regards the Cross respecting Salvation, they have virtually no understanding at all as it regards the Cross and Sanctification. As a result, the modern church simply does not know how to live for God. That's the reason it staggers and stumbles from one scheme to the other, all purporting to hold the answer, but which, in reality, do not.

The Cross of Christ alone holds the answer for Salvation and for Sanctification. When one considers that the meaning of the New Covenant was given to the Apostle Paul (Gal. 1:12), which, in effect, is the meaning of the Cross, and considering that ninety percent of all of his fourteen Epistles deals with this particular subject, we should consequently understand how important all of this is.

The modern church is somewhat like a man or woman who would attend law school and stay there for years but never learn anything about Law. The modern church simply doesn't know God's Prescribed Order of Life and Living. As a result, and as stated, it stumbles from one fad to the other.

That Sunday night the Lord helped me to see the condition of the church, and in no uncertain terms.

THE PROBLEM IS SIN

Satan has done everything within Hell's power to hide the real problem from the church, which is sin:

1. The Word of Faith people, which is no faith at all, claim that sin should not be mentioned. If it is mentioned, they claim, this will create a sin consciousness in people and they will thereby sin. So, the way to stop Christians from sinning, they claim, is to never mention sin. That's strange when we realize that the Apostle Paul mentioned sin seventeen times in the Sixth Chapter of Romans alone. Quite possibly, and I speak sarcastically, Paul was not as enlightened as these modern Faith giants are!

2. The Seeker Sensitive crowd claims that sin should not be mentioned because it may offend people. As a result, pews have been filled with people who have never truly been Born-Again and, as it regards the message that they are presently hearing, they never will be Born-Again.

3. The church, some say, has entered a new dimension. The old methods won't work anymore. So, sin should not be mentioned, Hell should not be mentioned, and anything that is

negative should not be mentioned. Everything should be looked at as sweetness and light. It's God's, they say, new way.

Irrespective of all of this, sin continues to take its deadly toll, in fact, worse than ever. The modern church is in worse condition spiritually than it has been at any time since the Reformation. That's quite a statement but it happens to be true! There is only one answer and that is, *"Jesus Christ and Him Crucified."* Every single Revival that the church has ever had in its two thousand year history has found itself back at the Cross. All Revivals begin at the Cross and, if the modern church is to have anything that even remotely resembles Revival, it must come back to the Cross. That is what *"The Spirit is saying unto the Churches."*

LET MY PEOPLE GO

Concerning the demand that Pharaoh was to let Israel go, the Scripture says the following:

"And afterward Moses and Aaron went in, and told the Pharaoh *(according to many authorities, the Pharaoh at that time was 'Menephthap,' the son and successor of 'Rameses II'; history records that he was a weak individual, but, because of certain events, had an exalted opinion of himself; the close of Chapter 4 presents the people worshipping in believing joy; the close of Chapter 5 sets before the reader the same people filled with unbelieving bitterness; the Glad Tidings of Salvation is one thing; the struggle against the power that tries to keep the soul in bondage is quite another)*, Thus says the LORD God of Israel, Let My People go, that they may hold a feast unto Me in the wilderness. *(If it is to be noticed, the Holy Spirit, in giving Moses direction regarding the Sacred Text, in no way recognizes the splendor of Egypt. The character of the Message that Moses was to deliver to Pharaoh was not calculated to compromise or pacify.)*

WHO IS THE LORD?

"**And Pharaoh said, Who is the LORD, that I should obey His Voice to let Israel go? I know not the LORD, neither will I let Israel go.** *(Satan will not easily allow his captives to go free; and God permits the bitter experience of Satan's power in order to exercise and strengthen Faith. Mackintosh says: 'When we contemplate Israel amid the brick kilns of Egypt, we behold a graphic figure of the condition of every child of Adam's fallen race by nature. There they were, crushed beneath the enemy's galling yolk, and having no power to deliver themselves. The mere mention of the word 'liberty' only caused the oppressor to bind his captives with a stronger fetter, and to lade them with a still more grievous burden. Consequently, it was absolutely necessary that deliverance should come from without.' Nevertheless, Pharaoh will soon find out exactly 'Who is the Lord!')*

THE SACRIFICE

"**And they** *(Moses and Aaron)* **said, The God of the Hebrews has met with us: let us go, we pray you, three days' journey into the desert, and Sacrifice unto the LORD our God; lest He fall upon us with pestilence, or with the sword.** *(This simple statement tells us, even as given to Moses by the Lord, that it is the Cross only which holds back the Judgment of God. In other words, the only thing standing between man and Hell is the Cross of Christ)*" **(Ex. 5:1-3).**

It didn't matter that it was God Almighty Who had given instructions to Pharaoh that he was to let Israel go. The Evil One did not buckle easily. In fact, Moses and Aaron had to come before Pharaoh seven times before he finally relented, and then only because of the death of his firstborn.

God's Word has point blank demanded that you, as a Believer, be free from the domination of the sin nature (Rom. 6:14; 8:1-2, 11; Gal. 6:14). To be sure, the Scriptures we have just given are most definitely the Word of God, but let us say it again, Satan does not fold his tent and leave because we have quoted the Word to him. He will try our metal and the Lord will allow him to do so. Let us say it again:

"Satan will not easily allow his captives to go free; and God permits the bitter experience of Satan's power in order to exercise and strengthen Faith."

Many Believers, when they meet head on with opposition, instead of Satan folding and running, they fold and run. Let us be clear so that no one will misunderstand.

To be sure, if you the Believer, do not quit, total and complete victory will be yours, and we speak of Victory over the world, the flesh, and the Devil. However, it will not come easily and it probably won't come quickly, but, if you keep believing, it will come.

THE OPPRESSION DOUBLED

The response of Pharaoh to the demand of Moses was that he doubled the workload of the people, in fact, to a killing pace. Satan will, no doubt, do the same thing to the Believer who has embraced the Message of the Cross, endeavoring to discourage him to the place that he will throw over his newfound Faith. The Scripture says:

"And the king of Egypt said unto them, Why do you, Moses and Aaron, let the people from their works? get you unto your burdens. *(They will now find that the burdens are increased. As the Children of Israel, it seems that many do not too very much mind being slaves to Satan, until the burdens become so heavy that they cannot be borne. Invariably, that will happen!)*

"And Pharaoh said, Behold, the people of the land

now are many *(the Israelites)*, and you make them rest from their burdens.

"And Pharaoh commanded the same day the taskmasters of the people, and their officers, saying,

"You shall no more give the people straw to make brick, as heretofore: let them go and gather straw for themselves. *(Oftentimes, the setting to carry out the Will of God will result in Satan's anger, with opposition being increased.)*

AT THE MENTION OF SACRIFICE, THAT IS, THE CROSS

"And the tale *(number)* of the bricks, which they did make heretofore, you shall lay upon them; you shall not diminish ought thereof: for they be idle; therefore they cry, saying, Let us go and sacrifice to our God. *(At the mention of sacrifice, Pharaoh increased the pressure and the workload, almost to a killing pace. When the Believer first begins to hear the Message of the Cross, he will find the opposition of Satan greatly increasing. This will be confusing at first, but the Believer should take heart. The enemy does this because he knows the Believer has now found the source of victory; therefore, he seeks to move the Believer's Faith from the Cross to other things, by discouragement, etc.)*

"Let there more work be laid upon the men, that they may labor therein; and let them not regard vain words. *(Pharaoh regarded the offering of 'Sacrifices' as 'vain words.' Regrettably, much of the modern Church does the same, as it regards the Cross.)*

"And the taskmasters of the people went out, and their officers, and they spoke to the people, saying, Thus says Pharaoh, I will not give you straw.

"Go you, get you straw where you can find it: yet not ought of your work shall be diminished. *(Even though you have to get the straw yourselves, you must turn out just as much work as previously.)*

"So the people were scattered abroad throughout all the land of Egypt to gather stubble instead of straw. *(It is good for a man to learn painfully the nature of sin's dominion, and his absolute helplessness in the grip of that monarch.)*

AWAKENED CHRISTIANS TO THE MESSAGE OF THE CROSS

"And the taskmasters hasted them, saying, Fulfill your works, your daily tasks, as when there was straw. *(The first move of Israel toward deliverance plunged her into deeper misery so that the people would have preferred being left quiet in their slavery. This is oftentimes the spiritual experience of awakened sinners, or even awakened Christians to the Message of the Cross.)*

"And the officers of the Children of Israel, which Pharaoh's taskmasters had set over them, were beaten, and demanded, Wherefore have you not fulfilled your task in making brick both yesterday and today, as heretofore? *(Satan wanted them to be willing to remain as slaves in Egypt. He almost succeeded!)*" **(Ex. 5:4-14).**

THE LEADERS IN ISRAEL TURNED AGAINST MOSES AND AARON

Oftentimes when the Believer accepts Christ and the Cross as the only answer for man's dilemma, whatever that dilemma might be, his friends and close relatives, and even his church, could very well turn against him. It happened here with Moses and Aaron. Because of the increased workload, the leaders among the Israelites began to turn against Moses and Aaron, in effect, blaming them for their difficulties. The Scripture says:

"Then the officers of the Children of Israel came and cried unto Pharaoh, saying, Why do you deal thus with your servants? *(Instead of crying unto the Lord, these leaders of the Israelites turned unto Pharaoh for relief. So often we as modern Believers follow suit. We appeal to man instead of God.)*

"There is no straw given unto your servants, and they say to us, Make brick: and, behold, your servants are beaten; but the fault is in your own people. *(The natural man ever prefers to lean upon an arm of flesh than be supported by Him Who is invisible.)*

"But he *(Pharaoh)* said, You are idle, you are idle: therefore you say, Let us go and do Sacrifice to the LORD. *(It is the 'Sacrifice' which rankled Pharaoh, even though he would not have been aware as to what exactly it all meant. The Cross always rankles Satan.)*

"Go therefore now, and work; for there shall no straw be given you, yet shall you deliver the tale *(number)* of bricks. *(We should learn that it's not Scriptural for us to make plans and then ask God to bless those plans. If God makes the plans, they are assured of blessing. So, leave Pharaoh alone, and depend exclusively on the Lord for all that is to be done.)*

DISCOURAGEMENT AND OPPOSITION FROM HIS OWN BRETHREN

"And the officers of the Children of Israel did see that they were in evil case, after it was said, You shall not minish *(reduce)* ought from your bricks of your daily task.

"And they met Moses and Aaron, who stood in the way, as they came forth from Pharaoh:

"And they said unto them, The LORD look upon you, and judge; because you have made our savor to be abhorred in the eyes of Pharaoh, and in the eyes of his servants, to put a sword in their hand to kill us. *(Moses was no doubt prepared for the rebuff which he had himself received from Pharaoh, for the Lord had plainly said that He would harden the king's heart. But, so far as the inspired record informs us, nothing has been told him that he would meet with discouragement and opposition from his own brethren. A real testing was this for God's servant, for it is far more trying to be criticized by our own Brethren, by those whom we are anxious to help, than it is to be persecuted by the world)"* (Ex. 5:15-21).

DELIVERANCE

To be sure, despite the opposition, the Children of Israel would ultimately be delivered. The opposition in brief was as follows:

• **Pharaoh did not yield despite the demand.** Just because we claim Faith in Christ and the Cross doesn't mean that Satan is going to give ground immediately.

• **Pharaoh doubled the workload.** Satan may very well double the opposition against you, the Believer, once you embrace the Message of the Cross. He does such to try to discourage you and make you quit.

• **We find that the leaders of the Children of Israel turned against Moses,** in effect, blaming him for the problems instead of Pharaoh. It may very well be that one's own loved ones, family, friends, and even their church, may turn against them when they embrace the Message of the Cross. Men love their *"works,"* and the Cross eliminates all of that.

However, if the Believer will not give in, will not lose his Faith, will keep believing even if he fails, to be sure, he is now on the right road and ultimately total and complete victory will be his.

WHAT DO WE MEAN BY VICTORY?

We mean that the sin nature no longer rules in our lives (Rom. 6:14).

The Bible, in fact, doesn't teach sinless perfection. If a person rightly understands himself, which he definitely will when he understands the Cross, he will be the first to realize that sinless perfection is not presently in the offing. That will come, but only when the Trump sounds (I Cor. 15:51-58).

When we speak of the sin nature ruling the Believer, we are speaking of a recurring sin, whatever it might be.

Some of you holding this book in your hands have had something in your life for months, even years, that has recurred, whatever it might be, over and over again, with you having to ask forgiveness many times. Thank the Lord, God will always forgive when we properly confess our sins to Him, etc. (I Jn. 1:9), but that's not the way the Lord intends for the Believer to live.

WHAT IS THE SIN NATURE?

It is what Adam and Eve became immediately after the Fall, whereas, their nature before the Fall had been that of Righteousness and Holiness, in other words, the Divine Nature. However, when they fell, their nature became that of sin and in totality. It was that totally and constantly.

The Lord intended for sons and daughters of God to be born into the world, but with the Fall of Adam, offspring could be born only in the likeness of Adam. Concerning all of this, the Scripture says:

ADAM'S DESCENDANTS

"This is the book of the generations of Adam *(corresponds with the phrase, 'The Book of the Generation of Jesus Christ,' Who was the Last Adam [Mat. 1:1])*. In the day that God created man, in the Likeness of God made He him *(the 'Likeness of God' is the 'Glory of God' [II Cor. 4:6]. Through the Fall, man lost that glory; however, at the First Resurrection of Life, every Believer will regain that glory [Rom. 8:17])*;

"**Male and female created He them** *(refers to the fact that homosexuality is a grievous sin before God)*; **and blessed them** *(the blessing was lost as a result of the Fall, but has been regained in Christ)*, **and called their name Adam, in the day when they were created** *(Adam, in the Hebrew, is the word for humankind in general besides the specific name for the first man)*.

IN THE LIKENESS OF ADAM

"**And Adam lived an hundred and thirty years, and begat** *(fathered)* **a son in his own likeness** *(God originally intended for mankind to procreate 'sons and daughters of God' into the world; due to the Fall, sons and daughters could be brought into the world only in the likeness of their original parent, Adam, a product of his fallen nature; it is called 'original sin')*, **and after his image** *(means that Adam no longer had the Image of God; the 'likeness' and 'image' are now after Satan [Jn. 8:44])*; **and called his name Seth** *(even though Seth was not the Promised One, still, he represented a ray of hope; through him, rather his line, the Promised One would come)*:

"**And the days of Adam after he had begotten Seth were eight hundred years: and he begat sons and daughters** *(the intimation is, Adam was able to father children, and Eve to conceive, for some eight hundred years. Exactly how many children they brought into the world we aren't told. But it had to be many)*:

"**And all the days that Adam lived were nine hundred and thirty years; and he died** *(the family history of this, the Heavenly Race, is marked by death; no matter how long a member of the family lived, yet three words attend the name: 'and he died')*" **(Gen. 5:1-5).**

As a result of Adam's Fall, all born into the world, which includes every single person who has ever lived, with the exception of Jesus Christ, were born with a sin nature. This means that with every person born, his or her nature was that of disobedience of the Word of God, iniquity, transgression, sin, etc. In fact, before a person comes to Christ, he is ruled by the sin nature 24/7. That's the reason the person has to be *"Born-Again"* (Jn. 3:3).

THE SIN NATURE IS NOT REMOVED WHEN
THE BELIEVING SINNER COMES TO CHRIST

While it is not removed, it is, in fact, made dormant. It's sort of like an electric appliance that is unplugged. So what causes it to be revived?

The Believer, in effect, now has three natures. They are:

1. The human nature;
2. The sin nature; and,
3. The Divine Nature.

The latter is obtained when you first come to Christ, and then the war begins, which is between the sin nature and the Divine Nature. In fact, that war will continue until the Trump sounds or until you die.

The sin nature is revived in the Christian because the Christian places his or her faith in something other than the Cross of Christ. That being done, the Holy Spirit residing in the heart and life of the Believer is now greatly hindered in what He can do. Inasmuch as He works exclusively within the parameters, one might say, of the Finished Work of Christ, He demands total Faith in Christ and the Cross on our part. When our Faith is placed elsewhere, this is a direction in which He cannot work. That being the case, we are left on our own, meaning that now we are trying to live for God by self-effort, which is woefully inadequate.

Such a Believer will then begin to fail the Lord with a predominate sin taking place within his or her life, and doing so over and over again, which is what we mean by a recurring sin. That's when the sin nature is then ruling the Child of God, which makes life miserable, to say the least. That's what Paul was talking about when he said, *"Oh wretched man that I am! Who shall deliver me from the body of this death?"* (Rom. 7:24).

The only answer to the situation is for the Believer to come to the understanding that Scripturally his victory is totally in Christ and the Cross and in no other manner. He is then obligated to place his Faith exclusively in Christ and the Cross, which then gives the Holy Spirit latitude to work in his life. Then and then only can the recurring sin be defeated and stopped.

THE APOSTLE PAUL

That's what Paul was talking about when he said to the Galatians:

"**Behold** *('mark my words!')*, **I Paul say unto you** *(presents the Apostle's authority regarding the Message he brings)*, **that if you be circumcised, Christ shall profit you nothing.** *(If the Believer goes back into Law, and Law of any kind, what Christ did at the Cross on our behalf will profit us nothing. One cannot have it two ways)*" **(Gal. 5:2).**

The great Apostle then said:

"**Christ is become of no effect unto you** *(this is a chilling statement, and refers to anyone who makes anything other than Christ and the Cross the Object of his Faith)*, **whosoever of you are justified by the Law** *(seek to be Justified by the Law)*; **you are fallen from Grace** *(fallen from the position of Grace, which means the Believer is trusting in something other than the Cross; it actually means, 'to apostatize')*" **(Gal. 5:4).**

That's why Paul also said:

"**For Christ sent me not to baptize** *(presents to us a*

Cardinal Truth), **but to preach the Gospel** *(the manner in which one may be Saved from sin)*: **not with wisdom of words** *(intellectualism is not the Gospel)*, **lest the Cross of Christ should be made of none effect.** *(This tells us in no uncertain terms that the Cross of Christ must always be the emphasis of the Message)*" **(I Cor. 1:17).**

THE DELIVERANCE OF ISRAEL BY AND THROUGH THE CROSS

I have debated in my spirit whether to include the first thirteen Verses of the Twelfth Chapter of Exodus because it is quite voluminous, considering the Text plus the notes from THE EXPOSITOR'S STUDY BIBLE; however, one of the reasons that so many people do not understand Christ is because they do not understand the Old Testament Types, etc. The first thirteen Verses of this Twelfth Chapter proclaim, beautifully so, Who Jesus is and what He did for us. Anything that opens up Christ to us is of tremendous worth, as should be obvious. So, despite the volume, I have elected to copy the first thirteen Verses in totality.

THE BEGINNING

"And the LORD spoke unto Moses and Aaron in the land of Egypt saying *(this Chapter is a perfect picture of Christ, the True Pascal Lamb)*,

"This month shall be unto you the beginning of months: it shall be the first month of the year to you. *(The person doesn't really begin to live until he comes to Christ; as well, the Believer doesn't really begin to enjoy the 'more abundant life' afforded him by Christ until he learns God's Prescribed Order of Victory, which is Faith in Christ and the Cross exclusively, which then gives the Holy Spirit latitude to work, thereby bringing about the Graces of the Fruit of the Spirit [Rom. 8:1-2, 11; Gal. 5:16-25].*

All Believers have 'more abundant life' [Jn. 10:10], but all Believers are not enjoying more abundant life and, in fact, cannot until they learn God's Prescribed Order of Victory, which is the Cross [I Cor. 1:17-18, 21, 23; 2:2; Gal. 6:14; Col. 2:14-15].)

A LAMB FOR AN HOUSE

"**Speak you unto all the congregation of Israel, saying** *(another great lesson learned here is the fact that neither Moses nor Aaron introduced any legislation of their own, either at this time or later. The whole system, spiritual, political, and ecclesiastical, was received by Divine Revelation, commanded by God, and merely established by the agency of the two brothers. This proclaims the fact that Salvation is all of God and none of man. This problem presents itself when man attempts to insert his means and ways into that which God has devised, which, in fact, the modern Church is now doing)*, **In the tenth day of this month they shall take to them every man a lamb, according to the house of their fathers, a lamb for an house:**
* *(In the Fourth Chapter of Genesis, it is a lamb for each person.*
* *Now it is a lamb for each house.*
* *Upon the giving of the Law, it would be a lamb for the entirety of the nation.*
* *But when Jesus came, He would be the Lamb for the entirety of the world [Jn. 1:29].*

"*The offering up of the Lamb in Sacrifice was a Type of Christ, and what He would do at the Cross, all on our behalf. The lamb represented innocence and gentleness. The Prophets represented the tender compassion of God for His people under the figure of the Shepherd and the Lamb [Isa. 40:11], and ultimately the intention of God for His people used the lamb as an important symbol; therefore, the Lamb was a worthy symbol of our Saviour, Who, in innocence, patiently endured suffering as our Substitute [I Pet. 1:19].)*

A LAMB WITHOUT BLEMISH

"And if the household be too little for the lamb, let him and his neighbor next unto his house take it according to the number of the souls; every man according to his eating shall make your count for the lamb. *(Every person had to partake of the Passover. This was mandatory. Even though the lamb represented the entire house, it had to be partaken by each and every individual in that house. It is the same as it regards Salvation, which is always very personal.)*

"Your lamb shall be without blemish *(Christ was without blemish, Who the lamb represented, 'holy, harmless, undefiled' — a 'lamb without spot' [I Pet. 1:19])*, a male of the first year *(meant to portray the virile manhood of Christ; in other words, He didn't die in the throes of old age, but rather in the prime of manhood)*: you shall take it out from the sheep, or from the goats *(the 'goats' then represented were different from our goats presently; then they were very similar to the sheep, actually, with their long flowing mane, even more beautiful than the sheep)*:

KILL THE LAMB IN THE EVENING

"And you shall keep it up until the fourteenth day of the same month *(they were to select the animal on the tenth day, and then kill it on the fourteenth day; it was to be minutely inspected during these four days, that no trace of illness would be observed; representing Christ, it had to be perfect)*: and the whole assembly of the congregation of Israel shall kill it in the evening. *(The actual Hebrew says, 'between the two evenings,' which was about 3 p.m. This was the exact time that Jesus died on the Cross of Calvary [Mat. 27:46].)*

THE BLOOD ON THE DOORPOST

"And they shall take of the blood *(which represented the shed Blood of the Lord Jesus Christ)***, and strike it on the two side posts and on the upper door post of the houses, wherein they shall eat it** *(eat the Passover; in I Cor. 5:7-8, we have the Divine Authority for our regarding the contents of Ex., Chpt. 12, as typical of what our Blessed Saviour did on the Cross; at the deliverance of the Children of Israel from Egypt, the blood, which represented the shed Blood of Christ, was to be put on the side posts and the upper posts of the house; later, it would be applied to the Mercy Seat on the Great Day of Atonement; now, by Faith, it is applied to our hearts [Jn. 3:16; Eph. 2:13-18].)*

UNLEAVENED BREAD AND BITTER HERBS

"And they shall eat the flesh in that night *(in essence, Jesus was referring to this in Jn. 6:53-55; of course, He wasn't speaking of His flesh literally being eaten, but was speaking rather of our Faith in Him and what He would do for us at the Cross; our Faith must be in the entirety of His Finished Work)***, roast with fire** *(this spoke of the Judgment of God that would come upon Him as the Sin-Bearer, which was death, instead of us)***, and unleavened bread** *(this typi- fied the Perfection of Christ; He was Holy, harmless, and undefiled [Heb. 7:26], of which the lack of leaven was a Type)***; and with bitter herbs they shall eat it** *(the 'bitter herbs' were to remind the Children of Israel of the slavery which they had experienced in Egypt [Ex. 1:14]; as well, the Cross ever reminds us presently of that from which we were redeemed, abject slavery to Satan)***.**

PARTAKING OF ALL OF THE CROSS

"Eat not of it raw, nor sodden at all with water *(this* *speaks of accepting Christ, but without the Cross, which God cannot condone)*, **but roast with fire** *(speaks of the Cross and the price paid there)*; **his head with his legs, and with the purtenance thereof.** *(The purtenance pertained to the intestines, which were removed and washed, and then placed back in the animal and, as obvious here, to be eaten when the lamb was consumed. This speaks of partaking of all of the Cross. Sin goes to the very vitals; therefore, for sin to be properly addressed, and in every capacity, everything that Christ did at the Cross must be accepted, and without fail.)*

LET NOTHING OF IT REMAIN

"And you shall let nothing of it remain until the morning *(all of it must be consumed, referring to the fact that we must accept all of Christ, or else we will not have any of Christ; untold millions attempt to accept Christ as a good man, a great example, even a miracle worker, but they care not for the Cross; if Christ is to be had at all, He can only be had by and through the Cross; otherwise, we have 'another Jesus' [II Cor. 11:4])*; **and that which remains of it until the morning you shall burn with fire.** *(This tells us that Christ cannot be received in stages. He can only be received in totality. Burning the remainder 'with fire' once again points to the Cross. We must always remember, Christ is the Source, while the Cross is the Means.)*

IT IS THE LORD'S PASSOVER

"And thus shall you eat it; with your loins girded, your shoes on your feet, and your staff in your hand *(proclaims the fact that they were leaving Egypt; after the Law was given, and Israel was safely ensconced in the Promised Land, they were to eat the Passover resting, and for all the obvious reasons)*; **and you shall eat it in**

haste *(the same admonition, however, should hold true for the modern Believer, in that we should be eagerly awaiting the moment when the Trump of God shall sound and, thereby, we will be raptured away [I Thess. 4:13-18])*; **it is the LORD's Passover.** *(Concerning this, Pink says: 'The Death of Christ glorified God if never a single sinner had been saved by the virtue of it. The more we study the teaching of Scripture on this subject, and the more we lay hold by simple Faith of what the Cross meant to God, the more stable will be our peace, and the deeper our joy and praise.' The Passover was ever a Type of the Cross. In I Cor. 5:7, we read: 'Christ our Passover.' He is now 'our' Passover, because He was first the 'LORD's Passover.')*

I AM THE LORD

"For I will pass through the land of Egypt this night, and will smite all the firstborn in the land of Egypt, both man and beast; and against all the gods of Egypt I will execute judgment: I am the LORD. *(The words 'pass through' could be translated 'go through,' since the word used is entirely unconnected with the 'Passover.' According to Ex. 12:23, the Lord did not personally go through the land of Egypt that particular night, but rather that He used an Angel. The 'beasts' were included, because animal worship was an important part of the religion of the Egyptians. So, the Lord directed His judgment against every facet of Egyptian life and living.)*

WHEN I SEE THE BLOOD, I WILL PASS OVER YOU

"And the blood shall be to you for a token upon the houses where you are *(the blood applied to the door posts meant that their Faith and trust were in the Pascal Lamb; the blood then applied was only a 'token,' meaning that it was then but a symbol of One Who was to come, Who would* *redeem mankind by the shedding of His Life's Blood)*: **and when I see the blood, I will pass over you** *(this is, without a doubt, one of the single most important Scriptures in the entirety of the Word of God; the lamb had taken the fatal blow; and because it had taken the blow, those in the house would be spared; it was not a question of personal worthiness, self had nothing whatever to do in the matter; it was a matter of Faith; all under the cover of the blood were safe, just as all presently under the cover of the Blood are safe; this means that they were not merely in a savable state, but rather that they were 'saved'; as well, they were not partly saved and partly exposed to judgment, they were wholly saved, and because there is no such thing as partial Justification; the Lord didn't say, 'When I see you,' or, 'When I see your good works,' etc., but, 'When I see the blood'; this speaks of Christ and what He would do at the Cross in order that we might be saved, which pertained to Him giving Himself in Sacrifice, which necessitated the shedding of His Precious Blood [I Pet. 1:18-19])*, **and the plague shall not be upon you to destroy you, when I smite the land of Egypt.** *(Salvation from the 'plague' of Judgment is afforded only by the shed Blood of the Lamb, and Faith in that shed Blood)*" **(Ex. 12:1-13).**

"Keep yourself pure! Christ's soldier hear,
"Through life's loud strife the call rings clear.
"Your Captain speaks His Word obey;
"So shall your strength be as your day."

"Keep yourself pure! When lusts assail,
"When flesh is strong and spirit frail,
"Fight on — a fadeless crown your meed,
"Your body as your captive lead."

"Keep yourself pure! Thrice blessed he,
"Whose heart from taint of sin is free.

"His feet shall stand where Saints have trod,
"He with rapped eye shall see his God."

"Keep yourself pure! For He Who died,
"Himself for your sake sanctified,
"Then hear Him speaking from the skies,
"And victor o'er temptation rise."

"Oh Holy Spirit, keep us pure,
"Grant us Your Strength when sins allure;
"Our bodies are Your Temple, Lord;
"Be Thou in thought and act adored."

Bibliography

CHAPTER 2
Chambers, Oswald, *The Complete Works of Oswald Chambers*,
    Grand Rapids, MI, Discover House Publishers, 2000.

CHAPTER 6
Renan, Ernest, *The Life of Jesus*, London, England, W. Scott,
    1897.

CHAPTER 13
George Williams, *The Students Commentary on the Holy
    Scriptures*, Grand Rapids, Kregel Publications, 1949.

CHAPTER 16
Kilpatrick, William Kirk, *Psychological Seduction*, Nashville,
    TN, Thomas Nelson Publishers, 1990.
Gross, Martin, *The Psychological Society.*

CHAPTER 22
George Williams, *The Students Commentary on the Holy
    Scriptures*, Grand Rapids, Kregel Publications, 1949.

CHAPTER 25
The New Strong's Exhaustive Concordance Of The Bible.

CHAPTER 27
George Williams, *The Students Commentary on the Holy
    Scriptures*, Grand Rapids, Kregel Publications, 1949.

Seeker Sensitive Church   p. 224
    (Purpose Driven Life)

Sin Nature - p. 443